African Histories and Modernities

This book series serves as a scholarly forum on African contributions to and negotiations of diverse modernities over time and space, with a particular emphasis on historical developments. Specifically, it aims to refute the hegemonic conception of a singular modernity, Western in origin, spreading out to encompass the globe over the last several decades. Indeed, rather than reinforcing conceptual boundaries or parameters, the series instead looks to receive and respond to changing perspectives on an important but inherently nebulous idea, deliberately creating a space in which multiple modernities can interact, overlap, and conflict. While privileging works that emphasize historical change over time, the series will also feature scholarship that blurs the lines between the historical and the contemporary, recognizing the ways in which our changing understandings of modernity in the present have the capacity to affect the way we think about African and global histories.

More information about this series at
https://link.springer.com/bookseries/14758

Dawne Y. Curry

Social Justice at Apartheid's Dawn

African Women Intellectuals and the Quest to Save the Nation

palgrave
macmillan

Dawne Y. Curry
Department of History
University of Nebraska-Lincoln
Lincoln, NE, USA

ISSN 2634-5773 ISSN 2634-5781 (electronic)
African Histories and Modernities
ISBN 978-3-030-85403-4 ISBN 978-3-030-85404-1 (eBook)
https://doi.org/10.1007/978-3-030-85404-1

Cover illustration: F42PIX / Alamy Stock Photo

This Palgrave Macmillan imprint is published by the registered company Springer Nature Switzerland AG.
The registered company address is: Gewerbestrasse 11, 6330 Cham, Switzerland

To five South African women who showered me with laughter and love during my Fulbright year (2017–2018) and beyond:
Gloria Bosman
"Rev." your music and humor have always been medicine to my soul!
Refilwe Kgare
"Ref" we'll always be 'Funkin for Jamaica!'
Mamagowa Letaba
"Weirdoo" u were an unexpected, treasured gift!
Keketso Petlane (Keke)
"Road dawg" you never fail to humor the "Tina" in me!
Brenda Sisane
"Dr." Sisane, Sundays at Kaya FM were always spiritually uplifting!

Acknowledgments

This book is the fulfillment of an incredible journey into South Africa's past. Researching the intellectual histories of African women during the country's segregation era pushed me to new scholarly limits and exposed a rich corpus of political thought generated by an important cadre of African women who dared to envision a new societal order in their quests to save the nation. A year-long US Fulbright Scholar Award to South Africa (2017–2018) afforded me the opportunity to continue necessary and engaging research and build upon University of Nebraska-Lincoln (UNL)-funded internal grants, but also to really think about how the archival documents and the testimonies interconnected. The Hallmark House in Doornfontein, Johannesburg, provided me the space for rumination. I often occupied the seat in the lounge near the corner in front of the big picture window where I journaled, took notes from articles and books, and thought deeply. I was such a resident 'occupant' of that seat that people literally asked me if it was okay to sit there! And if someone else was sitting there, friends told the 'trespassers' to get up, that's Dawne's seat! Thanks to all of the residents and staff at the Hallmark House that I met—Tsholo, Sihle, Ntobeko, Shylet, Enge, Ayanda, Zandisile, Lawrence, and others who made my stay more pleasant. Of course, I cannot leave out Hakeem Adewumi who was also on a Fulbright. I adopted him as my son and he adopted me as his mother. Thanks, son, for all of our adventures especially the Mpumalanga trip, the flat tire, and the potholes!

I also wish to thank several people within and outside the historical profession for their support. First and foremost, my mother deserves all the recognition for instilling the value of education in me at a young age. I never knew that a daily ritual—coming home from school, putting on my play clothes, and doing my homework at the kitchen table—would lead to this path I continue to embark upon. Nwando Achebe, Iris Berger, Robert R. Edgar, Robert Trent Vinson, Cherif Keita, and Holly Y. McGee, I have benefited immensely from your scholarship and collegiality of which I admire. University of Nebraska-Lincoln colleagues have enriched my experience since joining the Department of History. My current chair James Le Sueur—our journey started long before UNL. We originally met at the National Archives of South Africa in Pretoria; little did I know then in 2001 that we would be colleagues five years later! Special thanks also goes to Margaret Jacobs for our many discussions over lunch! Kenneth J. Winkle, the first Chair of the Department of History at UNL I ever had—thanks for your willingness to offer sound and judicious advice during my nearly sixteen years at Nebraska. Amelia Montes, my deepest gratitude to you for your careful review of my Fulbright proposal. We rendered harsh critiques that helped us both to land Fulbright Awards the very same year!!! Our weekly conversations while you were carrying out your research in Serbia and I in South Africa were spiritually and intellectually beneficial. Breana Garretson, what a pleasure knowing you. You continue to be a bright spot at the University. Thanks for the laughter, girl; we have plenty of memorable moments! Looking forward to more from our 'favorite' place!

Angela B. Lee continues to support my endeavors even after almost five decades of friendship. Thank you. Linda Mitchell Fauntleroy and Perry Fauntleroy you already know how I feel about you both—you two are rays of sunshine. Laura Munoz—thanks for your advice throughout this process; you always let me know that you were just a text and a phone call away. Natasha M. Crawford—I owe you a big thanks for taking care of my space and my car while I was on that Fulbright!! Special thanks is also due to 'The 7 to 11 Crew'—my writing comrades Cynthia Willis-Esqueda and Kwakiutl L. Dreher whose tenacity with a nightly schedule save Saturdays was inspiring and productive. Mary S. Willis, one half of the Sisters Willis, thanks for the advice throughout the revision process and beyond. Heather Doxon thanks for all the laughs and advice over the years! Mostly, thanks for trusting me to be your professor during your educational career.

Karen Kassebaum there are so many things to say so I will sum them up here. Thanks for the laughs, debates, and conversations. Parks M. Coble—you are truly a great mentor, a colleague, and a friend. I appreciate your humor, tough love, and stories about the past. You made such an impression on my mother that she asks about you frequently. I will never forget the day I called home. My mother picked up the phone; I said 'hello, how are you?' Without missing a beat, my mother who was more interested in knowing this answer, "Did you do what you were supposed to do for Parks?", that she didn't even bother to ask me how I was doing! I knew then I was in trouble and that you both would keep me in line and focused on my important work. But you all had another member on the team, Karen who more than met the challenge.

Special thanks to the archivists and librarians at the University of the Witwatersrand, the National Archives of South Africa, the Institute of Commonwealth Studies, Hampton University Archives, Spelman College archives, and those at other repositories.

My undying gratitude also belongs to Nomvula Sikakane and Mpumelelo Bhengu for their industry. They enhanced the women's narrative through their translation skills.

Last, but certainly not least, I give thanks to the South African women whose courage, foresight, and legacy made *Social Justice at Apartheid's Dawn: African Women Intellectuals and the Quest to Save the Nation* a reality. In the words of South African multi-award winning poet, actress, presenter, and producer Lebogang Mashile, "the book's female subjects told their stories". Mashile explains why Africans needed to 'Tell [Their] Story':

After they've fed off of your memories
Erased dreams from your eyes
Broken the seams of sanity
And glued what's left together with lies,
After the choices and voices have left you alone
And silence grows solid
Adhering like flesh to your bones
They've always known your spirit's home
Lay in your gentle sway
To light and substance
But jaded mirrors and false prophets have a way
Of removing you from yourself
You who lives with seven names

You who walks with seven faces
None can eliminate your pain
Let it nourish you,
Sustain you
And claim you
Tell your story
Let it feed you
Heal you
And release you
Tell your story
Let it twist and remix your shattered heart
Tell your story
Until your past stops tearing your present apart
"Lebogang Mashile: Tell Your Story"

https://www.lyrikline.org/en/poems/tell-your-story-4123 date accessed 29 May 2021

Contents

Acronyms

Aborigines Rights Protection Society	ARPS
Adelaide Casely Hayford	ACH
Adelaide Charles Dube	ACD
African Democratic Party	ADP
African Methodist Episcopal	AME
African National Congress	ANC
African National Congress Women's League	ANCWL
African Political Organisation	APO
All-African Convention	AAC
Alexandra Bus Owners Association	ABOA
Alexandra Emergency Transport Committee	AETC
Alexandra Health Committee	AHC
Alexandra Standholders Protection and Vigilance Association	ASPVA
Alexandra Tenants Association	ATA
Alexandra Women's League	AWL
Alexandra Workers Union	AWU
American Board of Commissioners of Foreign Missions	ABCFM
American Council of Learned Societies	ACLS
American Committee of the Bantu Youth League	ACBYL
American Missionary Association	AMA
Bantu Purity League	BPL
Bantu Tenants Association	BTA
Bantu Women's League	BWL
Bantu World	BW
Bantu Youth League	BYL
Booker T. Washington	BTW

British East India Company	BEIC
Cecilia Lillian Tshabalala	CLT
Champaign County Ministerial Association	CCMA
Civil Rights Movement	CRM
Comparative Black History Program	CBHP
Communist Party of South Africa	CPSA
Congress of Racial Equality	CORE
Daughters of Africa	DOA
East London	EL
Elizabeth Rheinallt-Jones	ERJ
Executive Committee of the Comintern	ECCI
Federation of South African Women	FSAW
Food and Canning Workers Union	FCWU
Fourth International	FI
Free African Society	FAS
Garment Workers Union	GWU
Highlander Folk School	HFS
Historically Black Colleges and Universities	HBCU
Ilanga lase Natal	ILL
Industrial Commercial Workers Union	ICU
International Workers of the World	IWW
James Weldon Johnson	JWJ
James Yapi Tantsi	JYT
John Rosamond Johnson	JRJ
Joseph Ephraim Casely Hayford	JECH
Katie Makanya	KM
London Missionary Society	LMS
Madie Hall Xuma	MHX
Michigan State University	MSU
Natal Native Congress	NNC
National Association of Colored Women	NACW
National Association for the Advancement of Colored People	NAACP
National Council of African Women	NCAW
National Council of Negro Women	NCNW
Native Advisory Boards	NAB
Native Affairs Commission	NAC
Native Affairs Department	NAD
Native Economic Commission	NEC
Natives Representative Council	NRC
New African Movement	NAM
Orange Free State	OFS
Pan Africanist Congress	PAC

Pietermaritzburg	PMB
Phelps-Stokes Fund	PSF
Port Elizabeth	PE
Public Utility Corporation	PUTCO
Social Science Research Council	SSRC
South African Indian Congress	SAIC
South African Institute of Race Relations	SAIRR
South African Police	SAP
Stallard Commission	SC
Transvaal African National Congress	TANC
Transvaal	TRV
Umteteli waBantu	UWB
United Nations	UN
United Negro Improvement Association	UNIA
United States	US
University of Nebraska-Lincoln	UNL
University of the Toilers of the East	KUTV
Women's Brigade	WB
Women's Political Council	WPC
Women's Social and Political Union	WSPU
World Council of Churches	WCC
Young Women's Christian Association	YWCA

List of Figures

List of Tables

CHAPTER 1

Introduction: The Journey, the Genealogy, and the Historiography

In the thick of the South Africa's segregation era in the 1930s, Natal native Cecilia Lillian Tshabalala submitted two editorials, "Our Great Women Where Are They?" and "Arise, O Ye Daughters!" to a prominent print medium. These calls to arms captured the immense political moment at which she, and her other female contemporary leaders, stood during the insurgency of African nationalism. This pioneer, who even wrote her own hymnals which became a mainstay of her organization, the Daughters of Africa (DOA), possessed an interesting résumé. She was a member of Alexandra's Women's Brigade, the Alexandra Women's League, and the African Democratic Party (ADP), and was a reappearing columnist in the *Bantu World*, one of the country's most popular Black presses. Whites mostly owned and edited African newspapers, however as Les Switzer points out, the mediums had a large Black readership. In the case of the *Bantu World*, it operated as a training ground for fledgling African journalists and those who gained skills in printing, typing, clerking, and advertising among other knowledge that the paper offered.[1] For Tshabalala, and other African women, the *Bantu World* provided a platform for them to proselytize on a larger scale.

Social Justice at Apartheid's Dawn is their intellectual coming-out party. This much-needed work addresses how this important female cadre devised different strategies to wade through South Africa's segregationist waters. From 1910 to 1948, they established political organizations, wrote

D. Y. Curry, *Social Justice at Apartheid's Dawn*, African Histories and Modernities, https://doi.org/10.1007/978-3-030-85404-1_1

editorials, composed hymnals, traveled, created poems, established schools, and lectured throughout the country. By undergoing these activities, African women contributed to existing theories on race and nation and expounded on them. They also played prominent roles in interrogating South Africa's historical past and shaping its contemporary present. In a study that brings their ideas to the fore, and to highlight their greatest bequeath, a blueprint to save the nation, these activist intellectuals coalesced around the transnational currents of race, gender, and nation to challenge segregation, to define notions on nationhood, to marry street politics with written and oral commentaries, to interpret South African society's racial politics, and lastly, to speak to other men and women across Africa.

Of all the book's featured women, Tshabalala interrogated the term nation as a social, racial, and geographical construct openly at a meeting in Pimville, Soweto. Tshabalala did more than theorize as this narrative shows; she created the DOA to serve as a model for the democratic, egalitarian nation that she envisioned using a syncretic blend of traditional African cultural practices and western ideologies. Tshabalala wanted her community, the baby race, she describes in 'Arise, O Ye Daughters!' to emulate other nations or, as Tshabalala put it, walk like them.[2]

Newspapers often provided snapshots of Tshabalala, the organizational founder, and member of several Alexandran organizations; however, these images added to my growing confusion. Printed mediums capture her seemingly innocuous in dresses draped by pearls while the autobiography of former Johannesburg Senator and lawyer describes her as militant who donned a tight-fitting black beret when she commanded the church women, and beer brewers that comprised the Women's Brigade (WB).[3] Both images seared an indelible impression in my mind. "Who would I meet during my research—the classy, refined, and respectable woman, '...[the] boisterous [person] who could at any moment burst into laughter or a loud command'[4] or the descendant of Zulu royalty of the Mshengu clan?" Like the contestants on the popular multi-year run game show, *Truth or Consequences*, I wanted the real Tshabalala to stand up.

Tshabalala grew up near Durban; spent eighteen years in the United States; attended Hampton University; established two women's organizations; pursued studies at the New Britain Normal School in New Haven, Connecticut; and wrote editorials in the *Bantu World*. Despite having this information several facts eluded me. I did not know her parents' names nor her birth and death dates. That changed when I consulted the section of 'At Home and Field' in the *Southern Workman*, a monthly journal that Hampton's founder and former president, Union army officer General Samuel Armstrong had established in 1872, which read: "one girl [who] (Tshabalala) comes to Hampton direct from Zululand (Kleinfontein) is a former student of Fanny Mabuda who ... [teaches] at the Umzumbe Mission Station [in] South Africa. She came to Hampton with four other African males in 1912."[5]

In 1868, following the American Civil War, Black and White leaders of the American Missionary Association (AMA) established the fabled institution situated on a former plantation called 'Little Scotland' not far from Fort Monroe. Hampton University had as its motto, "The Standard of Excellence, An Education for Life".[6] Prominent graduates included the likes of Booker T. Washington (BTW), who learned the nuts and bolts of industrial education from its principal proponent Armstrong. When my brother Ricky, my cousin Bobby, and I walked from the parking lot to the Huntington Building where Hampton houses its African Art Gallery and its Archives, I kept wondering if Tshabalala had taken this same path over a hundred years ago. My thoughts were soon interrupted when we entered the Huntington Building and marveled at the art. Amid the beautiful displays of artifacts, an ominous sign read, "no photos allowed." Our trepidation heightened so much that we aborted our thoughts. I viewed the room for the next fifteen minutes and then bid Ricky and Bobby farewell to approach the reading room.

Before, I could even plug in my laptop, take out a pencil, or glance at my notes, one of the archivists, Mrs. Poston, greeted me. She explained the rules that governed Hampton University's archives: no pens, no digitizing, no drinking, and no eating. The most important commandment dictated that I, other patrons, upheld was the wearing of latex gloves. I followed these rules to the letter, and with a pencil, I made my requests. Mrs. Poston reviewed the forms and then proceeded to ask me several questions about Tshabalala. I provided different iterations of her last name (Tshabalala, Chabalala, Shabalala) to assist with the research.

As quickly as Mrs. Poston had arrived to provide me the guides to conduct research, she left to wade through the selected documents. Mrs. Poston disappeared for a few minutes, but to be honest, her absence felt like an eternity. I thought that I was finally going to put to bed unanswered questions about Tshabalala's personal details. I was so wrong on that note, and here is why! Mrs. Poston came back to the reading room with a file. Professional as ever she said, "Dr. Curry can you tell me more about this lady?" I said, "Yes, she was born in Kleinfontein, and she came to Hampton University in 1912. She said, I think this is your lady, but she didn't graduate from here." "I said oh. May I review the file?" "No, we can't give out information on former students. You will need to get a notarized letter from a family member." "Seriously!! I thought how am I going to do that for someone who was a student over a century ago, and who has been dead presumably since the early sixties? I went home empty-handed, and crestfallen."

It took a year before I licked my wounds and mustered up the courage to submit another request. At the time, I was beginning my tenure as a US Fulbright Scholar to South Africa (2017–2018)—a year-long research award to address how African women were intellectuals who contributed to political thought before apartheid—this was the question that had its genesis going back to my grad school days at MSU. Twelve days after my original correspondence on 19 September 2017, another one of Hampton University's archivists, Ms. Andreese Scott wrote back and addressed some of my lingering queries. Eight years after the discovery of gold on the Witwatersrand, Daniel and Chandlia Tshabalala welcomed their daughter Lillian to the royal Mshengu clan from which she descended on 28 September 1888. They had no idea at the time that one of their children would travel the world and the African continent. Tshabalala registered as a junior, having already completed some of her necessary credits at Umzumbe College. Her tenure in Hampton, however, was short-lived. Tshabalala left the Tidewater area in her traveling wake just twelve months after matriculation (1912–1913).

Lures of a New England institution and the opportunities to conduct social work in African American churches in the same area possibly led to her abrupt departure. This part of her intellectual journey is annotated with photographs and articles that appear in the *Bantu World*, *Ilanga laseNatal*, *The Brooklyn News*, and *The New Amsterdam*, among other African and American newspapers. They typically immortalized the DOA founder with headshots; however, one visual provides a full body pose of Tshabalala in a knee-length dress with accoutrements of a smile, decorative jewelry, and a handbag. Another documents the leader with four African-American youth, two of whom are draped by her arms.

Tshabalala's quest for social justice gathered further momentum when she was seized by the desire to visit the Chautauqua's religious conferences in upstate New York. Like the Mary Church Terrell-led National Association of Colored Women (NACW), which Tshabalala modeled the Daughters of Africa (DOA) on their prominent example, these attendants also influenced her political outlook and appreciation for cross-cultural alignment.[7] The conference represented what the Daughters became a mix between a democracy and a tradition built upon African oral, and religious culture.

My visits to the National Archives of South Africa (NASA) in Pretoria unearthed several under-mined historical documents that chronicle the DOA's development and its evolution. This was not an easy task. Sometimes research on the DOA was filed under unsuspecting headings or obvious ones. 'Native Organizations' contain files like different pieces of correspondence; the DOA's push to become a charitable political body; its communication with South Africa's Native Commissioner and other officials or they possess flyers that announced the organization's celebration of 'Red Letter Day' or the hymns the leaders and membership sang or even wrote.[8]

My first scholarly introduction to Tshabalala's bus boycott activism came from political scientist Alfred Stadler and social activist Baruch Hirson. Stadler's rendition of the 'long walks' offers a brief homage to Alexandra's militant female citizenry and its stance during the forties with this observation, "the contribution of women can be scarcely exaggerated."[9] While Stadler does little to insert how women impacted each historic event, Hirson goes a little further with his work, *Yours for the Union*. Hirson heavily depicts male activism, but he also engages with women's involvement as this statement attests: "the activities of The Daughters of Africa, ... and the Alexandra Women's Brigade, formed at the time when Lilian Tshabalala [headed the body] are known."[10]

Discussions of how Africans intellectualized segregation, the economy, and transport are often left out of the well-cited Xuma Papers. When placed against the male voices of ANC President Alfred B. Xuma's memorandum, and novelist Modikwe Dikobe's short story, 'We Shall Walk', the Alexandra Women's League's treatise demonstrates even further how personal papers, secondary literature, and popular culture marry.[11] Even with Xuma's presence of mind to archive the memorandums, he falls short in this significant way. Like Hirson, Xuma fails to identify female participants linked to Tshabalala, the AWL, or the Women's Brigade. Parallels could have been drawn out had these groups been place side by side. This study also challenges the secondary literature of Alfred Stadler (1979), Philip Bonner and Noor Nieftagodien (2008), Eddie Roux (1943), and John Nauright (1990) by treating women and men as intellectual actors, and contributors to broader discussions on the economy, and segregation.[12]

Mina Tembeka Soga also had worldly experience as an attendant at the international Madras conference held in India, and its post-session events in the United States and Europe. By the time, she had arrived on American soil in 1939, Tshabalala and, another contemporary, Sibusisiwe Violet Makanya had already returned to South Africa. During the year of the Chicago World Exhibition (1893), parents Philip Rulumente and Novili Aylmer Soga welcomed their daughter Mina into the world. She was one of fourteen children born onto them. Queenstown embraced this Christian family and offered it a highly, active commercial center at their reach. The closely knit community lay straddled in the middle of the Eastern Cape and situated on a large farming district. Soga's father served the community as an *induna* (Chief), a position that not only gave him authority but also welcomed income. His local role grew even larger when he, a firm believer in education, turned part of the family home into a makeshift school that welcomed youth from around the village.

Soga anxiously welcomed the opportunity to participate and learn, however, there was a problem, tradition dictated that the eldest child attain education.[13] This standard practice rankled Soga, who as a younger member of the family had to wait her turn. She made sure that opportunity arrived sooner rather than later. Bouts of crying, protestations, and displays of envy eventually earned her the much-coveted slate which she used to write the alphabet.[14] Soga went on to receive formal education at the Scottish Presbyterian Mission before stepping foot on the world stage at the age of forty-five. The South African lived well into her nineties, just missing the century mark by four years (1893–1989).

A conspicuous trail of presidential addresses, organizational minutes, and letters yet to be fully mined illuminate Soga's political life. Sometimes, these scholarly gems appeared in files dedicated to the National Council of African Women, a body she helmed from 1939 to 1954, under 'Urban Affairs' among other subheadings or featured in the personal archives of prominent men. John David Rheinallt-Jones (JDRJ), the former South African Institute of Race Relations (SAIRR) Director, bequeathed his papers to the University of the Witwatersrand (Wits). Of the many documents is Soga's interpretation of the 'Patterns of Segregation', and the letters she exchanged with the Rheinallt-Jones litter his file.

Despite the plethora of archival materials that feature the NCAW, Soga's identity as a president is absent. Nombonisa Gasa makes several observations about this organization in her anthology *Women in South African History* with these remarks: male leaders feared that the body's alliance with the National Council of Women (NCW) led to their increasing independence and radicalization; the body lessened its political impact by not connecting the dots between the anti-pass struggles and other issues; and lastly, people viewed the group as an ineffectual body, however there is no inclusion of the organizational paper trail that Soga left behind that this book illuminates. Another concern is the need to extricate Soga from the organization to concentrate on the person and her ideologies. Seabury's biography, the article by Nico Botha, 'Towards the Engendering of Missiology', and Keona Mashala's dissertation provides different accounts of the NCAW's long-term leader. Seabury traces her childhood, her travels to the international Madras Conference, and the post-meeting lectures that she conducted in the United States, Canada, and Europe, all of which took place from 1938 to 1939. Seabury also includes discussion on Soga's reintegration in South Africa. Botha concentrates on her religious and ideological philosophies; however, several items are missing from her chronicles. Mashala's dissertation fills in some important gaps as she delves deeply into Soga's performance as NCAW President during the apartheid era.[15]

Based on the extant corpus of organizational documents, personal correspondence, presidential addresses, Seabury's book, Botha's article, and newspaper coverage, the NCAW and Soga deserve their own respective monographs on par with Shireen Hassim's *The ANC's Women's League*, and Robert R. Edgar's account of *Josie Mpama/Palmer in Get Up and Get Moving* which both appear as part of the Ohio University Short Histories Series. Such studies propose to bear different interpretations of an African woman at the center of a burgeoning movement of African nationalism, at the nascent stages of Black internationalism, and at the crossroads of feminism, womanism, and pan-humanism at the same time. For example, in order for Soga to transcend and intersect these boundaries, she sought the financial help, and intellectual manpower of leading White figures at a time when the government worked hard to disenfranchise and exploit her people.

I first 'met' Nhlumba Bertha Mkhize at the Campbell Collections (formerly Killie Campbell); an archive housed in a Dutch-style home formerly called Muckleneuk situated along Gladys Mazibuko Road in Durban. This white-covered house set within a deep brown wooden trim stood on a sloping hill. Flora and fauna bounded the house, which was once owned by Sir Marshall Campbell, a sugar planter and Natal politician. Although both of Campbell's children, William and Killie Campbell, converted their childhood home into a repository, it was the latter that maintained a vast archive that accounts for many of the site's holdings (photographs, indigenous newspapers, oral histories, manuscripts, and other sources) which she bequeathed upon her death in 1965. While the archives housed a digitized database, and published guides, the card catalog, an analog of the past became my very best friend.

I found so many notable entries on African women. Some of them I had never heard of before like Albertina Mnguni. She was at one time the Secretary of the Daughters of Africa. As a member of the South African Institute of Race Relations (SAIRR), Mnguni conducted piecework which entailed finding extremely impoverished individuals, particularly those suckling, to distribute milk to fortify their emaciated bodies. During her tenure as the DOA's secretary, Mnguni carried out similar projects, which along with the body's goal for the African nation to know one another was one of the reasons she joined Tshabalala's organization. Mnguni traveled the rural areas with Nhlumba Bertha Mkhize, the subject of another discovery I found on a typed note card.

Campbell Collections housed taped and transcribed versions (in English, and isiZulu) of interviews that historians Heather Hughes, Julia C. Wells, and D. Manson conducted independently with Mkhize in 1979. The two-part interview is layered with nuances of Mkhize's complexity as a person. She was an educator, a tailor, a leader, an activist, and a Ba'hi adherent. Discussion of Mkhize's political affiliations, her protest activities, the American Board missionaries, the activities of other leaders, and her family history takes center stage in this chronicle of her life. Mkhize controls the riveting narrative from the very beginning. A photograph of the family home ignites the discussion that she carried out with two westerners in her physical and metaphorical home.

Book chapters and articles offer short allusions to this important freedom fighter who used her positions as a DOA leader and an ICU member to effect change. Peter Limb's study on the African National Congress' early years provides some insight into this under-researched historical figure, but it fails to tease out the multiple philosophies that she espoused. Mkhize was a complex figure who understood the significance of forming female comradeships across the color line when she pursued labor politics with Ray Alexander or Helen Joseph, another struggle stalwart, whom she worked with collaboratively. The Africanism that Mkhize advocated for possibly represented the same principles that the ANC endorsed with the Freedom Charter that its leadership and members composed in Kliptown,

Soweto, in 1955. Of its many lines, this quote garners the most attention for the organization's daring led to the immortalization of this widely disseminated line of the Freedom Charter, "South Africa belonged to all who live in it, black and white." Mkhize held its principles close to her vest and in her arsenal when she partnered with some of the most prominent females of her politically, exciting time. Before Mkhize set the political stage on fire, this last born of two boys and two girls experienced tragedy at the tender age of four when her father passed away in 1893.

Devastated by her husband's passing, Mkhize's mother uprooted the entire family and moved them to her birthplace, Inanda. Inanda already enjoyed fame. American missionaries Daniel and Lucy Lindley had established the all-female Inanda Seminary going back to 1856. Having this highly reputed educational institution within her children's orbit allayed the concerned mother's fears since Mkhize's father's birthplace offered little in terms of education. Tshabalala and Makanya were both alums of this fabled institution. Other storied landmarks existed in Inanda, in fact, it was the home of Mahatma Gandhi and Dr. John L. Dube, two prominent leaders who had established the Ohlange Institute and the Phoenix Settlement approximately fifteen miles inland from Durban respectively in 1901 and 1904. The children's education was so superior that Mkhize ended up teaching math, geography, and grammar. Her teaching came with a strongly held belief that Africans needed to learn English, the world's lingua franca so that they could attain jobs in Durban's thriving metropolis.

As much as teaching represented Mkhize's passion, the love to educate was not enough to pay mounting bills so she turned to tailoring. Not long after that, Mkhize began to understand the theories that governed labor politics, especially after the Latvian emigrant Ray Alexander turned her on to the mysteries of its nuts-and-bolts. Mkhize garnered another ideological home when she turned to the Ba'hi faith. She found its adherents' belief in the equality of all races, creeds, and sexes alluring and representative of what she professed as an activist, as a leader, and as a woman. Mkhize stayed true to her ideological form in that her politics represented and manifested the philosophies that she and the Ba'hi religion professed. Anti-pass demonstrations illustrated the ways in which Mkhize employed pavement politics to attain the Ba'hi faith's guiding principles. Not carrying the passes represented a push for equality in terms of Africans' ability to enter the urban areas without government-mandated documentation.

Tshabalala joined Mkhize by having her own ideological turn from being a diehard liberal to an ardent leftist when she joined Hyman Basner, Paul Mosaka, Gaur Radebe, and others in forming the interracial African Democratic Party (ADP) as an alternative and parallel organization to the ANC, in 1945. Josie Mpama/Palmer's dogma also shifted during the last decades of her life when she switched sociopolitical streams from the red-Marxist ideals of Communism to the monotheistic religion of Christianity. Sibusisiwe Violet Makanya went from indirectly endorsing the Adaptation Model in her capacity as the Purity League's secretary to doing a major theoretical shift following her travels throughout Natal, the Transvaal, and in the United States.

In the final analysis, all these different and disparate roads led to my life-long mission to unearth the experiences of African women by juxtaposing their achievements, and notions, alongside African men, and each other. *Social Justice at Apartheid's Dawn* demonstrates that African history does not end exclusively on the continent or within its various nations, instead it is a composite of holistic experiences woven together from different parts of the world where they made, chronicled, or defied history. Healy-Clancy, Iris Berger, Thozama April, Athambile Masola, and others have begun addressing the lingering underlying problem of African women's muted or partially recognized intellectual thoughts. My quest to save the nation began with Tshabalala, whom as the root of my genealogical tree led me to other unsung or well-known African women. Maybe this book secures as the modicum of equity and justice that my subjects fought for and in some ways failed to attain or partially experienced during the segregation era. These defiant women privileged religion, gender, and pan-humanism in their bequeathed instructions to the next generation. They lay out the problem and discuss resolutions that mirror some of the artistry of contemporary South African poets, and musicians. The theme of Mashile's opening poem, 'Tell Your Story,' is also contained in the work of not only Adelaide Charles Dube, but also Nonsitzi Mgqwetho (Chap. 4). The former reminds her readers of the glorious African past and the symbolic, functional, and generational tie to the land while the latter expounds upon the discussion by focusing on the embodiment of a multi-composited African identity interrupted by outside colonial forces. They all yearn for a past and a future that is sentimental, representational, and afro-futuristic at the same time. Ordained by ancestral powers, these women all took an oath to serve as griots—the people's historical custodians. Mashile makes this point even clearer in 'You and I,' in which she writes, 'We are the keepers of dreams/We mould them into light beams/ And weave them into life's seams.'[16]

Outline of the Book

Research landed me on three continents—Africa, North America, and Europe—to facilitate this outline created from consultations at the National Archives of South Africa in Pretoria, South Africa, the Historical Papers, Cullen Library, University of the Witwatersrand, Johannesburg, South Africa, Campbell Collections in Durban, South Africa, Spelman College, Hampton University, Howard University, and other historically black colleges and universities (HBCUs) and the London Institute of Commonwealth Studies. Chapter 1, 'The Journey, the Genealogy, and the Historiography', plots out the intellectual map that I blazed by following the scholarly bread crumbs that Tshabalala left behind. It also discusses where she and her contemporaries sit within the literature. For example, studies on South Africa's segregation period typically feature race by devoting considerable attention to its structural implications. This approach has its academic value as it allows for the construction and deconstruction of the activities of policymakers, prominent White activists, and proponents of segregation, however, it negates the subaltern, and their politics and the juxtapositions they form between men and women and the latter themselves.

Chapter 2, 'The Roots of Segregation, Apartheid's Menacing Predecessor', discusses the origins and the evolution of the policy of segregation in South Africa. The chapter opens with the observations of South Africans (African, White, and Asian) and African Americans regarding separate residential enclaves, race-designated institutions, and the intimacy of the policy within modes of travel, hospitals, elevators, and other areas where race mattered and where the government amplified difference.

Chapter 3, 'Wake Up! The Nation Must Be Saved', scrutinizes the different reasons why African women concluded that the African nation faced impending threats from the government and its policies due to its increasing debilitation. During this racially charged period, and the insurgent rise of African nationalism, African women from various social, economic, and political backgrounds answered my queries in many compelling ways. Some like Daughters of Africa (DOA) founder Cecilia Lillian Tshabalala wrote editorials in the widely read African newspaper, *Bantu World*, at the zenith of her power in the 1930s and 1940s.

Chapter 4, 'Activist Intellectuals and the Quest to Save the Nation', explores how Africans employed narratives, poems, musical compositions, and editorials to address the physiological and physical impact of segregation. This chapter offers several possibilities for saving the nation even at a time when governmental policies, intra-racial tensions, and political disabilities threatened liberation. Tshabalala sparked this line of inquiry and led me to archives across the world and within the African continent.

Chapter 5, 'Travel Narratives of Globetrotting African Women', charts African women's overseas experiences to illuminate how they computed and dissected issues of race, gender, and nationality on foreign soil. Their narratives provide early case studies of Black women's internationalism both within and outside the African continent.

Chapter 6, 'Oral and Written Resolutions to Segregation and Transport', examines the different ideological strands of gender, nationalism, socialism, and community development that political bodies in Alexandra and Johannesburg represented. Each intellectual thread addresses social justice at apartheid's dawn dissimilarly in terms of their respective approaches, but also alike in their extrapolation of larger societal issues through the lens of transport and the problems borne by segregation. Tshabalala's narrative is threaded yet again around the mostly middle-class DOA that she led.

Chapter 7, 'Daughters of Africa and the Politics of Religious and Literary Sampling', chronicles Tshabalala's quest to save the nation through social healing, proselytization, and musical compositions which she used to teach, to galvanize the nation, and to defy the segregationist that refutes Hirson's assertion that theory and Tshabalala never mixed.

Chapter 8, 'The National Council of African Women and the Minutes of a Moral Agenda', examines the multi-faceted approach to challenging segregation not only at its core, but also its base through programs that tackled low-income families, and health disparities, and that promoted racial collaboration.

Chapter 9, 'Blueprints for the Nation They Left Behind', intersperses theory, and the women's words to chart the distinct ways that these activist intellectuals left behind a roadmap to save the nation. These militants did this by crawling under the blanket where the twin evils of race and segregation cuddled together to threaten African people at apartheid's foreboding dawn.

Notes

1. Les Switzer, and Donna Switzer, *The Black Press in South Africa and Lesotho: A Descriptive Bibliographic Guide to African, Coloured and Indian newspapers, newsletters, and magazines 1836–1976* (Boston: G. K. Hall & Company, 1979), 7–8.
2. Arise, O Ye Daughters!, *Bantu World*, June 27, 1936, 9.
3. Miriam Basner, *Am I an African? The Political Memoirs of H. M. Basner* (Johannesburg: University of Witwatersrand Press, 1993), 153.
4. Ibid.
5. "Miss Tshabalala," *Southern Workman*, 1912, Hampton University Archives, Hampton, Virginia.
6. History-Hampton University, https://home.hamptonu.edu/about/history/, date accessed 31 October 2020.
7. Meghan Healy-Clancy "The Daughters of Africa and Transatlantic Racial Kinship: Cecilia Lilian Tshabalala and the Women's Club Movement, 1912–1943," *Amerikastudien/American Studies* 59, 4 (2014): 481–500.
8. Katie Mooney, Amadodakazi – Baradi Ba Africa (Daughters of Africa) Overview and Archival Records at NARSSA, unpublished paper, 2–3.
9. Alfred Stadler, "A Long Way to Walk: Bus Boycotts in Alexandra, 1940–1945, in Philip Bonner" (ed.), *Working Papers in Southern African Studies* (Johannesburg: Ravan Press, 1981), 232–233.
10. Baruch Hirson, *Yours for the Community: Class and Community Struggles in South Africa, 1930–1947* (Johannesburg: University of Witwatersrand, 1989), 139.
11. Meghan Healy-Clancy, "The Self, the Nation, and the World: The Scale of Clubwomen's Work," 24th Biennial conference of the Southern African Historical Society, University of Botswana, Gaborone 27–9 (June 2013), 19.
12. See Alfred Stadler, "A Long Way to Walk: Bus Boycotts in Alexandra, 1940–1945," in *Working Papers in Southern African Studies*, 228–257. Johannesburg: Ravan Press, 1981, Philip Bonner and Noor Nieftagodien, *AleXandra: A History* (Johannesburg: Witwatersrand University Press, 2008), Eddie Roux, *Time Longer Than Rope: A History of the Black Man's Struggle for Freedom in South Africa*, 2nd Edition (Madison: University of Wisconsin, 1967).
13. Ruth Isabel Seabury, *Daughter of Africa* (Boston: Pilgrim Press, 1945), 1–20.
14. Ibid.

15. Ruth Isabel Seabury, *Daughter of Africa* (Boston: Pilgrim Press, 1945), Nico Botha, 'Towards the Engendering of Missiology:' The Life-narrative of Mina Tembeka Soga, *Missionalia*, 31, 1 (2003): 11–16 and Keona Mashala, Were Women Hidden from South Africa's Political History?: A Life History of Mina Thembeka Soga, MA thesis, University of Johannesburg, Johannesburg, South Africa, 2020.
16. 'You and I,' A Poem by Lebogang Mashile, https://www.poemhunter.com/poem/you-and-i-227/, date accessed 26 March 2022. Mashile's predecessors understood why the nation needed saving. Mgqwetho offered one problem in this rebuilding mission. She attacked her people for their complicity in stabbing their very own continent, and for sowing divisions among themselves. DOA leader Angeline Khumalo Dube cautioned her organizational flock to pay attention to the political horizon. Social Justice at Apartheid's Dawn explains how these thinkers, educators, organizational founders, poets, composers, and editorialists became woke to use today's parlance. They, through their different blueprints of poems, presidential addresses, newspaper columns, musical compositions, and pronouncements, describe their rising political consciousness and their escalating dread over the looming fate of South Africa's policy of segregation.

CHAPTER 2

The Roots of Segregation, Apartheid's Menacing Predecessor

Before future NCAW President Mina Tembeka Soga left the United States after a nation-wide tour full of speeches, dinners, network opportunities, and first-hand encounters with racial discrimination, she expressed this about her own nation and what going home meant for her.

> 'Ruthie,' [referring to her chronicler Dr. Ruth Isabel Seabury] she said suddenly, 'you keep praying for me. It's going to be very hard to crawl back under the blanket.' 'The blanket?' I said in astonishment. 'The blanket,' she replied firmly. "It is the symbol of Africa's past. To the white man it represents the old order and life in the kraal. To me it means the segregation in which I have always lived."[1]

During a widely attended Johannesburg conference, Soga crawled back under the blanket to render these observations. On a panel with SAIRR leader Dr. Oscar Wollheim, Soga in her official organizational capacity and as an African woman and as a public thinker opens her remarks with comments rendered by Jan Christian Smuts, the renowned South African statesman, politician, military, and war hero who served as prime minister from 1919 to 1924 and again from 1939 to 1948.

Smuts eschewed isolation, but also failed to endorse integration as an alternative to the unequal relations of power that segregation brokered. Instead, he continued his unwavering support of segregation, a policy

D. Y. Curry, *Social Justice at Apartheid's Dawn*, African Histories and Modernities, https://doi.org/10.1007/978-3-030-85404-1_2

built on the mastery, and overlordship of the country's White minority population.[2] Smuts' top-down approach met fierce and measured opposition from Soga and Wollheim who joined his fellow panelist by speaking about the social, economic, and geographical segregation that colored relations between the country's diverse populations. Wollheim covers several issues, but his discussion focuses principally on education and economics while Soga addresses segregation on a more intimate level through travel, in particular, the embarkation counters where Africans bought tickets at the racially designated windows.

Even when Africans and Whites served as part of the buying public, money failed to equalize them. Wollheim points out that Whites failed to see beyond their own adoption of colorism. Africans suffered even further when White counterparts did several things like break into the front of the lines on Africans' designated side or railway and bus attendants overlooked Africans to serve their European-descended patrons first. Wollheim states that in some towns:

> the black man must wait till all likely European passengers have been served and I go further and say till the server has overcome his dislike for serving Africans. While this battle wages within he "busies" himself over a piece of paper, or newspaper, or chats with a "pal" or anybody else who is around, determined not ever to glance at the anxious black face at the small third-class window. Then at the last possible moment, a frowning face with a rough voice asks, "what do you want?" Sometimes he walks back to the other fellow to ridicule the solemn face anxiously waiting to be served. Ultimately the ticket and change are flung back to him as much as "Don't bother me again."[3]

Africans had purchasing power, yet their roles as the buying public were lost on business owners, and their respective employees who often chose to continue social mores rather than oppose them.

United Nations (UN) Diplomat and Nobel Peace Prize recipient Dr. Ralph Bunche carries on this discussion from a different vantage point. His elocution centers on enclosed public space within elevators, movie houses, and clubs among other examples. From September 1936 and February 1937, Bunche's trip coincided with Robeson. Bunche chronicles his exploits in an itinerary that encompassed Johannesburg, Bloemfontein, Pretoria, Cape Town, and Thaba Nchu among other urban and rural South African communities that dotted South Africa's mountainous, deserted, savannah, and other topographically featured landscapes. One of his journal entries documents the role of technology in the maintenance of segregation in another example that captures the intimacy of this policy.

Bunche went to the Exploration Building situated along Fox Street across from Johannesburg's Stock Exchange to meet FOA Ballinger. Ballinger initially came to South Africa as an envoy sent by the British Independent Labour Party (BILP) to assist ICU Clements Kadalie as an advisor, but by the time he had arrived the organization already suffered from deep-seated, irreconcilable tensions. The newly emigrated Briton made his time in South Africa count. He became an author and interpreter of South Africa society with his work, *Race and Economics in South Africa* (1934). Ballinger and his wife Mary Ballinger fought tirelessly for equal rights, a goal they sought with the FOA. From the beginning of apartheid in 1948 to the Sharpeville Massacre in 1960, Ballinger served as member of the Senate who represented the Transvaal and the Orange Free State.[4] The day Bunche visited Ballinger, he initially took the African American on an elevator labeled for Whites but:

> When [Bunche] later came down with [his host], however, he brought [him] down in the non-European one, explaining that "Europeans often use it too." Later [Bunche] came back with Masole, [an African], and walked into the European elevator. The operator, a German Jew refugee—an old man with a Prussian moustache—glared, said nothing, but made motions toward the elevator on the other side. [Bunche] said that's all right, when Masole hesitated about stepping in, and the old guy took us up. Later, [Bunche] came back alone, and after another hesitation, he took me up, but was obviously flabbergasted. Electrically powered elevators typically ferried White riders while Africans, Coloureds, and Asians, the group the government derisively referred to as Non-European, accessed self-operating ones or they climbed, or descended flights of stairs (Fig. 2.1).[5]

Other instances of segregated conditions surfaced at the Empire Exhibition. The event originally began in London, but thereafter spread to Johannesburg where it appeared for the first time outside of the European city where it was inaugurated in 1936.

The public festivity, which celebrated the gold mining capital's Jubilee, ran from September 1936 to January 1937. Geographer Jennifer Robinson explains that this 'wonder city' or 'glorious new city within a city' reflected and shaped the social relations and spatial practices [of Johannesburg].[6] She further elaborates by explaining that "… the spaces of the exhibition provided opportunities for meeting and interaction, as well as for the imposition of various segregationist strategies and norms. These overlay

Fig. 2.1 Segregation signs. (https://theconversation.com/book-review-selling-apartheid-south-africas-global-propaganda-war-49380 date accessed 25 June 2021. This photo is symbolic of the racial segregation that existed within South Africa. As deemed by the government, the country was composed of Africans, Coloureds, and Asians of different ethnicities and origins whom the state labeled as non-Europeans to indicate their alleged inferiority in its socially constructed racial schema)

the wider practices of racialization which were already part of the conventions of the 'exhibitionary complex'. Staging difference, through the lenses of ethnography, science, and museology, drew on a series of tropes including evolutionary narratives, hierarchizing exhibits according to their relative assigned importance, often juxtaposing the old and the new, or the traditional and the modern and frequently consigning traditional and indigenous cultural practices to a timeless existence in the past."[7]

Carried out to commemorate Johannesburg's Jubilee celebration, the Empire Exhibition established parameters for admittance based on race. Coloureds and Asians initially had no limitations while Africans only attended on specified days. Once revenue began plummeting to deafening levels, things changed dramatically. Reluctant organizers began to admit Africans daily, including holidays. This privilege came with an important proviso that in the end upheld segregation's iron-clad tenets. Turnstiles remained to demarcate racial separation and to connote difference.[8] Johannesburg's nightlife mirrored the Empire Exhibition's practices. Australian émigré Jack Phillips owned a popular after-hours club that fell under three different names. Coloureds patronized the Ritz-Palais, Africans, the Inchcape Hall, and the elderly, the Majestic. An amassing number of incentives lured club-goers, who by their willingness to enjoy nightlife entered their own 'exclusive, private venue' indicated by the color-coded lighted globes that simultaneously summoned them.[9]

Near segregation's end, Maggie Resha, the wife of the highly decorated ANC leader Robert Resha, joined the staff at Pretoria Hospital, a year before the Nationalist Party took control over the South African government and instituted apartheid in 1947. Resha's tenure at this medical facility highlighted one frame of her adventurous and committed life in South Africa's liberation struggle. Some of her political awakening occurred in this racially segregated hospital where the institution's sterile walls incubated and festered the discrimination of the country's policy in microscopic form. She breaks down segregation's mechanization and even concedes her own surprise of the policy's functionality within a medical facility:

> The first thing that struck me was the segregation then in operation—nothing in my training had prepared me for this discovery. Although the hospital was under one central administration, it was divided into two sections: one for 'Europeans', another for 'non-Europeans', but with the added oddness, however, that all matrons as well as all doctors to the so-called 'non-European' section were white, and that the 'European' section was staffed exclusively by whites as well. Most trained nurses commuted to work at 7:00 am. Those who did not have homes in the townships were accommodated at the hospital. They paid a monthly rent. Four nurses usually shared one room. Although the place was kept clean, because there were cleaners, it was disgusting. It had no ceilings, no floorboards, no carpets, and it had horrible steel doors. We usually had our meals in the quarters reserved for pupil nurses, which was a stone's throw away from the hostel. Our food, which was different from that of the patients, was sufficient, but it was terribly unappetizing.[10]

Race and space reared their heads yet again in Resha's testimony. Four African nurses occupied one room they all rented. The filthy, improperly built hostel provided little if any privacy for its female occupants. That luxury failed to enter the minds of officials who considered the living standards appropriate for Africans whom they considered anything but human. Moreover, they viewed this option as doing them a favor since some African nurses failed to have homes within the many peripheral townships.

They already performed this practice for migrant African men who lived in rooms with as many as eleven other men on harden, concrete bunks.

Although the hospital contained separate racially designated areas only employed White staff gained permission to cross the imaginary color line. White nurses attended to the medical needs of African patients in their separate section, but this was not the case for African medical personnel who could only devote their expertise to infirmed Blacks. Officials continued to carry out demoralization to its basest level and to the nth degree through food. Meals created a hierarchical arrangement based on limited and unappetizing culinary selections. Even butcheries apportioned food by race. In his autobiography, *Kaffir Boy*, Mark Mathabane recalls how the family purchased cattle heads, entrails, hooves, bones, meat, and other entities not desired by Whites who had the option of receiving higher graded portions of succulent beef, and other meats.[11] The state even continued this unfair and unhealthy dietary practice on Robben Island where political prisoners like Asians received better food options, sugar with their tea, and long trousers whereas Africans wore short, cropped pants, and consumed mealie-based porridge.[12] Resha's account follows a chorus of assaults that the South African government leveled to catalyze the social death of Africans, but as the Alexandra squatters' movement conveys, segregation's appearance in South Africa consisted of nuanced configurations based on different analytics of power.

Instead of Alexandran residents accepting the squatters who moved to the township on orders of the Johannesburg City Council (JCC), dwellers opposed their presence, ostracized them, issued threats, and complained. Their discontent reached the public's discerning eye. One member of the Alexandra Health Committee was interviewed by a *Rand Daily Mail* correspondent. Angered over the JCC's decision to remove the Alexandran squatters from Orlando, an unidentified member complained that the body had "dumped them on the township's doorstep". A group of property owners also chimed when they urged the Alexandra Health Committee "to dump its filth where it dumps its filth".[13]

Tensions between these parties erupted over how the squatters arrived in Alexandra, over the struggle for basic amenities, over health and sanitation concerns, and over the squatters' occupation of the township's public squares. Each side drew a solid line in the political sand with the ideologies and the needs of subordinate (squatters) and the dominant (township residents) violently colliding. These opposing groups created a different form of sequestration than that mandated by the government. Instead of segregation between Black and White, it existed between Alexandra's permanent dwellers and its temporary ones. Alexandra properly occupied a subordinate liminal space within Johannesburg's urban areas.[14] But with the squatters taking up dwelling, it became the dominant community that Baduza and his entourage, Abner Kunene (magistrate), Lucas Bokaba (treasurer), and Marks Rammitloa (secretary), dared to defy.

Baduza's creation of a 'territory within a territory' replete with geographical boundaries, stationed sentries, and identification cards separated Alexandra proper inhabitants from the tenants (leasers of rooms owned by landlords), subtenants (leasers of rooms occupied by renters), rural migrants, and families that made up his squatting community. Philip Bonner and Noor Nieftagodien address the conflict among Alexandra's dwellers, but they conceal the geographical relationship that the subordinate dominator (Alexandra proper dwellers) and the land-deprived squatters had.[15] The main residential and temporary living areas mirrored each other spatially and because of this parallelism, they reveal how two spaces created a symbiotic geographical relationship. In Alexandra's 'Freehold' where Africans and Coloureds could own land within Johannesburg, squatters and residents replicated the relations of power by mimicking what the dominant White mainstream did within the larger society through the prism of semi-autonomy.[16]

South Africa's emigrant Indian community presented another iteration of segregation. Indians began arriving when the Dutch controlled Cape Town from 1652 to 1684. They initially came to the country to work as slaves on Cape Town's farms or in the Lodge, the site where Dutch East India Company (VOC) officials lived and carried out business. Other streams of Indian migrants came later in the eighteenth and nineteenth centuries to serve as indentured workers on Natal's sugar plantations or simply paid their way ('free' or passenger Indians) to visit South Africa. While immigration ended in 1914, the year of the First World War, the Indian population had reached 219,000 people by 1936.[17] Feeling the weight of their commercial and numerical threat, as many Indians owned businesses and competed with Whites, the government enacted the 1946 Asiatic Land Tenure and Indian Representation Act.[18]

Colloquially known as the 'Ghetto Act', this law designated areas within Natal for Indian occupation. Mirroring early policy initiatives, the 'Ghetto Act', like the Jewish ghettos that emerged in Europe under German leader Adolph Hitler, revealed several things about how the state constructed and deconstructed race in terms of its buffering of difference and its containment of sameness. An increasing number of scholars insert the word apartheid in place of ghetto to examine America's inner cities. In particular, Douglas S. Massey and Nancy Denton's analysis not only illustrates how segregated conditions gave rise to ghettos, but also shows how this policy fostered a culture of poverty.[19] Alexandra's categorization of ghetto initially resided with race, but that changed to incorporate other identity markers such as permanent and temporary, resident and squatter, dominant and subordinate, perforated space, and political exclave, and legal and illegal.[20] These terms all defined the African and Coloured community that not only occupied the township, but that also conveys a different configuration of power among the subaltern. Another Asian community, the numerically smaller Chinese started coming to the country around the seventeenth century. Many were prisoners and exiles sent from Batavia and then onward to the Cape Colony where eventually they migrated to South Africa's larger metropoles. In a gripping and telling memoir, Journalist Ufrieda Ho's work *Paper Sons and Daughters* provides one explanation of what it was like growing up Chinese in South Africa. She writes:

> My parents, like so many other Chinese parents, thought that the Chinese school was the best educational option for their children. The small school did not have the money for extras like swimming pools, a proper science laboratory or student exchange programmes. But the extras did not matter too much because Chinese parents placed a higher premium on retraining some of our 'Chineseness' at a school that would promote Chinese culture, language and with it the ethic and discipline that they expected from us… . Even without the extras, I was well aware that our school was not the worst. Only a few kilometres away from our school in Bramley were schools in Alexandra township that did not even have the luxury of enough school desks for everyone or glass in some of their windows… . Stigma and silence came to be so much a part of our lives because we existed outside of the law essentially. So we got these dual identities—one we owned up to in our inner circle of community and family and another that we claimed or managed when we were in the company of 'others.'[21]

Like the other examples given, the segregation that emerged in Alexandra, in other parts of Johannesburg and in Durban, and the rest of the country represented a microcosm of the state's larger policy whose roots trace back to several centuries.

The Roots of Segregation

In 1652, ninety Calvinist settlers under the leadership of Jan Van Riebeeck established the Netherland's first permanent settlement at the tip of the African continent.[22] Amiable relations between the Europeans and the indigenous Khoisan that had been brokered when the Dutch used the Cape as a refreshment station gradually weakened. Problems arose when the Dutch who married their Bantu-speaking neighbors began to enslave them. Tensions continued to mount as the threat of cattle theft and other unauthorized transactions escalated. In a move to shore up his community's protection, and to avoid reduction in their food supply, Van Riebeeck used topography to mark out the colonists' territory, and to entrench the country's first sign of de facto segregation. In later years, land and space further divided Whites from Blacks.

Authorities began breaking up 'enormous and unwieldy' reserves to form 'smaller ones' as early as the nineteenth century.[23] When an amassing number of African refugees from different ethnicities encroached upon the British stronghold in Natal, Diplomatic Agent for Native Tribes Sir Theophilus Shepstone responded in a much more systematic way than Van Riebeeck had done with the almond hedge bush that he planted as a geographical marker, and as a barrier. Shepstone quelled the reverberation of this demographic alarm with a definitive blow. The Briton turned Cape Colony émigré, set aside ten reserves for African occupation outside of Durban in his capacity. Shepstone's administrative style served as a proto example of Indirect Rule that another Britain Lord Frederick Lugard devised and imposed in Northern Nigeria where he retained the traditional African political structures of the Islamic emirs. From that group an African intermediary reported both to the European colonial official and to his people, when the United Kingdom officially raised the Union Jack in 1901. Historian David Welsh writes that the Shepstonian Reserve System was "the precursor of the later policy of 'segregation', which in turn [was] called 'apartheid,' 'separate development,' and 'separate freedoms in South Africa'".[24] Instituted in 1848, Shepstone's Reserve System tainted South African fabric for years to come. The 1894 Glen Grey Act is just one example of many that bear its imprint.

With individual land ownership privileged and communal sharing of land under increasing siege, the indigenous Xhosa population had no other alternative but to concede or at least appear to acquiescence. The Glen Grey Act went on to force able-bodied African men into a cash-wage economy. Africans had to earn European currency to pay for the hut and poll taxes that the dominating power imposed on all homes in villages and on African males sixteen and older. While all of this was going on, White-owned land companies ran by absentee landlords controlled a whopping fifth of South Africa's total land area.[25] Heartening as this situation was, the government sped up its plan, and began to insert land into politics yet again when officials formed the Zulu Land Delimitation and the Lagden Commissions respectively in 1902 and 1903. Commission members conducted surveys to issue proposals on how best to demarcate, and to delimit the voluminous land that Africans of various ethnicities fought to stave off an encroaching Afrikaner, and British threat.[26]

The ball kept rolling with three measures that politically changed the segregationist game and earned the state a well-engineered checkmate. The first of this unholy trinity, the 1913 Natives Land Act, demographically erupted, and racially divided Africans, who, like those who lived in Shepstone's Durban, resided on the outskirts of the major cities. South Africa's numerically overwhelming African population (93%) ended up consigned to 7% of the most unfertile and remote land. Officials engaged in geographical engineering in another way under the Stallard Commission (SC).[27] This body emerged following consistent and steady protests that Africans launched over hazardous labor conditions and extremely low wages in the early 1920s. The Stallard Commission supported racial segregation as long as White privileges remained solidly intact. Members reached a riveting, landmark decision in a statement that became branded as the Stallard Doctrine:

> The masterless native in urban areas is a source of danger and a cause of degradation of both black and white. For that reason, [Natives—men, women, and children—should only be permitted within the municipal areas only if their presence is demanded by the wants of white people.][28]

Not long after the formation of the Stallard Commission, officials passed the 1923 Natives Urban Areas Act. That law dramatically altered conditions of residency when it laid down the foundations for urban segregation and created townships. The term township assumed different names depending on language. Townships are referred to as *lokasies* in Afrikaans and *izilokishi* in the Nguni languages of isiZulu and isiXhosa. These segregated enclaves sprung up all over the metropolitan (Johannesburg, Cape Town, Durban, and Pretoria) and rural (Sharpeville,

Zolani, Bultfontein, and Kuruman) peripheries. Alexandra differed in that township a multitude of ethnicities intermingled freely whereas in the sprawling township of Soweto, and its more than twenty locations, the state implemented divide and rule by separating Africans from each other, for instance, the AmaXhosa lived in one part, and the AmaZulu in another, and so on. Before the forced removals in Alexandra, and the destruction of Sophiatown, Coloureds lived among Africans until the government created their own enclaves in Diepkloof and Eldorado Park among other places. Native Advisory Boards (NAB) heavily monitored them.

Eslanda 'Essie' Robeson's visit to South Africa coincided with Prime Minister Hertzog's administration and Bunche's stay. The anthropologist and Civil Rights activist journaled constantly about her experiences. Her annotated notes provide a bird's eye view of segregated South Africa near the throes of its twilight in the mid-thirties. Of the many topics she featured, townships drew substantial attention. They represented the geographically manufactured racial hot spots that the government created to separate the country's various populations. During an excursion to Cape Town, Robeson unleashed copious details on Langa Township.

Langa earned its name from a dissident of the Hlubi clan named Langalibalele who earned the British's extreme ire when he refused to register the guns of his people. Langalibalele fled to neighboring Basutoland (present-day Lesotho) instead of honoring their request.[29] The British eventually caught, arrested, and sentenced this rainmaker to Robben Island, the former leper colony, bird sanctuary, and naval base that turned into an Alcatraz-like island for political prisoners. Langa Location became a residential reality when its namesake began living on 'Uitvlugt', a nearby farm that adjoins Pinelands after developing in different stages from 1898 to 1927. Langa, which means 'sun' in isiXhosa, emerged when the state moved African people from Ndabeni Location near Maitland to its present location on the Cape Flats, a sandy stretch of land situated on the outskirts of touristy Cape Town.[30] Forced removals occurred because of the state's quest to satisfy the 1923 Natives Urban Areas Act which called for compulsory segregation and the regulation of Africans into the cities. Everyone in Langa was:

> … African, except of course the superintendent, the hospital matron, and the Sister-Africans from every corner of the Union who have found work, or hope to find work, in Cape Town and environs. It is a little village in itself: bungalows set out in rows, forming rough streets; three small schools, and

> a tiny hospital. There is no paving of any kind, in fact the last two miles of road from Cape Town are of unpaved dirt and deeply rutted. The bungalows are of one, two, three, and four rooms. There are no baths, no toilets, no water of any kind in the houses. There are community taps and toilets at the back, serving large groups of houses. If tenants fall behind in their rent, they are evicted and put in prison.[31]

Robeson continues her observations by making comparisons between South Africa and the United States. She writes:

> As a Negro citizen of "democratic" America, segregated colored sections of cities are not unknown to me. But these still further segregated locations are something different altogether. The Colored people in South Africa, as in America, are allowed to live in certain sections within the city proper, or in the immediate outskirts of the segregated Colored sections, or in any part of the cities whatsoever, they must live in the locations and in the reserves, which are special areas for them, entirely removed from the cities) as in the case of Langa seven miles outside Capetown … .[32]

The traveling mother, wife, and activist harps on about conditions within Langa, however she misses several opportunities to make comparisons that went beyond Black and White, but that included South Africa's Indian, Khoisan, and Coloured communities, and America's indigenous peoples some of whom occupied the Pine Ridge Reservation or the Navajo Nation respectively in Utah, New Mexico, and Arizona among other locations. South African Rilda Matta, who appears in Chap. 5, captures the indigenous populations she witnessed in New York and the surrounding areas during her visit to America to initially study cosmetology.[33] Despite these criticisms, Robeson skillfully situates South Africa and the United States within a conversation that incorporates the environment. She teases out how the physical landscape serves as an extension of the dominant power's oppression.

The South African government clearly used containment, a political tool later used during the Cold War between the Soviet Union and the United States, to prevent the Domino Effect with countries falling to the power and spell of Communism. South Africa's application also involved geopolitics, however, on a much smaller scale, and specifically to 'contain' and to 'keep out' racial sameness and difference. Occurring long before the Truman Doctrine, which typically defines the start of the Cold War in 1947, the South African landscape emblazoned the separation of African,

Coloured, and Asian communities. Several goals were sought through the promulgation of legislative measures that promoted and codified segregation. Governmental officials wanted each race group to develop along its own cultural lines. They also wanted to preserve the 'purity' of Whites and to prohibit miscegenation through all social costs and legislative measures.

Issues of permeability and legibility emerge through these examples. Micro-contained communities multiplied as newer and even more modern townships sprung up all over the country. Problems, however, did emerge. Sometimes the nation's statistically smaller White community felt imprisoned by the same legislative measures put in place to monitor or regulate African mobility, to enforce racial segregation, to extract cheap labor, and to manipulate identity politics. Africans, Coloureds, and Asians sometimes passed as another race so that they could move socially up the hierarchical ladder. Seeing the flexibility that other race groups had, Hertzog did everything he could to save 'his' nation, the two White minority populations whose power he sought to consolidate.

Hertzog's Bills

Hertzog had begun the idea of an equal 'White nation' going back to his 'Two Streams' speech some twenty-four years before in 1912. He sought to capitalize on the spoils of the Treaty of Vereeniging which brought two deadly enemies, the British and the Afrikaners (Boers, Dutch descendants), together when they united around the lingering 'Native Question'. These bitter opponents decided to withhold the political and civil rights of Africans despite the fact that they participated on both sides during the turbulent war which saw the death toll mount, the abuse of Afrikaner, and African women and children skyrocket in the concentration camps, and a series of scorched earth campaigns that devastated crops, and future agricultural production. In 1909, the state passed the South Africa Act. This measure laid down the parameters for a union between the British colonies and the two Afrikaner Republics. It also instituted a set of draft laws which had as its goal to disenfranchise Africans at a more horrific and accelerating level.[34]

When the dueling White populations formed a Union in 1910, the move served only to "[u]nite… the White races and was against Blacks; for the color bar clause struck the death-knell of Native confidence in what used to be called British fair play".[35] South Africa's Coloured and African populations never forgot how both sides (the British and the Afrikaners) demanded and used their labor, combatant, and reconnaissance skills, and swelling numbers during those horrific wars. During a CPSA meeting held in the twenties, Potchefstroom native T. W. Thibedi reminded his captive audience of this glaring oversight when he posed this question, "Was your property returned to you after the war? No! You were poor people when the war was over, and you are being kept poor [now]?" European descendants reneged on deals that saw them draw out the 'Native Question'.[36] A rapidly growing African population lured to Johannesburg, Kimberley, and other cities for the promise of monthly and weekly pay in the mines, and the mechanized assembly lines failed to settle things.[37] Instead concern among Whites rose, forcing Hertzog to hunker down on the vision contained in his rabble-rousing 'Two Streams Policy' speech. During his fifteen-year tenure which spanned from 1924 to 1939, the method to Hertzog's political madness reared its discriminatory head when two important, but extremely controversial bills sailed through Parliament near the end of his controversial and earth-shattering administration.

Hertzog felt the sting of a large-scale settlement of first-generation immigrants—women who moved to the towns independently and men who left home to pursue the financial lures of the city—took place in the 1930s and 1940s. The Second World War and the Great Depression further heightened the movement of people, unemployment reached staggering numbers, and poverty decimated the rural areas and forced many African women to migrate to the cities where they ended up as domestic laborers. They came in droves from poorly industrialized rural areas where poverty not only wreaked havoc, but also forced them to leave and to seek greener pastures. African women who ended up working as domestics in White suburban homes sent remittances to fill up empty bellies at home.[38]

African men also left their families and sent money home. Many had already begun their migrant lives with the discovery of diamonds and gold on the banks of the Orange River and on a Transvaal farm in 1867 and 1886, respectively. Need for labor, and the push for African men to strike it rich while the mineral iron was hot, led to them living in poorly outfitted hostels during the tenure of their contract which could be six or more months at a time. Their sweeping and increasing migration in the early twenties had an adverse impact on the decimating problem of poor Whites many of whom had Cornish, Afrikaner, and Lithuanian heritages. Approximately 63,000–92,000 African people "... overflowed out of the backyards, the passages, the verandahs, outhouses and lavatories for which they were paying ridiculous rents. [T]hey spilled onto the veld, [and] into … [places]," such as Benoni, Alberton, Soweto, and Alexandra and set up cities of tents.[39] Makeshift shanties caused problems of regulation for the state, which was already concerned over the increasing influx of Africans into the urban areas. A quandary developed in their midst.

Officials were torn between maximizing African labor in the mines and industries for profit and taking care of financially strapped Whites who desperately tried to eke out a living for themselves in an ever-expanding economy that appeared to lock them out from the country's precipitous growth. In 1922, they took matters into their own laboring hands. Angered by the mine owners' decisions, White workers launched a rebellion that consumed the Rand. Fully armed workers took Jeppe, Benoni, Brakpan, and Johannesburg hostage until the country's top leader Smuts put an end to their rising dissent with a battery of military muscle. Troops, tanks, bomber aircraft, and artillery finally quelled the rebellion, but not the incessant fear of the alleged 'Black peril' (*Swart Gevaar*).[40] As much as this movement called for the unity of Whites with slogans like "Workers of the world unite, and fight for a White South Africa", racist undertones loomed, and crept into the politic of the revolt.[41] While Whites had the power to unionize or protests like they did on the Rand, the government prohibited Africans from doing the same as pained by the Industrial Conciliation Act (ICA). This discrepancy in policy failed to turn the tide for Africans; if anything, Hertzog sped up measures to institute an even more comprehensive segregation policy, but he faced recalcitrant opposition from various sides.[42]

One of his critics was none other than the fiery and blunt 'Aunt Josie (Mpama/Palmer)' who wailed against African, Coloured, White, and Asian women for not opposing these laws in large, commanding numbers. An entry in the *South African Worker* (*Umsebenzi*), a prominent CPSA newspaper that reported on issues of labor, and class, illustrates her deep disappointment in her female compatriots:

> We, women, should come on to the field as strugglers for only with our help can our men fight successfully against this new bill. Only by joint struggle can we compel Grobler and Co. to withdraw this new slave law.[43]

In another move to appeal to the prime minister, D. D. T. Jabavu met with Hertzog, and other government officials in Cape Town, the same year of the AAC's inauguration in Bloemfontein and the return of Rilda Matta after spending three years in America (Chap. 4) in 1935. Jabavu helped to establish the AAC before Hertzog's bills moved from the Parliament floor to the political landscape. Further opposition came from the Non-European Convention (NEC) which also met in Kimberley during the same year. The NEC hosted a diverse array of participants from all over Southern Africa. Representation came from the ANC, APO, South African Indian Congress (SAIC), the Native Voters Association (NVA), the Bantu Union, and religious and welfare societies.[44] Hertzog worked in concert to promote White unity while further eroding the rights of Africans. This caused great alarm:

> the creation of a unified 'white nation' under the rubric of 'South Africanism' was the mirror image of the subordination and exclusion of Africans from civil society. Indeed, the success of each was conditional, to at least some extent, on the fulfilment of the other.[45]

Hertzog's Bills were only part of an insidious problem that was enveloping South Africa. Nazism and Fascism were also spectacularly on the rise. Hertzog's support of Adolf Hitler and Benito Mussolini concerned the CPSA even more so when the Grey shirts and other like-minded gangs combed the streets and attacked Communists.[46] Another issue pertained to the Second World War which represented an important harbinger and a barometer of the country's surging pulse, and of vociferous African dissatisfaction that was reaching a thunderous crescendo. When the world's demand for gold, platinum, uranium, and steel reached a premium high, South Africa easily met this global demand even when the country's labor supply initially waned until other sources emerged. A growing body of women began to commute to the war factories, and other fight time industries, and an additional 650,000 African immigrants landed on the Rand to assume many of the cheaply paid jobs needed to fuel the increasing demand for rapidly mechanized outputs.[47]

Mushrooming numbers spelled trouble for the South African government. A V-Day message printed by the CPSA's Central Committee encapsulates the sentiment of the dramatic historic moment. Mass demonstrations on South Africa's rebellious and boisterous streets during autumn when the beauty of the purple-blossoming jacarandas adorned the trees set the mineral-rich Witwatersrand on blazing fire. As president of the ANC Transvaal branch Constantine (CS) Ramahanoe, the husband of Daughters of Africa leader Violet Ramahanoe, spoke about these events occurring in May 1945 with a cautionary tale:

> While we celebrate the defeat of the Nazi-Fascist military power and the eradication of the festering sore of that infectious and poisonous Nazi ideology, let us not forget that the battle for the home front has still to be won; that we still have Fascists in our midst, and that in South Africa racial oppression is still the order of the day; that the noble ideals for which many gallant sons of South Africa made the supreme sacrifice—Freedom, Peace, Progress and Security—have not been realised. Our heroes will have sacrificed in vain if the lofty and righteous aims for which the war has been fought are not fulfilled. They have done their duty, and it is now for us to complete the job that they began.[48]

The world stage reached South Africa yet again when Ramahanoe dispatched an urgent cable to the country's former war hero Smuts. He was attending the World Security Conference (WSC) in San Francisco, California, where delegates from over fifty nations had gathered. Attendants sought to create a body that would maintain global security. Increasing steam for this type of world-wide organization swelled following the alliance of Germany, Italy, and Japan (Axis Powers) against Britain, France, Russia, China, and the United States (Allied Powers) during the Second World War. During their tenure in San Francisco, Smuts, and his colleagues put the finishing touches on the United Nations (UN) Charter which carried this important Preamble: "We the people of the United Nations determined to save succeeding generations from the scourge of war."[49] Ramahanoe brought the plight of the world to Smuts' doorstep when he made a strong plea for him, and other dignitaries in attendance:

> ... to accept the principle of equal rights for all men and women everywhere. Colonial mentality herrenvolk practices menace to world security, prosperity, and peace especially in a country where millions [are] barred from the franchise, freedom of movement, skilled employment because of their race and colour. Will you raise on our behalf the proposal to outlaw race and colour discrimination anywhere in the world's a Fascist practice? We believe such an understanding to be a basic foundation for lasting world peace.[50]

Smuts failed to help matters. Not only did he contribute to the draft of the UN's preamble, and its charter, his position stood in stark contradiction to the policies he promulgated and supported on the South African home front where despite engaging in liberal paternalism granted extensive concessions to a voting White electorate. He wantonly violated Article 1, Number 3 which reads in abbreviated form, "... promoting and encouraging respect for human rights and for fundamental freedoms for all without distinction as to race, sex, language, or religion".[51] Thus, Smuts had the opportunity to make a difference within his home country instead, he continued his unflinching support for segregation and its mutations under the larger, governmental umbrella from which it originated.

All this spelled disaster for South Africa's majority population. They began registering their grievances with an incipient rise of bus boycotts, squatting campaigns, pass protests, worker strikes, and intellectual pronouncements that consumed and inundated South Africa's segregation era and affirmed Jabavu's contention that this bubbling dissent was just the tip of an emerging political iceberg. Africans "[seethed] like molten volcanic lava in the breasts of these inarticulate people" whose tools they used to their advantage.[52] The nation faced increasing danger, and people like Soga, Tshabalala, and other activist intellectuals on deck sought to redress their grievances in militant form and in fiery verse.

Notes

1. Ruth Isabel Seabury, *Daughter of Africa*, 129.
2. Mina Tembeka Soga, Patterns of Segregation, South African Institute of Race Relations, Head Office Memoranda (1948) File 1, Historical Papers, Cullen Library, University of the Witwatersrand, Aa12.15.7, 12/48.
3. Dr. Oscar Wollheim, South African Institute of Race Relations, Head Office Memoranda (1948) File 1, Historical Papers, Cullen Library, University of the Witwatersrand, Aa12.15.7, 12/48.
4. William George Ballinger, https://www.sahistory.org.za/people/william-george-ballinger, date accessed 13 May 2021.
5. Robert R. Edgar, *An African American in South Africa*, 159–160, and this photo shows differentiation in technology. The right side shows a mechanized way to ascend the stairs while the left side shows the converse. https://theconversation.com/book-review-selling-apartheid-south-africas-global-propaganda-war-49380, date accessed 18 May 2021.
6. Jennifer Robinson, Johannesburg's 1936 Empire Exhibition: Interaction, Segregation and Modernity in a South African City, *Journal of Southern African Studies*, 29, 3 (September 2003): 761.
7. Ibid., 761–762.
8. Robert R. Edgar, *An African American in South Africa*, 175, and Jennifer Robinson, Johannesburg's 1936 Empire Exhibition: Interaction, Segregation and Modernity in a South African City, *Journal of Southern African Studies*, 29, 3 (September 2003): 759–789.

9. Robert R. Edgar, *An African American in South Africa*, 180.
10. Maggie Resha, *Mangoana O Tsoara Thipa Ka Bohaleng, My Life in the Struggle* (Johannesburg: Congress of South African Writers, 1991), 30.
11. Mark Mathabane, *Kaffir Boy: The Story of a Black Youth's Coming of Age in Apartheid South Africa* (New York: Free Press, 1986), 62.
12. See Fran Lisa Buntman, *Robben Island and Prisoner Resistance to Apartheid* (Cambridge: Cambridge University Press, 2003).
13. "5,000 Squatters Erect Shelters in Alexandra: Health Committee Condemns Action of Council," Rand Daily Mail, January 8, 1947, 25, and Dawne Y. Curry, 'Their World Was a Ghetto': Space, power, and identity in Alexandra, South Africa's squatters' movement, 1946–1947 in Wendy Z. Goldman and Joe W. Trotter (eds.) *The Ghetto in Global History: 1500 to the Present* (New York: Routledge, 2018), 278–279. Of Baduza's lieutenants, most information exists on Rammitloa, who after being a petty hawker, trade unionist, and squatter leader turned to writing short stories and poems under the pseudonym Modikwe Dikobe. Alexandra's backdrop of protest—a consumer boycott in 1917, and a series of bus strikes in the 1940s—made the township highly attractive as a literary subject. Alexandra had other things going for it. The township maintained its own local authority, the Health Committee; ran a sewage disposal system; operated a skeleton staff clinic; and offered a bus line. Compared to Alexandra proper, the squatter encampment was a slum of epic proportions. But that did not stop Baduza from making Alexandra a significant spoke in the wheel of land dispossession and excessive poverty.
14. Dawne Y. Curry, 'Their World Was a Ghetto': Space, power, and identity in Alexandra, South Africa's squatters' movement, 1946–1947 in Wendy Z. Goldman and Joe W. Trotter (eds.) *The Ghetto in Global History: 1500 to the Present* (New York: Routledge, 2018), 278–279. See also Alfred W. Stadler, Birds in the Cornfield: Squatter Movements in Johannesburg, 1944–1947, *Journal of Southern African Studies*, 6, 1 (1979): 360–372.
15. Ibid., 279–282, and Philip Bonner and Noor Nieftagodien, *Alexandra: A History* (Johannesburg: Witwatersrand University Press (2008), 90–96.
16. Dawne Y. Curry, 'Their World Was a Ghetto', 290.
17. Ibid., 279–280.
18. Maynard Swanson, "The Asiatic Menace": Creating Segregation in Durban, 1870–1900, *The International Journal of African Historical Studies*, 16, 3 (1983): 403.
19. Dawne Y. Curry, 'Their World Was a Ghetto', 279–280. See Douglas S. Massey and Nancy A. Denton, *American Apartheid: Segregation and the Making of the Underclass* (Cambridge: Harvard University Press, 1998).
20. Dawne Y. Curry, 'Their World Was a Ghetto', 280.
21. Ufrieda Ho, Paper *Sons and Daughters: Growing Up Chinese in South Africa* (Athens: Ohio University, 2011), 104–105.

22. Marco Ramerini, English text revision by Dietrich Köster, The Dutch in South Africa, 1652–1795 and 1802–1806, https://www.colonialvoyage.com/dutch-south-africa/#:~:text=The%20Dutch%20settlement%20history%20in%20South%20Africa%20began,ships%20under%20the%20command%20of%20W.G.%20de%20Jong, date accessed 1 January 2021.
23. "Timeline of Land Dispossession and Segregation in South Africa 1900–1947," https://www.sahistory.org.za/article/timeline-land-dispossession-and-segregation-south-africa-1900-1947, date accessed 22 December 2020. The Glen Grey Act, https://www.britannica.com/biography/Cecil-Rhodes/Policies-as-prime-minister-of-Cape-Colony#ref137760, date accessed 11 November 2020.
24. David Welsh, *The Roots of Segregation: Native Policy in Natal* (1845–1910) (Cape Town: Oxford, 1971), 23–25.
25. Timeline of Land Dispossession and Segregation in South Africa 1900–1947," https://www.sahistory.org.za/article/timeline-land-dispossession-and-segregation-south-africa-1900-1947, date accessed 22 December 2020. The Glen Grey Act, https://www.britannica.com/biography/Cecil-Rhodes/Policies-as-prime-minister-of-Cape-Colony#ref137760, date accessed 11 November 2020.
26. Ibid.
27. Leepo Modise, The Natives Land Act of 1913 Engineered the Poverty of Black South Africans:

    a Historico-ecclesiastical Perspective, *Studia Historiae Ecclesiasticae*, 39, 2 (2013): 359–378.

    See Natives Land Act of 1913, http://psimg.jstor.org/fsi/img/pdf/i0/10.5555/al.sff.document.leg19130619.028.020.027_final.pdf, date accessed 8 April 2021, Natives Land Act of 1913, https://www.sahistory.org.za/article/natives-land-act-1913, 8 April 2021.
28. South African History Online, "State Policies and Social Protest 1924–1939," https://www.sahistory.org.za/article/state-policies-and-social-protest-1924-1939, date accessed 17 December 2017.
29. South African History Online, Langa Township, https://www.sahistory.org.za/place/langa-township-cape-town, date accessed 9 April 2021.
30. Ibid.
31. Eslanda Robeson, *African Journey* (New York: The John Day, 1945), 37–38.
32. Ibid.
33. Rilda Marta(sic), Trip to the United States Full of Excitement, *Bantu World*, June 29, 1935, 12.
34. Leonard Thompson, *History of South Africa* (New Haven: Yale University Press, 2000), 157.
35. Brandy S. Thomas, "Give the Women Their Due": Black Female Missionaries and The South African-American Nexus, 1920s-1930s,

B. A. Thesis, The Ohio State University, Columbus, Ohio, 2011, 15. Thomas writes that The Christian Express later renamed the South African Outlook reprinted the speech in its newspaper.

36. Robert R. Edgar, *Josie Mpama/Palmer*, 54.
37. Philip Bonner, "African Urbanisation on the Rand Between the 1930s and 1960s: its Social Character and Political Consequences," *Journal of Southern African Studies*, 21, 1 (March 1995): 116–118.
38. Ibid.
39. Dawne Y. Curry, 'Their World Was a Ghetto', 277 and Olive Schreiner, "The People Overflow: The Story of the Johannesburg Shanty Towns," pamphlet, 1947, 46.
40. Rand Rebellion 1922, https://www.sahistory.org.za/article/rand-rebellion-1922, 3 June 2021.
41. Ibid.
42. Saul Dubow, The Passage of Hertzog's Native Bills, Part One. In: Racial Segregation and the Origins of Apartheid in South Africa, 1919–36 (London: Palgrave Macmillan, 1989), 131. https://doi.org/10.1007/978-1-349-20041-2 6, date accessed 11 January 2020.
43. "African Women Must Be Organized We are Prepared to Move," *South African Worker*, June 26, 1937, Robert R. Edgar, *Get Up, Get Moving*, 178.
44. Timeline of the African National Congress, https://www.sahistory.org.za/article/african-national-congress-timeline-1930-1939#:~:text=A%20Non-European%20Convention%20is%20held%20in%20Kimberley%20to,and%20welfare%20societies%20from%20all%20over%20Southern%20Africa.
45. Saul Dubow, The Passage of Hertzog's Native Bills.
46. Brian Percy Bunting, *Moses Kotane, South African Revolutionary: A Political Biography* (London: Inkululeko Publications, 1975), 67.
47. World War II, Britannica, https://www.britannica.com/place/South-Africa/World-War-II Second World War and its impact, 1939–1948 https://www.sahistory.org.za/article/second-world-war-and-its-impact-1939-1948, date accessed 16 March 2021.
48. Brian Percy Bunting, *Moses Kotane*, 124.
49. Preamble UN, https://www.un.org/en/about-us/un-charter/preamble, date accessed 12 May 2021.
50. Brian Percy Bunting, *Moses Kotane*, 124.
51. Chapter 1: Purposes and Principles, https://www.un.org/en/sections/un-charter/chapter-i/index.html, date accessed 15 January 2021.
52. Brandy S. Thomas, "Give the Women Their Due," 16.

CHAPTER 3

Wake Up!: The Nation Must Be Saved

'Wake Up Daughters, it's Dawn!' exclaimed the illustrious Natal president of the Daughters of Africa (DOA) (*Amadodakazi aseAfrika*, *Baradi baAfrika*) Angeline Khumalo Dube (AKD) (Fig. 3.1) in an emphatic clarion call issued to the people she championed. Cecilia Lillian Tshabalala countered with her own insistence. The DOA founder (*umbumbi*) employed imagery and the Bible to drive home her point when she reminded her organizational flock that "just like the 10 virgins, may [they] all come with [their] lamps and bottles full of oil to light up Africa with [their] righteous work. … After telling them of their social responsibility, Tshabalala shouted as if speaking to the world at large when she said, Wake up daughters and be heard and get your house in order."[1] AKD's five commanding, but chilling, words and Tshabalala's biblical and metaphorical passage signaled the alarm for the ensuing trouble that lay on the political horizon.

These statements and commentaries were made in the mid-thirties when the world still reeled from the Great Depression, jazz, and African-infused sounds of Marabi and the rhythmic melodies of acapella captured South Africa's thriving entertainment scene, and Prime Ministers James Munnik Barry Hertzog and Jan Christian Smuts flexed their power hard and long enough to make segregation a national policy. For thirty-eight intense years (1910–1948), the ruling White minority of Afrikaners (Dutch descendants, the British, and other European nationalities) made it nearly impossible for the numerically advantaged and ethnically diverse

D. Y. Curry, *Social Justice at Apartheid's Dawn*, African Histories and Modernities, https://doi.org/10.1007/978-3-030-85404-1_3

Fig. 3.1 Angeline Khumalo Dube. (Ezama AmaDodakazi eNanda, *Bantu World*, 8 January 1937. Angeline Khumalo Dube served as the Daughters of Africa President in Natal for three consecutive times. In this capacity, she put important issues on the table for discussion and action. Among them were the youth, urban vices, and unity across ethnic lines.)

African population to attain any political and civil rights; if anything, they were on a serious mission to erode the limited freedoms that precariously existed.

Problems piled up so much that they could no longer be overlooked. Africans ended up living in the reserves, in locations, or in townships far away from places of employment instead of the same massive tracts of land that they had collectively worked on, harvested, and communed over multiple generations. Hut and poll taxes also ran Africans off their traditional lands straight into a cash-wage economy. No longer could they render payment with cowrie shells or other monetary representations, they had to pay the imposed taxes with European currencies. Their economic independence further plummeted when laws like the 1913 Natives Land Act outlawed squatting on White-owned farms and further pushed them into earning meagre wages.

When the capitalistic boom of mining Johannesburg's illuminating gold and Kimberley's sparkling diamonds hit these areas, a migratory African workforce catapulted the excavation of these shiny, elusive metals and stones into the stratosphere. Africans dug deep into the earth's cavernous belly while so-called Coloureds and Whites maintained skilled positions because of the color bar outlined in the 1911 Mines and Works Act. Even when the demand for African labor exceeded the levels of supply, officials went on a tear to control the influx of African men into the cities by regulating their movement with the carrying of identity documents called passes beginning in the nineteenth century around 1890. African women, by contrast, bobbed and ducked long enough to stave off this imposition up until the mid-twentieth century. The looming threat, however, continued to serve as a persistent, rallying call for resistance, and mobilization. Some African women turned to Reverend Dr. John L. and Nokutela Ndima Dube's indigenous newspaper *Ilanga laseNatal* to issue billboard-like amber alerts as one article entitled 'Women Were in Danger' (*Ingozi Besifazane*) read. Angeline Khumalo Dube's push for African women *ukuvuka* (to wake up) along with mounting legislative measures and African alienation from the land represented strong indications that the African nation needed saving at apartheid's dawn. "When the White people arrived, (Angeline Khumalo Dube shared) we got lost and said that all they do is what is right, and then that all we believed in was wrong. What our parents did to us, we no longer do to our children. This is the time whereby we roll up our sleeves and get ready to correct all those wrongs. Take a stand woman and save the nation!"[2]

Luckily for scholars, and successive generations, this book's African female subjects left behind a blueprint for future considerations, modifications, and emulations. They were activist intellectuals who "[were] not only attached to the ideological but also to the material conditions of society. Their writings emanated from the society that they belonged in. … [In fact,] they [wrote] truth to power irrespective of the consequences."[3] South Africa's segregation era created "a complex of signs and practices which [organized] social existence and social reproduction" through legislation, geography, race, and space.[4] In response to the country's prevailing mood, and Africans' declining political and economic power, African women produced a discourse that articulated and embodied a message, a view, or an attitude that [inscribed] their ideals of nation, race, and citizenship.[5] They bore witness to similar systems of oppression; to 'emancipated' Black people, to different cultures; and to their beings as Africans.

From this well of opportunities, ideas, and life experiences, African women intellectualized about their society's fate. They quested to save the nation first, by defining it.

What Is the Nation?

After eight years of being back in South Africa and living eighteen years in the United States, Tshabalala spoke before a distinguished body of teachers in Pimville, one of Soweto's sprawling townships. She delivered her speech at a time when subsistence struggles against higher bus fares, housing shortages, and food crises began to skyrocket in the forties. Events in Cape Town matched Johannesburg's accelerating rise of protests in support of 'bread and butter issues'. Elizabeth Mafeking, whom the apartheid regime considered a national threat, worked with others in her capacity as a labor activist to weaponize their consumer strikes and food programs. Pimville was witnessing its thirty-fifth year of existence when the buzz of activity heightened in different locales. Africans from the infectious hotspots of Newtown and the so-called Coolie Location began to inhabit Pimville, this 'underdeveloped farm' once called Klipspruit.[6]

Authorities forcibly removed dwellers in these racially mixed working-class neighborhoods when the Pneumonic Plague began debilitating the country in the early twentieth century. In 1905, a year after the pandemic, the Rand Plague Committee published a report that cited the details of 113 cases that explosively broke out.[7] "Authorities razed the Coolie Location [of Jeppestown, Fordsburg and Braamfontein] on April 8 by burning it to the ground. A total of '1,600 Asiatics, 142 Coloureds and 1,358 natives' were relocated to a camp 12 miles from the center of Johannesburg ... to a township that later become known as Soweto."[8] Pimville replaced the name Klipspruit when authorities honored "a man (Howard Pim) who had dedicated a large part of his life to the 'upliftment' of Africans in Johannesburg".[9] Six years after Pimville became Johannesburg's first municipal location, Tshabalala set foot on its storied doorsteps.

Tshabalala seized the immensity of the moment to explain the DOA's evolution. The discussion ended up becoming a confessional. In 1930, "upon [her] return from the United States, [she] found the African nation suffering like a piece of overcooked corn. [She] knew then [that she] had to do something to rebuild it."[10] Setting up a major women's political organization was one way that Tshabalala went about completing this objective, another was to theorize. Everywhere she went throughout the country, Tshabalala engaged in deep analytical conversations. Pimville was no different. Tshabalala gauged the pulse of her assembled listeners and asked this poignant question, "what is the nation?" She taunted her assembled listeners for a spell-binding moment. Suspense filled the air before she lessened its abeyance with a response textured in plain simple terms, but ensconced within human, social, and political geography. Tshabalala observed how Johannesburg's bustling streets, for example, create a mirage and an actuality at the same time:

> The nation ... represented people on the streets who wandered about destitute and some we can't recognize because they are so impoverished and malnourished by the squalor that enveloped them.[11]

Rather than single out one laboring category as trade unionist and activist Lilian Ngoyi would do years later by declaring that factory workers were the nation,[12] Tshabalala recognized and charged all strata with the community's collective and individual welfare. Africans participated in their own denigration when they overlooked (invisibility) the downtrodden or viewed (visibility) them through their prejudiced lens. Poverty cloaked people in darkness not only those beset by economic misfortunes, but also those interpreting their squalor. "If these people are not taken care of, Tshabalala contended, the nation will no longer exist [because] the nation must be built from the bottom up ... [in order to make] all segments of the black nation even stronger."[13] Tshabalala's explication of nation rested on the Southern African salvation, *Ubuntu*. Its phrase *ungu muntu ngabantu* "I am because you are" explains the significance of connections between and among all people, but also the social responsibility they all had with each other.

BYL founder Sibusisiwe Violet Makanya also prescribed to this philosophy; however, she uses the Zulu custom of *isivivane*, a heap of lucky stones, to express the same concept:

> The idea is when a person is known to be in need, those who pass along the road throw in their lot with the one in need by bringing in a stone and adding it to the pile as their token of help. They continue on their journey taking some of the good fortune with them.[14]

Makanya and Tshabalala both endorsed philosophies that captured the nation "as a soul, – a spiritual principle that [lay] in the past and in the present".[15] This differs from Benedict Anderson who argues in his seminal study that the nation was an imagined political community that bound people together.[16] Anderson concentrates on the nation's composition and identity markers like ethnicity, languages, and class while the aforementioned activist intellectuals focused on spirituality, and the politics of energy. Contemporary male-led African bodies provide another articulation.

Over a period of weeks from August to September 1903, Abner Sigudo, a non-exempted African (traditional religion believer), sparked an intense and rigorous debate with Stephen Nyongwana, the president of the Natal Native Congress (NNC), a body established by several mission-educated graduates and amakholwas (Christian converts) in the early twentieth century over the concept of nation. Formed to cultivate political awareness among Black people, the NNC represented all Africans, but particularly those accorded the status of exemption following their conversion to Christianity.[17] The NNC had a mouthpiece, *Ipepha loHlanga* (*Paper of the Nation*) which was the first non-missionary print medium ever launched in Pietermaritzburg (PMB) the same year of the NNC's establishment in 1901. *Ipepha loHlanga*'s four-page production incorporated the vast talent of its principal proprietors Chief Isaac Mkhize and James Majozi, and its first editor, Mark Radebe, a Lovedale graduate, owner of a drapery shop, a one-time Methodist minister, and activist in the Wesleyan church circles.[18] The organization's talented leadership and its institutional pedigree failed to stave off the stiff challenge that Sigudo issued to the NNC. He hurled his first caustic punch within the pages of *Ilanga laseNatal.* His question/statement, originally in isiZulu and translated to English here, read: "Am I not mistaken this body was formed by Africans who have renounced tradition for an alien culture?"[19]

Sigudo appears to act inquisitive, but the subtext reveals that he is really pouring fuel on a growing intellectual fire that gained increasing momentum twenty-one days later when Nyongwana, a confirmed *amakholwa* (Christian believer), issued a deft rebuttal. "My friend, I fear that if I don't expose the situation within the Congress or rather explain its purpose, he [meaning Sigudo] will destroy the organization since he has the audacity to use the whole page for his weak criticism."[20] Nyongwana's explication praised the NNC for bringing all Black people together, for representing them and for fighting for their civil and political rights regardless of their religious affiliation. The NNC did these things, because as Nyongwana maintains, the body represented the eyes, the ears, and the mouthpiece for the African people.[21] Nyongwana's analogy of the NNC as a complete person fell upon Sigudo's deaf ears. His criticism further accelerated with another scathing editorial. This time Sigudo outlines the nation, he defined. Sigudo's conception, which employs the biological construction of race, takes into consideration Colonial and Customary law in Natal. Sigudo considers issues of residency, and legality in this observation that refutes well-known colonial Natal Magistrate James Stuart, and historian Shula Marks who argue that religion had divided African people. He wrote:

> Okukuqala nga funa bonke abantu abamnyama lapa eNatal baqonde kahle abanga qonda ukuba siwu Hlanga myama izikumba zeli ziya fana zimnyama. Kodwa ke sa hlukenekabili ngomteto manga malungelo.
>
> first, people must understand that all blacks were the same whether they were exempted [Christian believers or traditionalists] or not. We all have the same skin. Our skin is black, but as Sigudo points out, race did not divide Natal's black people rather [they] were divided into because of [their] rights.[22]

Insisting that the division centered on rights, Sigudo offered a potential resolution to this lingering problem of identity politics within colonial Natal. He recommended that the NNC and John Khumalo's *Funamalungelo* (We Want Rights) join forces instead of having two separate bodies devoted to Black people.[23] Even with this suggestion Sigudo commits the same mistake as Nyongwana when he speaks for the people rather than privileging their voices. Tshabalala, however, offers an alternative discourse when she employs a bottom-up approach to nation-building. She used the widely read African newspaper, the *Bantu World* that Bertram Paver established in 1932, to weaponize its pages to create a national body politic.[24]

Bantu World catered to the upwardly mobile African and his aspirant counterpart. Reportage on sports, entertainment, news from around the world, region, continent, and community along with the discussion on beauty pageants, politics, obituaries, protests, featured subjects, and other topics that appeared in English or in indigenous languages. *Bantu World* garnered an extensive readership which amounted to at least 6000 subscribers at one time. Richard Victor Selope, an ardent ANC activist, and member of the Natives Representative Council (NRC), was the paper's editor for twenty years from 1932 to 1952. His tenure noted the incorporation of additional pages devoted exclusively to children, families, and women. Called 'Marching Forward', Reginald R. R. Dhlomo edited 'The Women's Supplement' where Tshabalala frequently appeared as a subject and as a columnist. Tshabalala mapped out her vision of a religious democracy and a pan-humanist model within the newspaper's black and white pages. The DOA captured what Tshabalala wanted to achieve nationally. Its branches spread throughout the Transvaal, Natal, and even in Southern Rhodesia (present-day Zimbabwe). Tshabalala's meteoric rise during the Negritude movement, a cultural explosion that promoted African aesthetics, and identity in the 1930s, occurred at a precipitous time when African women had been relegated to the peripheries in most male-led bodies like the ANC which refused to open its membership doors until the founding of the African National Congress Women's League (ANCWL) in 1943.[25] Up until that time the ANC had missed several important points. African women played prominent roles in building homes, raising future daughters and sons, preparing future leaders, and grasping the nation's success literally in their hands.[26] The ANC's rejection was a whopping slap in the face given African women's diverse roles and unique capabilities. In spite of waging a war to attain a modicum of equality, Tshabalala encouraged all African women to hold hands while they moved forward together to find resolutions not only to the 'Woman Question', but also to the peril and self-inflicted wounds that swarmed around them:

> We are in a very bad state as we always wait for things to be done for us at all times. The government is forcing women to carry passes. Observing the black nation over a period of months, revealed that it represented the filthiest of all Nations. In addition to all the orphans we have in our country, there are now 10,000 unemployed people in Natal only. How many people will the Government then feed? This nation is so used to being spoon-fed. There is no future nation.[27]

Safety, health, and well-being of those African women who dared to venture into the towns, those alluring dens of lust, and incestuous traps were of great concern to Angeline Khumalo Dube. During the same Vryheid speech, she expressed her disproval of the rapid rise in prostitution, alcoholism, and illicit brewing of *Skokiian* and other potent African concoctions. Wayward activity oftentimes carried over with employees in suburban homes when the mistresses failed to look after their maids. Like many African women engaged in employment in the prescribed, White-designated areas, domestics underwent routine bodily inspections to determine their bills of health. Searches gently or roughly occurred, in fact, the degree of intensity lay with the inspecting officers and the fallout from attempts to resist. Assaults immediately shot up, for example in the hotbed of Potchefstroom numbers swelled following the municipality's decision to regulate the occupants within homes. They had to pay for and obtain lodger's permits. African men faced their own challenges. Many turned to alcohol to numb the symbolic violence that they endured daily.

Protests surged. Black South Africans mounted grievances against the construction of beer halls within various African townships, the collection of poll taxes levied against males sixteen and older, the regulation of mobility, and soaring transport costs. Liquor raids also raised consternation. Situated in the former Transvaal's (present-day Gauteng Province) southern quadrant, Vereeniging, the future site of the 1960 Sharpeville Massacre, erupted when the police combed the streets to seize alcoholic contraband. The violence was so palpable that it fanned the flames of paranoia. During Ralph Bunche's visit with well-known White politician William George Ballinger, the African American learned of his host's fear that once the gold boom trickled and petered out, battles between Black and White would end spectacularly in bloodshed. Ballinger and the African populace had reasons to be alarmed. All over Johannesburg an open terror on Africans and their personhood occurred. Iconic Potchefstroom heroine Josie Mpama/Palmer documented the havoc with these thoughts:

> The past four weeks have been weeks of unrest in all locations … you are disturbed from your sound-sleep by police raiding for passes, poll tax, beer etc. Why have we got this attack on the locations? Simply because the location Councils have decided to open beer canteens, which is disapproved of by the masses. Our conclusion is this, that the police have decided to terrify you to such an extent that instead of boycotting the canteens, which is the general feeling, you will be so scared that the canteens will be opened without the least resistance. We will find that as far as our menfolk are concerned the present pass raids are to check up on the number of unemployed who are roaming about. We see that the Amendment to the Urban Areas Act is providing cheap labor for the farmers. This means that anybody who is not in the employ of a European will be forced to work as a for a farmer for whatever he wishes to pay.

Hysteria of Black men raping White women further exacerbated things. The notion of the 'Black peril' (*Swart Gevaar*) developed in Southern Rhodesia during colonialism and spilled over into South Africa where the perceived threat reached deafening and threatening levels. This assumed danger was so pervasive that the government cleared out several of Johannesburg's dilapidating slums for several reasons. The 1923 Natives Urban Areas Act legalized urban segregation and set in motion the downward spiral of African empowerment. Officials went from condoning slumyards to vilifying them.[28] Alexandra, for example, also faced increasing threats of expropriation amid the government's restructuring. Encircling White suburbs were growing at a rapid rate; however, the problem was that Alexandra and its square mile stood in the way of their expansionary plans. Others took issue with racially mixed Alexandra because:

> There is an ever-growing uncontrolled population of natives and coloured herded together, in the majority of cases under most unsanitary conditions, thus creating a breeding ground for disease and as it is only uncontrolled native township near the Main Reef Towns, it is the gathering place for the scum of the Reef, for the criminals of the Union, the brewers of skokiaan, the vendors of illicit liquor, and all that is bad in native life.[29]

According to the North Eastern Districts Protection League (NEDPL), "The time ha[d] ...arrived when abolition of the Township as a non-European residential area [wa]s the only possible solution to the problem from every point of view."[30] Attacks were not just germane to the urban metropoli, rural areas also experienced hard hits, financially and otherwise. Changes in land allocation altered traditional farming patterns and social interactions. A culture war around technology set the rural areas on an ideological collision course between modernity and habituation. Also, not helping matters was the rising and recurring migration of African men and women into the nation's urban centers. Rural areas suffered from the brain drains and reduced manpower that the cities inherited. Land alienation represented a problem of enormous proportions and long-lasting consequences. This subject reached the eyes of literary artists. In Chap. 4, Nontsizi Mgqwetho witnessed this demographic and ideological change that she pleaded with her people on several occasions to repatriate themselves politically and socially by returning to the confiscated and reallocated land they left behind. Another call to political arms came from Tshabalala.

The Call to Political Arms

While on a tour through townships near Colenso, a town named after Natal's first Bishop John Colenso, a fervent biblical scholar, and staunch supporter of the AmaZulu, Tshabalala observed the impact of the government's forced removal process first hand. Authorities sullied the fable lore of this town situated on the southern bank of the Tugela River, south of Ladysmith, and north of Estcourt in Natal, when they stormed houses and tossed out personal belongings. Priceless items endured damage, and the house occupants faced homelessness. Tshabalala told her audience that while Africans had their eyes wide open, they needed the government to make rules for the Black nation to adhere. But, while Tshabalala admonished Africans as a group, she turned her attention to African men. She argued, "If they continued to overlook women the nation will be in shambles today and for future generations to come."[31]

At a meeting held in Vryheid, the coal-mining and ranching town in northern KwaZulu-Natal where the body had one of its branches, Angeline Khumalo Dube echoed Tshabalala's sentiment. She spoke with a tone of lament and encouragement. The DOA's president in Natal pointed out where African women faltered, and how they could rectify the situation when she stated:

> we no longer look after our own kids, we just let them grow to fend for themselves just like animals in a jungle. Let us be more vigilant, keep an eye out for our children, and help them to be a greater force.[32]

Several DOA leaders and other speakers literally and figuratively put the adolescents on trial and found them guilty in the court of public opinion. Informal documentation of several examples of indiscretion and discourteous behavior littered the newspapers and peppered an array of speeches. The most egregious of all happened during a very rare visit to the Zulu Royal House. Tshabalala bore testimony to the children's deplorable behavior and blamed the parents for their lack of respect and decorum.[33] This extreme lapse in judgment imbued the nation with a conspicuous stain on its social fabric that other leaders frequently addressed. Visiting male ANC leader H. Selby Msimang, who throughout the years had lobbied for his people, expressed his concern over the nation's deteriorating state and its future inheritors with this commentary during one of the DOA's meetings:

> alcoholism amongst the youth, educated teachers and the children [was] somehow a punishment from God for being traitors and pretending to worship when we are empty shells. "Faith without action," he continued, "is dead." This is what the apostle says, and it is true.[34]

Because youth rampantly disrespected parents, and teachers alike, African women began to pray for straying, wayward, and discourteous youth. They eventually turned this serious matter over to the priests and called on the Lord for extra measure. The DOA addressed this issue in its litany. Excerpted here, and produced later in its entirety, the prayer offers a blessing and a wish, "May the sisterhood household of the African race devote its energies in working for its youth morally and spiritually, socially and otherwise."[35] The same church service that Pastor Sibiya spoke before and that DOA leader T. Dlamini chaired issued its support of the 'Ulusha Lisezwe' (the youth), while wearing their colorful uniforms. A Rhodesia DOA member Mrs. E. Mabeka spoke about the huge, powerful revival where attendants plead with God, and prayed for their children in different tongues but for one holistic nation.[36] The call for Africans to wear linen uniforms, to smear their bodies with ash, and to slaughter animals for sacrifice to appease the ancestors served as penance for the children's moral lack of judgment.[37] This suggestion raises key questions: firstly, was this ritual part of fending off a possible apocalypse on the scale of the Xhosa cattle-killing episode encouraged by Nongqawuse or the premonition of Eastern Cape prophet Nontetha Nkwenkwe of an impending flu epidemic; and secondly, was the performance needed to wash away the city's sins on the African community's insatiable flesh, respectively, in the late nineteenth and early twentieth centuries? Tshabalala, Sigudo, and others encouraged a different form of prophecy when they advocated for Christianity or traditional religions respectively. Both of these historical actors rightly concluded that Africans had strayed far away from any type of gospel. They did, however, differ on whether the God was Jesus or another entity.[38] This might provide one explanation for the unruly children that caused disruptions between themselves and the elders while Western influences may offer another possibility. Tshabalala turned to the Bible to arouse African women's consciousness amid a progressing siege at apartheid's dawn.[39] Gladys Casely Hayford's insightful poem 'Dawn' is appropriate to introduce and to analyze here because it further explains why the transition between night and day augured bad tidings.

GCH, who assumed the pseudonym Aquah Laluah, rose to prominence as a literary figure whose published works appeared in the *Atlantic Monthly* and the *Philadelphia Tribune* among other outlets. She was the daughter of prominent African activists. Her mother, Adelaide Casely Hayford, who hailed from Sierra Leone, was a cultural nationalist, a Pan-Africanist, a feminist, and a school founder. Casely Hayford spent most of her formative and adult years in Europe before returning to the West African nation for good (see Chap. 5). GCH/Laluah's father, Joseph Ephraim Casely Hayford, was widely recognized Gold Coast (present-day Ghana) barrister, a newspaper founder, a Pan-Africanist, and an author. Even while coming from this pedigree, GCH grew up a shy, sheltered soul who poured her heart out in her literary art. Her mother wrote this about the child she bore. "We had quite a lot in common, my darling one gial pickin and I. We were both premature, utterly negligible, puny little infants causing our parents a lot of anxiety and trouble. We were both Wednesday's children—full of woe. At an early age we both learned to suffer, but we possessed such iron constitutions that we survived.... Even when she was about to be stricken down with her short fatal illness in 1950, she wrote us a letter which was full of jokes and fun, radiating her joyous personality."[40] The poet's personality that her mother captures exemplifies the different interpretations that her poem 'Dawn' conjures up as a lyrical journey in melancholy (Africans) and in celebration (Whites). 'Dawn' explains in artistic beauty the paradoxes of this early morning ritual and why African women had a right to fear the impending future. Thus, her literary offering foretells of the exhilaration and anxiety ushered in by a new day:

Dawn for the rich, the artistic and the wise
Is beauty splashed on canvas of the skies,
The brushes being the clouds that float the blue,
Dipped in the breeze for paint and washed by dew.
But dawn to those who bathe the night in tears,
Squeeze sustenance from hard unyielding years,
Is full of strange imaginings and fears.
The dawn renews the terror of the day
Where harassing uncertainties hold sway;
And pain held in surcease through brief hours of rest
Roars up its head in its unceasing quest

To wear out body, brain and mind and soul
Till death is a resolve, and death a goal.
For those life holds no beauty, dawn no light,
For day is hopeless, dawn is struck with blight.[41]

On the eve of South Africa's seismic political shakeup, African women busied themselves by articulating ways to save the nation from the ensuing throes of a more virulent policy. They braced themselves just like GCH/AL who paints the landscape between the contrasts of anticipation and despair, but instead of relenting, South Africa's defiant corps formed part of a nascent women's movement that "nurtured an African nationalist body politic based on a new model for privacy and public life".[42] These activist intellectuals sought ameliorations within an existing system rather the overthrow of White minority rule. But, even with their good intentions and the myriad ways they tackled and grappled with governmental legislation nothing could stave off the growing tide of racism that gripped the South African climate when the policy of segregation passed its discriminatory baton to the system of apartheid.

Notes

1. C. L. Tshabalala, "Ayahlangana Amadodakazi aseAfrika eDannhauser," *Bantu World*, May 10, 1935, 13.
2. B. Mkhize, "Abona Ngehlo Elisha Amadodakazi ase Afrika (The Daughters Are Seeing Things Anew," *Ilanga laseNatal*, 3 March 1935, 18.
3. Ompha Tshikhudo Malima, Decoloniality and the Activist Intellectual, https://www.convivialthinking.org/index.php/2020/03/14/decoloniality-and-the-activist-intellectual/ date accessed 10 May 2021.
4. Anibal Quijano, "Coloniality and Modernity/Rationality". Cultural Studies, 21, 2-3 (2007): 168–178. doi:10.1080/09502380601164353, date accessed 21 May 2021.
5. Waskar Ari, *Earth Politics: Religion, Decolonization, and Bolivia's Indigenous Intellectuals* (Durham: Duke University Press, 2014), 9.
6. Pimville, Soweto, Johannesburg, https://www.sahistory.org.za/place/primville-soweto-johannesburg, date accessed 24 June 2021.
7. Charles M. Evans, Joseph R. Egan and Ian Hall, Pneumonic Plague in Johannesburg, South Africa, 1904, *Emerging Infectious Diseases*, 24, 1 (January 2018): 95-102.
8. Ibid.

9. Ibid., and Pimville, Soweto-Johannesburg, https://www.sahistory.org.za/place/primville-soweto-johannesburg, date accessed 24 June 2021.
10. Umbumbi wePimville, *Bantu World*, March 25, 1940, 8.
11. Lilian Tshabalala 'Miss L.C. (sic) Tshabalala's Career,' *Bantu World*, March 14, 1936, and Dawne Y. Curry, What is What We Call the Nation: Cecilia Lillian Tshabalala's Definition, Diagnosis, and Prognosis of the Nation in Segregated South Africa, *Safundi: Journal of South African and American Studies*, 19, 1 (2018): 55-76.
12. Cynthia Kros, "Urban African Women's Organisations, 1935-1956," *Africa Perspective* 3 (1980): 42.
13. Umbumbi wePimville.
14. Umehani Khan, A Critical Study of the Life of Sibusisiwe Makanya and Her Work as Educator and Social Worker in the Umbumbulu District of Natal 1894-1971, 115, https://researchspace.ukzn.ac.za/xmlui/handle/10413/16962, date accessed 4 February 2021.
15. Homi K. Bhaba (ed.) *Nation and Narration* (New York: Routledge, 1990), 19.
16. The Nation as Imagined Community, https://www.litcharts.com/lit/imagined-communities/themes/the-nation-as-imagined-community, date accessed 10 May 2021. See Benedict Anderson, *Imagined Communities: Reflections on the Origin and Spread of Nationalism* (New York: Verso, 1998).
17. Andre Odendaal, *Vukani Bantu! Black Protest Politics in South Africa to 1912* (New Jersey: Barnes & Noble Books, 1984), 33, 59-63. The body's leadership came from the Scotland and American Zulu Mission-educated Africans who attended these schools in Grouteville where Chief Albert Luthuli, the former ANC President, and the first African Nobel Peace Prize recipient (1967) resided.
18. Ibid., 59-63.
19. Abner Sigudo, "Kumhleli weLanga," *Ilanga laseNatal*, August 21, 1903, 11.
20. Stephen Nyongwana, "Kumhleli weLanga," *Ilanga lase Natal*, September 21, 1903, 11.
21. Ibid.
22. Abner Sigudo, "Kumhleli weLanga."
23. Andre Odendaal, *Vukani Bantu!*, 18-19, 61. Reports of the Funamalungelo's activities appeared in the vernacular newspaper *Inkanyiso laseNatal* (the *Natal Light*). First published in 1889 by Anglicans from Pietermaritzburg, Natal, in both isiZulu and English, the paper quickly emerged as the preeminent protest journal. From Estcourt, the

Funamalungelo branched out to the Driefontein Mission situated in the Klip River Division and then onto Edendale near Pietermaritzburg. The protest activities of the Funamalungelo consisted of petitioning the government for the clarification of its member's status as exempted Africans in addition to seeking relief from the discriminatory laws that affected them daily, but in spite of the organization's goals it floundered because of political impotence. Colonial officials did not respond to the petitions either in writing or by convening meetings with leaders of the Funamalungelo resulting in the formation of a new organization called the Natal Native Congress.

24. Meghan Healy-Clancy "The Daughters of Africa and Transatlantic Racial Kinship," 481–483.
25. Dawne Y. Curry, "What Is It We Call the Nation," 60. An ideology and cultural movement espoused and developed by Senegal's Leopold Senghor, French Guiana's Leon Damas, and the Caribbean's Aimee Cesaire, Negritude was a counterpoint to the negative impact of colonial rule and years of debasement. Like the American Harlem Renaissance, Negritude celebrated African culture. Shireen Hassim, *The ANC Women's League: Sex, Gender and Politics* (Ohio Short Histories of Africa) (Athens: Ohio University Press, 2015), 13-16.
26. "Liya Phuma Ilanga Nakuma Dodakazi AseAfrika," *Bantu World*, November 11, 1939, 3.
27. "Madodakazi Ase Afrika," *Ilanga laseNatal*, April 1, 1958, 13.
28. Susan Parnell, Race, Power, and Urban Control: Johannesburg's Inner City Slum-yards, 1910-1923, *Journal of Southern African Studies*, 29, 3 (2003): 615.
29. John Nauright, Black Island in a White Sea: Black and White in the Making of Alexandra Township, South Africa, PhD Dissertation, Queens University, Toronto, 1998, 98–101.
30. Ibid.
31. "Ingosi YaBesifazane Ezibalulekile zamaDodakazi AseAfrika, *Ilanga laseNatal*, March 6, 1948, 4.
32. "Ezani amadodakazi aseafrika?," *Ilanga laseNatal*, August 8, 1946, 12.
33. "Impendulo ka Mgqugquzeli we D. O. a. Ku Nkk. V. A. Khumalo wase St. Augustine's Dundee," *Ilanga laseNatal*, January 5, 1945, 11.
34. "Amadodakazi kwaZulu," *Ilanga laseNatal*, August 31, 1946, 9.
35. DOA Litany, *Bantu World*, March 25, 1940, 9.
36. "Ingosi YaBesifazane-Amadodakazi AseAfrika," 4.
37. "Amadodakazi kwaZulu," *Ilanga laseNatal*, August 31, 1946, 9.
38. Abner Sigudo, "Kumhleli weLanga."
39. C. L. Tshabalala, "Ayahlangana Amadodakazi aseAfrika eDannhauser," *Bantu World*, 10 May 1935, 13.

40. Esi Sutherland-Addy and Aminata Diaw, *Women Writing Africa: West Africa and the Sahel*, Adelaide Casely-Hayford: A Profile of Gladys (New York: Feminist Press, 2005), 213-216.
41. Gladys May Casely Hayford: Pioneer African Female Poet Of Harlem Renaissance And Cultural Luminary Of Her Day, https://kwekudee-tripdownmemorylane.blogspot.com/2013/11/gladys-may-casely-hayford-pioneer.html, date accessed 29 May 2021.
42. Meghan Healy-Clancy, Women and the Problem of Family in Early African Nationalist History and Historiography, *South African Historical Journal*, 64, 3 (2012): 450-471.

    Published online: 07 Aug 2012, Download citation https://doi.org/10.1080/02582473.2012.667830

CHAPTER 4

Activist Intellectuals and the Quest to Save the Nation

In his classic text, *Native Life in South Africa*, Solomon T. Plaatje, a prominent ANC leader, editor, journalist, translator, and documentarian, made this bold pronouncement, "By far the most outrageous of the monstrous crimes that characterized the South African Parliament's crusade against law-abiding Natives was the passage and enforcement of Law No. 27 of 1913 under the war hero, and the country's first Prime Minister Louis Botha, and within three years of a unified Republic." Plaatje's gripping account examines the distressing effects of [this] parliamentary promulgation by which "the South African native '[Awoke] on Friday morning, June 20, 1913, [to find] himself, not actually a slave, but a pariah in the land of his birth'".[1] Acclaimed poet Adelaide Charles Dube (ACD) echoes Plaatje's characterization of Africans by employing the term outcast to describe the liminal space in which they inhabited. 'Africa, My Native Land' highlights ACD's role as an *imbongi* (praise poet). In this four-piece stanza, the word lyricist and daughter of religious leader J. Y. Tantsi educates, extolls, and criticizes Africans at the same time. She calls upon the forebearers and upon the glory of another time when Africans had a home on the land that they had traditionally cultivated, settled, and communed:

It is here where our noble ancestors,
Experienced joys of dear ones and of home;
Where great and glorious kingdoms rose and fell

D. Y. Curry, *Social Justice at Apartheid's Dawn*, African Histories and Modernities, https://doi.org/10.1007/978-3-030-85404-1_4

Where blood was shed to save thee, thou
dearest Land ever known;[2]

The juxtaposition of Plaatje's and ACD's works is important for understanding how men and women viewed or interpreted the same issue. Each author aligned and disjoined in key ways. Plaatje, for example, distinguishes himself through the oral testimonies he documents during his tour of the rural areas whereas ACD uses her literary license to mediate between the earthly and spiritual worlds. The problem was that the 1913 Natives Land Act uprooted tradition for a falsehood when it initiated a different type of ownership and relationship with the land that defied the unwritten code of cosmology and physiology. Loss of land was not just about economics alone, but the return of the physical being with the spiritual soul. Both Plaatje and ACD understood the importance of reconciliation and repatriation in Africa's metaphorical return. This occurred when survivors laid bodies to rest, and generations communed on the same land and perpetuated secrets. Plaatje and ACD's offerings mirror the message of Maxeke's song *Phakama Afrika* when she, like them, issues a charge for her people:

God has created you	Ukwenzel' u-Thixo
a conviction himself	Idinga ngokakwe
receive it now and rise up	Lamkele ngoku uvuke
Rise, O Africa, Amen.	O' Afrika, vuka, Amen.[3]

God made a covenant with the African nation, but its inhabitants failed to honor their part in this sacred, redemptive bargain. Mind, body, and spirit got caught up in the throes of colonialism which through legislative measures rendered African people politically and socially disempowered. Amid their declining agency, a corps of Africans sought to right a historical and human rights wrong through prose and poetry. Chroniclers and poets bore testimony to the African nation's colossal forfeiture which they reclaim with their reflective words.

Solomon Tshekisho Plaatje

Plaatje grew up near Mafeking, the site of an incredible siege that lasted for 217 arduous, bloody, and combative days during the second Boer War (South African War, 1899–1900). Plaatje had begun journaling the intricate details of this military campaign at its onset in 1899. The war's belligerent sounds came alive through the vivid descriptions that litter his diary's pages. Plaatje illustrated his documentarian skills even further by reporting the effects of the 1913 Natives Land Act in his *Native Life in South Africa*.[4] Plaatje began working on this polemic piece while on board a vessel to England. Plaatje, J. L. Dube, and other ANC leadership journeyed to London to convince the British government, which was still closely tied to South Africa despite having self-governing status, to put a stop to this earth-shattering measure. Unfortunately, the assassination of Austria-Hungary's Archduke Franz Ferdinand, which thrust the world into its first global war beginning in 1914, spoiled those plans; however, it failed to stop Plaatje from writing about this South African tragedy which saw the light of day finally with its publication in 1916.

Plaatje's tour of the affected rural areas began when he and his entourage left the diamond mining capital of Kimberley on the early morning train. When the convoy traveled beyond Bloemhof in the TRV, one of the Afrikaans-speaking homelands, they found a throng of Africans crossing the River Diggings in full flight. They had reached the area two weeks before the group's impending visit. Plaatje believed that farmers had devious motives when they sought to capitalize on the opportunity to transform Africans from tenants to slaves. 'One Night with the Refugees' and 'Another Night with the Suffers' are two of the chapters in Plaatje's book that encapsulate this observation. They tell about the plight of an elderly man named Kgabale whose sons leave the earthen mines of Johannesburg every spring to help their father and their sisters to plow the fields in the Hoopstad District.

The family had made a respectable living from farming and maintaining livestock which allowed them over the years to pay the landowner 50% of the produce annually and all the levies that the government imposed. Problems started to develop when Kgabale wandered from place to place trying to find someone who could write. The elder gentleman wanted desperately to dictate a letter to his sons living in Johannesburg so that he could tell them what had happened. Three weeks before Plaatje visited the area, the farmer canceled Kgabale's verbal contract, thereby rendering him and his family as unpaid servants who 'earned' the privilege of squatting on his farm. Kgabale had seven days to produce his sons, but when a week expired with no word from Johannesburg, the landlord became even more abusive and demanded that they begin performing labor on his farm the very next morning. The elder family man prayed the entire night for his sons to end this nightmare which left him in a quandary.[5] Before the 1913 Natives Land Act, Africans had the option of moving to the next available farm, "but now, under the Natives' Land Act, no sympathetic landowner would be permitted to shelter them for a single day". Kgabale ended up in

Klerksdorp, the first capital of the former Transvaal in the Northwest Province, a defeated man. He lost evidence of his industry because land was:

> to the African what the sea is to the fish; it is essential to his life. Without it he becomes detribalized. More harm has been done to African life and morals, except in West Africa, by European land hunger than by any drink or trade.[6]

This push for drastic social and political change propelled the mass exodus and destitution that Plaatje describes in a work that serves as a haunting elegy and as an oral history at the same analytical time.

Trouble started and continued to plummet following a raging blizzard that began blanketing the night sky. Temperatures lowered to frigid levels causing the children's teeth to chatter as their shivering bodies stood by their mothers' sides. Of all that Plaatje and his entourage witnessed in this location, he makes a conscious effort to highlight the sick toddler whose mother transferred him from a cottage to a jolting ox-wagon when they 'left' the farm. Death began knocking on this toddler's door within two days.

> The little one began to sink as the result of privation and exposure on the road, and the night before we met them its little soul was released from its earthly bonds. The death of the child added a fresh perplexity to the stricken parents.[7]

Public roads turned into freeways that ferried more than vehicles, horse and buggies, and other forms of transport. Humans from all walks of life made makeshift homes alongside their inundated banks simply because:

> They had no right or title to the farmlands through which they trekked: they must keep to the public roads—the only places in the country open to the outcasts if they are possessed of a travelling permit. The deceased child had to be buried, but where, when, and how?[8]

The inability to inter loved ones at funerals forced Africans to carry out last rites in the following way:

> a wandering family decided to dig a grave under cover of the darkness of that night, when no one was looking, and in that crude manner the dead child was interred—and interred amid fear and trembling, as well as the throbs of a torturing anguish, in a stolen grave, lest the proprietor of the

> spot, or any of his servants, should surprise them in the act. Even criminals dropping straight from the gallows have an undisputed claim to six feet of ground on which to rest their criminal remains, but under the cruel operation of the Natives' Land Act little children, whose only crime is that God did not make them white, are sometimes denied that right in their ancestral home.[9]

Because they were unable to mourn publicly at funerals, Plaatje's subjects experienced disenfranchised grief.[10] "In the nineteenth century, religious denomination determined place of burial. In the twentieth century race and ethnicity became the dominant factor, reflecting the imposition of segregationary and apartheid laws."[11] Plaatje paints a tormenting portrait of the family's anguish in this oral obituary which explains how these victims died under the cover of darkness rather than how they lived under the prism of light. While nighttime allegedly provides safety, it did not guarantee funeral attendants a proper homegoing nor survivors reduced corporeal fear. These things heightened amidst the tightening of legislative measures that strangled African people. Plaatje's reference to criminals is a chilling and powerful inclusion. Hardened and soft offenders had, as prophesied by Ecclesiastes, the enfranchised liberty to return to the earth, but that was not the case for the casualties that the 1913 Natives Land Act made out of toddlers and older children. Plaatje does however, by telling this gripping narrative, restore his subjects' enfranchised grief by giving them a literary tombstone.

Nontsizi Mgqwetho, who appears later, also creates an oral obituary when she documents the continent's symbolic and physical passing in 'We Are Stabbing Africa'. The word lyricist cites several examples of 'death', "you scratch your head in search of a scapegoat", "Ntsikana warned you a long time ago", or "Money's the lighting bird-leave it alone".[12] Her poem supports her main argument that Africa's destruction and deterioration began the minute its various peoples refused to accept culpability for its condition, for not listening to an ancestor and for being driven by capitalist whims. She follows this public rebuke with this salvo for the nation: "Always remember where you come from: consult the sages if you seek solutions."[13] Adelaide Charles Dube explores this theme and others further in her poem 'Africa My Native Land'. Reprinted on the anniversary of King Dinzulu's burial, and during the year the government enacted the 1913 Natives Land Act, ACD's literary ode represents the earliest example of a poem written by an African woman.[14]

Adelaide Charles Dube nee Tantsi

'Africa, My Native Land' immortalizes a different vantage point than what Plaatje treats, but the two South Africans render similar messages in their indictments against the 1913 Natives Land Act. Adelaide Charles Dube's gripping account, which colorfully describes a metaphor about the land that drips with images of dispossession, violence, and mourning, begins in this literary, impressionistic way: "How beautiful are they hills and thy dales! I love thy very atmosphere so sweet. Thy trees adorn the landscape rough and steep. No other country in the whole world could with thee compare."[15] Rolling hills and lush valleys are set against a landscape littered with swaths of trees, and rugged, earthen spaces. The beauty and the majesty of the terrain are celebrated and sullied with historical allusions and longing sorrow.

The poem's rhythm follows the ascensions and declinations of past African kingdoms. While the poet does not mention names in this eulogy, and in this ode, her work does conjure up the military feats of Shaka, Moshoeshoe, Lobengula, Mzilikazi, and Manthatisi who all engaged in nation-building around the same time that the trekking Boers left the Cape for a homeland in the interior, and the redcoat British lustily eyed indigenous African land. Lore and legend of these state-building leaders grew to astronomical levels during the 'Mfecane'. Extensive drought, famine, deforestation, and dispossession shook Southern Africa from 1815 to 1840,[16] but as Plaatje describes, the 1913 Natives Land Act had similar ecological, demographic, and geographical import, something that ACD echoes in her poem's second stanza: "No longer can their off-spring cherish thee, No land to call their own—but outcasts in their own country!"[17] Xhosa poet Mgqwetho also wrote about this devastating piece of legislation to explain Africans' self-imposed fate:

> Today, you're a stranger in Africa, you go about clutching at straws: groom your Shield, this land of your fathers is now the playground of strangers.
>
> We perch like birds on branches: why are the houses of Africans burning? Even a polecat growls in its lair but a black has nowhere to stay.[18]

Land was vital as water, in fact, its composition represented a lived experience and a communal tradition. Its nutrients contained the ancestors' blood, which their successors used to regenerate, and to fertilize generations with sacrificial alms, and corporeal offerings.[19] Issues of sovereignty came under direct fire in the scorched-earth campaign that the 1913 Natives Land Act set ablaze. Rites of passage among Africans faced disruption. Passing land down to future generations represented a cyclical exchange that inhabitants engaged with the earth's inheritors. Legacy and heritage faced irreparable damage. Africans mortgaged their futures by allowing their continent to become "the playground of strangers", as Mgqwetho describes.[20] As two of the main components of the nation, the deficiency of these items ultimately led to Africans experiencing social death. Historian Orlando Patterson coined this term to highlight the deprivation that African Americans encountered as a result of American slavery. Chattel owners and South Africa's segregationists treated African Americans and Africans as if they were dead or non-existent.[21]

Adelaide Charles Dube reverses this process in her role as a master griot who like Plaatje and Mgqwetho passes down oral tradition. They all provide a different form of genealogical history than that usually offered by men who focused exclusively on the narratives of clans. She traces the past to the present by unearthing 'the bones' in this literary exhumation: "Despair of thee I never, never will, Struggle I must for freedom—God's greatest gift—Till every drop of blood within my veins. Shall dry upon my troubled bones, oh thou Dearest Native Land!!!"[22] A passage found in *Women Writing Africa: The Southern African Region* provides the best summation for the meaning, and further contextualization of Adelaide Charles Dube's profound, metaphorical words read above:

> The reference to "my troubled bones," marks allegiance to an ancestral religion, alluding to the importance of burial in one's home ground and to the rupture between the ancestors and their offspring through the alienation of the land.[23]

This quote connects nicely with Plaatje's observations in *Native Life in South Africa*. It underscores the relationship between land and mourning practices that the 1913 Natives Land Act disrupted. The metaphor and the analogy represent the fortification of the body, and the disintegration of the corpse, and the realm in which the spirits reside.[24] 'The bones' and the land encode the people's DNA—the molecules that fertilize the planetary energies that guide and support the universe and its spiritual language, which she deciphers in this forceful assault. Plaatje is no different, and no less relentless in his critique. He engages in a different form of decryption. People's bodies, facial expressions, and other etchings serve as the 'living bones' of his subjects. ACD's and Plaatje's work encapsulates the biblical scripture found in Genesis which states, "All living creatures go to the same place [because] We are made from earth, and we return to earth."[25]

Reuben Tholakele Caluza

Renowned musician, composer, and nationalist proponent Reuben Tholakele Caluza offers another interpretation that fits within this analysis. "In the wake of the [1913 Natives Land] Act, his uncle applied to purchase a farm that was not earmarked within the 8 percent of land set aside for black occupation; he was denied."[26] This descendant of a stanchly devoted Christian Zulu family grew up in the isiZulu-speaking area of Natal. Caluza followed his pedigree. Several of his uncles played the organ. "Caluza picked up this skill, honing his musical abilities before developing as a composer and choir leader during his student years at the Ohlange Institute."[27] He also studied and graduated from Hampton University and Columbia University. This accomplished composer's meteoric rise occurred amid the development of a burgeoning intelligentsia that used scholarship, culture, and politics to push for modernity during the New African Movement (NAM) that began in the 1930s and lasted until 1960.[28] Caluza added to the growing dissent against the segregationist government's policies as his debut song written when he was seventeen years of age, *Umteto We Land Act* (*The Land Act Song*) attests:

> We are children of Africa
> We cry for our land
> Zulu, Xhosa, Sotho
> We are mad over the Land Act
> A terrible law that allows sojourners
> To deny us our land
> Crying that we the people
> Should pay to get our land back
> We cry for the children of our fathers
> Who roam around the world without a home
> Even in the land of their forefathers.[29]

Like Adelaide Charles Dube, Plaatje, and Mgqwetho, Caluza refers to the spirits' unsettlement. He is also cognizant of the disrupted rite of passage because the land and souls changed hands. With Africans no longer possessing this birth and tenure right, the cosmological energies that charted their spiritual cartographies fragmented amid the violent and diplomatic passification of their people. Death became part of living life with the inability of the soil and the spirit to interface. For that reason, ACD's 'troubled bones' kept rattling and Caluza's subjects lamented over the fact that the outsiders put a price tag on their traditional lands. Mgqwetho substantiates these assertions when she turns the table on African themselves to discuss the various ways that they 'stabbed' their own continent.

Nontsizi Mgqwetho

This "physically unappealing, a bulky woman with 'matchstick legs', and may possibly have been unmarried, is a self-description of one of the nation's first African women to write explicitly in isiXhosa".[30] Mgqwetho submitted several poems to *Umteteli waBantu* (UWB), a multi-lingual print medium established by the Chamber of Mines and the Native Recruiting Corporation (NRC) following the labor strike that swept the Rand in the early twenties.[31] Mgqwetho ended up writing ninety-five poems and three articles from 23 October 1920 and 4 September 1926; and two more poems appeared after a two-year gap on 22 December 1928 and 5 January 1929:

> The poems are complex in form. In one sense they are very obviously praise poems: they are largely non-narrative; comprise series of epithets and images about their subjects; and offer commendation, advice, and criticism.[32]

Jeff Opland's and Isabel Hofmeyr's *The Nation's Bounty: The Xhosa Poetry of Nontsizi Mgqwetho* brings this elusive literary figure and her poems from newspapers to analytical life in a volume that captures the soul she poured out with each and every stanza that dripped of her outspoken consciousness.[33] Duncan Patrick's article 'My Pen Is the Tongue of a Skilful (sic) Poet' grapples with the different personas she assumes as a poet who in the position of an *imbongi* defies gender-prescribed boundaries in this role traditionally held by men.[34] Mgqwetho speaks frequently to her avid readers which she does through the power of own creative hand: "Your poetry goes to the core / And the peaks of the nation swivel / As you sway from side to side." "Woman, the winsome song of your voice / Sets Africa's walls vibrating, / Utterly shaming all the lads."[35]

Her provocative poems often signed by her isiXhosa clan name 'Cizama' fueled a seismic and catalytic reverberation that played out on the pages of *UWB* and *Imvo Zabantsundu*, a newspaper established by John Tengo Jabavu in the Eastern Cape's King Williams Town. Her first poem with that byline was sent from Crown Mines where it reached the reading public on 23 October 1920.[36] Mgqwetho's work treads closely to Adelaide Charles Dube and Plaatje but also diverges from her contemporaries. She syncs with the 'Africa, My Native Land' poet and *Native Life in South Africa* chronicler when she employs her literary art as a political tool. The brunt of her attacks affronted the ANC, the very organization Plaatje helped to form.[37] Mgqwetho disliked that the ANC failed to bring Black people together which the frustrated poetess who further critiqued the body for this major depressing oversight. She wrote:

> Take the ANC
> We once praised it till our ribs burst
> Now we go round in search of it
> Has anyone seen where it's gone?[38]

One of Makanya's closest friends and ICU colleagues Bertha Mkhize had her own reservations about the ANC; she commented, "All those people in the African National Congress are too slow in fighting against the laws that hold us down. They just want to wait a bit in order to win the favor of the Europeans."[39] Mgqwetho chastises Black people collectively with this fierce diatribe she encloses in

> 'We're Stabbing Africa': "We split into factions, betray our own people, And Africa leaves as we claw at each other. We'd be all at sea if we ruled ourselves: our cry for self-rule is vapid! Zulu and Xhosa! Sotho, Swazi, Mfengu! To help other nations you shun your own people in your desperate quest for honour and status. They gather from you all our closest secrets. Let me ask you this question: when will it all end?"[40]

Mgqwetho questions the integrity of Africans whom she believed had sold themselves to the highest political bidder for self-gain, and for personal acclaim. This push for social and political aspirations betrayed ubuntu and the collective African humanity it espoused.

Mgqwetho backed up her lyrical assault on more than one occasion with forays into politics. Several issues rose up. She came out in full support of the Maxekes (Marshall and Charlotte) when others accused them of being government collaborators. When the pass laws became an issue yet again for African women, Mgqwetho registered her grievances and hit the pavement in defiance.[41] Her participation carried on a tradition that women of all races had started going as far back as the nineteenth century when Alice Victoria Kinloch penned a letter to the New Age with the signature, 'A Native of South Africa'. Dated 30 September, the correspondence describes the operation of the pass laws that gripped Natal in the late nineteenth century.[42] Pass laws date way back to 1709, when slaves who left their masters' homes carried signed documents that granted them permission to be away.[43] Between 1916 and 1984, the pass laws impacted over 1,774,500,030 Africans.[44] Initially, the state only required men to possess and produce these documents, but as time went on the threat loomed large over women.[45]

Beginning in the early twentieth century when women of various persuasions delivered 5000 signed petitions to Prime Minister Louis Botha's office in 1912. When that move failed to garner a response from the state, several women formed a delegation and went directly to Cape Town where the seat of Parliament resided. They sought a meeting with Native Commissioner Henry Burton. Despite gestures of sympathy, and empathy, Burton failed to do anything which compelled these dissenters to gather at the famed Waaihoek Location, an area that began housing a 'non-White Coloured' population in Bloemfontein in 1861.[46] Things continued to spill over and to heighten at resounding levels so much so that Bloemfontein eventually erupted the same year as the cataclysmic Natives Land Act in 1913.

Bloemfontein's swelling unrest chronicled the combative stand and intrepid travails of twenty-three-year-old Katie Louw, Mrs. A. S. Gabashane, and Mrs. Kotsi. Louw was a Wesleyan minister's wife, Gabashane, the nuptial partner of a prominent African Methodist Episcopal (AME) Church activist, and Kotsi registered with the same credentials as her peers. Six hundred women, led by a flag-draping and a very stout warrior Mrs.[47] Pankhurst, marched up Maitland Street at 9 am. Chattering and shouting comprised the movement's sonic volumes while its visual splendor included "emblems of liberty in the shape of the Union Jacks attached to walking sticks, knobkerries, and broom handles. Women were seen jumping up springboards."[48] Similar Kodak moments immortalized the anti-pass campaign (1919) of which Mgqwetho participated and of which Maxeke and her BWL spearheaded. Maxeke saw this problem all along with the passes:

> the pass laws had turned thousands of beloved sons into criminals and now sought 'to degrade the honor' of women. It was high time that the voice of the Bantu woman was heard.[49]

Under Tshabalala's leadership, the Daughters took a definitive stand. Its members argued that the passes gave rise to criminality as this isiZulu statement conveys: "*amapasi lawa andisa ubugebengu nje.*"[50] Despite successfully defeating the state's attempt to regulate their influx into the cities through the dreaded pass, the threat of its imposition continued to loom over African women. The warning materialized and became a reality when the government passed the 1954 Natives Law Amendment Act and required every African to carry passes.

Mgqwetho's personal involvement in protest activities surfaces in a poetic contribution dated 13 December 1924 which carries this insinuation, "What a fool I was sucking up to the whites! / Next thing I knew the cops had the cuffs on me."[51] Handcuffs symbolized criminalization, and blackness, something that Mgqwetho had thought up until that time had protected her given the good relations that she had brokered with White people. The arrest disabused her of such a notion, while also highlighting the disabilities that Africans faced despite their aspirations to attain social and political advancements within segregated South Africa.[52] As Mgqwetho further illustrates consorting with Whites led to multiple untreated wounds.

Commercialization of human bodies left everyone traumatized as this verse reveals: "When we trade our own people to whites for profit, we inflict a deep wound on Africa. I'm not one to shy from saying so: your public behaviour bears eloquent witness."[53] Mgqwetho requests a blessing and offers up a resolution in the poem's conclusion: "God bless Africa! Patch the network of cracks in the wall up with clay, so the surface appears chameleon-coloured, a sign to inspire our respect for each other."[54] Mgqwetho strongly implies that the cracks in the wall developed from the violent stabs that slavery, colonialism, ethnic tensions, and eroding customs produced. Clay sealed the holes while also reinforcing the notion that everything Africa needs to succeed exists within the soil on which the continent stands.

Mayibuye! I Afrika! Awu (Oh, Bring Africa Home!) is another of Mgqwetho's offerings. The poem first appeared in UWB, the same year that the government passed the 1923 Natives Urban Areas Act which increased the percentage of land for Africans to 13% while also legalizing urban segregation. At the time of the elegy's publication, South Africa was in the midst of severing its ties with Great Britain. An alliance formed between the National Party (NP) and the Labour Party (LP) sought to attain that goal by creating a new South African flag and by making Afrikaans, a West Germanic language that derived from seventeenth-century Dutch speakers, an official tongue. This all-consuming Pact government brokered between Smuts and Hertzog also curtailed black economic freedom by prohibiting the formation of unions.[55] Mgqwetho belted out a provocative piece against this intense backdrop:

> … first two stanzas show a desperate cry for Africa's restoration after being "consumed and scattered by birds". Through "wailing" and "imploring" the "Garden of Africa" their voices have become hoarse; they have appealed to other nations but in vain. Although a foreign enemy came in and caused havoc, looking to other nations for help will bear no fruit, but is merely an "appeal to phantoms."[56]

Africa gets scorned in this important way, "All the earth's nations profit from you, they come from the north, they come from the south, from the east and from the west." To satisfy the demand for raw materials following the Industrial Revolution that swept the European continent during the late eighteenth and early nineteenth centuries, France, Great Britain, and other metropoles turned to Africa to meet this supply. Africans experienced social death all over again. Europe's economic chokehold strangled Africa and its people. The continent began to spiral precipitously downward. South Africa represented one of its causalities. Mgqwetho prescribes a remedy amid this political and social turmoil as this stanza exhibits:

> We call to you from Table Bay, we call to you from Algoa Bay, we call to you from Grahamstown, clutching satchels crammed with half-jacks; we drink suicidally calling you home, we cover your eyes and declare you blind, you go right back to where you came from as we call you home from the depths of depravity.[57]

Mgqwetho harks back to South Africa's development as a country with the inclusion of these sites. Table Bay birthed Cape Town, a sprawling South African city situated on the Atlantic Ocean and ensconced between Table Mountain and squatter settlements of corrugated iron and other materials strewn together to create housing structures and lavish houses and complexes situated on cliffs overlooking the Atlantic Ocean. The country's first taste of colonialism took place on Table Bay when the Dutch turned a stopover into a permanent settlement while Algoa Bay, which is situated in the Eastern Cape, was named originally Angra da Roca (The Bay of Rocks) by Portuguese explorer Bartholomew Diaz when he 'discovered' the area and planted a white cross on nearby Saint Cruz Island in 1488. Grahamstown, the other site she mentions, began as a frontier garrison strategically positioned near the AmaXhosa along the rapidly flowing Kowie River near the wooded slope of the eye-catching Suur Mountains.

Landing on the African continent created different stories of origin. Mgqwetho implies that social death began the minute Europeans arrived. They brought with them their own forms of depravity that ended up tainting pre-existing African moralities.[58] Arrival and settlement initiated new chapters in African, European, and global history. The former submitted, allied, or confronted the ensemble of Europeans who, as the latter, hammered, passified, or ruled Africans for centuries.[59] Colonialism's impact hit hard. Toddler Flora Zeto entered America after an auspicious rescue from the heavily foliated Congo bush. Samaritans found and took the bundle of joy to the nearby Lukunga Mission station where Clara Ann Howard, a Spelman graduate, and African American missionary, worked. Zeto was a casualty of a devastating proxy war brought on by the economic struggle between King Leopold II and his Congolese army and Zanzibari Arab slave traders who wreaked havoc on the area. Between 1892 and 1894, fighting erupted in eastern Congo for control over the area's vast wealth in minerals and ivory. Even when the two warring sides reached an agreement, destruction lay in their militant wakes. Zeto lost her biological parents but gained an adoptive one in Howard.[60] Soga brings out another observation about European arrival and subsequent colonization that supports Mgqwetho's criticism:

> Behold me in this awkward dress of the West. It doesn't become me particularly, or go with me, yet the white man led us to believe when he came to Africa that everything African was heathen, and without intending to do so he confused us. We began to believe that everything Western—even the things of the white man—was Christian. If we wore clothes just like his, we would be more civilized—and perhaps more Christian. If we could speak the language of the white man so as never to make a mistake, we would be more civilized—and perhaps more Christian. So millions of my people have assumed that by changing their dress they could take on Christianity. They have changed the exterior, but the heart is not changed. Christianity must be based on a changed heart. And for that the African must be at home with his God.[61]

Erroneous beliefs like the ones Soga describes lay at the heart of arrival and immersion narratives. Mgqwetho and other activist intellectuals point to these conversations as foddering fuel to convince Africans to redeem and to reclaim themselves from the framing of the continent's image by the West. Nineteenth-century prophet Nongqawuse best reflects an attempt at an exorcism or a purgation that Mgqwetho solicits.

Historian Helen Bradford recounts the well-rehearsed tale of this controversial figure in Nombonisa Gasa's anthology, *Women in South African History*.[62] Bradford considers different explanations for Nongqawuse's historical condemnation: vilification in European and African sources; the concentration on Xhosaland as the principal site of contact; the exclusion of other indigenous documents or the use of oral traditions (praise poems). This 'Maiden of Scatter' is rescued by Bradford in two principal ways. She examines Xhosaland as the movement's epicenter. Bradford also moves beyond this area's borders to explore the cattle-killing episode "as part of a religious, and spiritual movement [that] reached transnational shores and poured over to seven African countries before it hit Russia, India, and Europe".[63] "Bradford does what Nongqawuse failed to do, and what Mgqwetho calls for when she asks Africans to drink suicidally [to call the Europeans] home" rather than partake in the destruction of stock, and crops to drive them out as Nongqawuse allegedly prescribed. Mgqwetho's *Mayibuye iAfrika*, Adelaide Charles Dube's 'Africa, My Native Land,' and even Plaatje's *Native Life in South Africa* foreshadowed the thinking of future African liberationists.

Guinea-Bissau leader Amilcar Cabral's incisive 'Return to the Source' is one of a series of speeches that resonates with these activist intellectuals for the following reasons. Cabral critiques an emerging and established bourgeoisie class that alienated themselves from their traditional cultures and mores. He urges them to embrace their indigenous roots once again.[64] Mgqwetho, who stands as the example for this comparison, calls for Europeans to do the same thing when she invoked the 'source' motif when she suggested that Europeans depart by beginning where their origin stories started at Table Bay, Algoa Bay, and other points of entry on the African continent. Mgqwetho issues this bold deportation order for several reasons. When the Scramble for Africa erupted on the continent, Great Britain, France, Portugal, and other nations were in a race to attain colonies in Africa. Several catalysts initiated the Scramble—France's dispatch of three missions in 1879, Great Britain's checkmate with its occupation of Egypt in 1882, and German Chancellor Otto von Bismarck's change of mind when he threw his country's hat into the ring and began to acquire African territories.[65] Long after the ratification of the 1885 Treaty of Berlin which partitioned the continent into different spheres of European influence, a new race for Africa's social and political redemption began.

As the need to fuel mercantilism grew, various European powers began settling colonists on African land which ultimately displaced its original inhabitants. For example, the British removed the Nandi from their original habitats to build a railroad that joined British East Africa—Kenya, Uganda, Zanzibar, and Tanganyika. The same thing happened to Kenya's Kikuyu when they removed them from a highly arable area to desolate, far-removed places. British settlers soon began to occupy this reserved territory, popularly called the White Highlands from 1902 to 1961. Haphazard and life-altering relocations disrupted centuries-old communal partnerships that Africans possessed with the earth and its resources. Adelaide Charles Dube's haunting pleas in 'Africa, My Native Land' is an attempt for her to reconcile her 'troubled bones'. Mgqwetho's poetic offering screams for the African nation to repatriate by turning to its ideological and spiritual roots.

Through all of this radical, demographic, and social change, Mgqwetho and Plaatje respectively asked the same question, "What have [they] done to so offend God?" or "... what have [they] done to deserve this rude unsettlement and persecution?"[66] Their words echoed. In more recent times, the ever-popular struggle song, *Senzeni na*, asks the same question with these lines, "what is our sin, is it because our skin is black?"[67] Blackness takes on a whole new meaning when it turns pain into a Pan-African experience. African descended people in the Caribbean, the United States, the continent, and elsewhere share a history of enslavement and colonization which inflicted pain upon the affected populations. Deborah Walker King contends, "Black pain is a sign of racism's insidious ability to assert power and maintain control over those it claims."[68] Exorcism further happens when Plaatje, ACD, Maxeke, Caluza and Mgqwetho employ their pens in acts of social purgation. Pain emerges as cathartic exercise whereby the poet or composer undergoes a confessional and a baptism at the same time. Souls reckon with the past and reconcile to attain the future. Pain is also a testament, an elegy, and an appeal as the poets' parting remarks convey these significant and contrasting thoughts: Adelaide Charles Dube ends with a vow, "Till every drop of blood within my veins Shall dry upon my troubled bones, oh thou Dearest Native Land!" Mgqwetho, on the other hand, ends with one word, "Camagu!" (Peace!).[69] Rattling bones, piercing stabs, and hovering death are the forms of imagery they all conjure up. Land is a multi-purpose metaphor that each employ to issue spiritual readings between the soil, the nation, and the blood. Maxeke (Fig. 4.1) continues this dialogue on the nation's rise and its impending reconciliation. In an article written in the African newspaper *Imvo Zabantsundu*, professor and ANC activist Z. K. Matthews, the husband of Frieda Bokwe Matthews (see Chap. 4), describes Maxeke, another one of South Africa's activist intellectuals, in the following way:

> a stout lady with a striking face, with sharp penetrating eyes which could strike terror into those who crossed words with her and yet be gentle and kind to those who needed her sympathy.[70]

Fig. 4.1 Charlotte Mannya Maxeke
Maxeke utilized her musical background to deafen the homesickness that paralyzed her in the United States. Through every 'I' she dotted and every 'T' she crossed, Maxeke's vulnerability seeped through her letters. In those personal exchanges, Maxeke exposes her yearning for her South African homeland, an objective which differed from her male contemporary Plaatje who captured the bellicosity that he witnessed during the Battle of Mafeking.[71]

https://www.sahistory.org.za/dated-event/charlotte-maxeke-politician-and-founder-bantu-womens-league-south-africa-born, date accessed 6 June 2019

Charlotte Mannya Maxeke

Maxeke's (Fig. 4.1) long interest in politics stemmed from several sources, but specifically from the different ideological influences she encountered while traveling, living in a foreign country (England, 1896–1897; United States, 1897–1901) and witnessing the events and measures that defined her own. As part of the sixteen-member African Choir that descended upon Jolly old England, Maxeke and her sister met trailblazing British suffragist Emmeline (Emily) Pankhurst. Her sister Katie Mannya describes this British pioneer as a "small woman whose hairpins were constantly falling out of her thick black hair and whose purple eyes glowed with enthusiasm" founded the Women's Social and Political Union (WSPU) in 1903.[72] Pankhurst lived to see England confer voting privileges for women the final year of her life in 1928. Pankhurst's success with organizing perhaps represented one of the motivations that inspired Maxeke when she directed a mass gathering in Johannesburg to protest the Women's Suffrage Bill (WSB). At the time Maxeke held the reins of the BWL. The body expressed "[its]… emphatic disapproval of the introduction of the proposed principle" based on these grounds: the appearance of a largely anti-Black European public; and the need to concentrate solely on the enfranchisement of African men inhabiting the entire union.[73] Women's suffragism failed to appear as a consistent campaign item on the BWL's roster, however, the issue conveyed the body's willingness to pursue graduated ameliorations even if meant advancing men first.

In *Beauty of the Heart*, Zubeida Jaffer writes, "Under Charlotte's leadership the BWL bombarded government with petitions against pass laws and sexist inspections of domestic workers. They were also vociferous when it came to workers' rights especially those of women."[74] Gasa alternatively asserts that "the BWL's wings were somewhat clipped because as an organisation [it] fell under the auspices of the ANC in the time of the complex issue of membership".[75] Jaffer's quotation highlights African women's agency while Gasa implies that the BWL's affiliation with the ANC prevented the full execution of their power. Maxeke more than compensated for this lack of relationship as she built on the extensive connections and networks, she had across international lines.[76] Furthermore, Maxeke never let the BWL's fire flicker if anything, the organization kept pushing forward discussions and activities that promoted young girls. She even incorporated a quote from the isiXhosa

Christian prophet, evangelist, and hymn composer Ntsikana to drive home the importance of the girl child. The revered 'Mother of Politics' proclaimed most passionately this, "If we want our nation to be upright, a girl has to be respectable, [to stand out through good habits and purity] and be groomed by [faithful] women as it was done during Ntsikana's times."[77] This eulogy paid homage to Ntsikana, a proud proponent of the isiXhosa language, but it also serves as a refutation. Segregationists believed that African women represented lascivious beings without a moral compass or a sanitary regimen. They were a large reason that Whites feared the swarming 'Black peril' that descended upon the nation's cities and inner slums. Maxeke sought to turn the tables on this nation-wide smear campaign with this comment that calls for morality as a marker of respectability and beauty as a signal of self-appreciation:

> ... let me say this to you girls, it is the beauty of the heart and good behavior that will last until you go to the grave. Beauty is adorable when accompanied by other good things. Try to exercise self-control over yourselves.[78]

While attending Wilberforce University, Maxeke took classes with the well-renowned intellectual Du Bois who issued this complimentary statement regarding his protege: in a foreword contained in a pamphlet entitled 'Charlotte Manye (Mrs. Maxeke): What an Educated African Girl Can Do':

> I regard Mrs Maxeke as a pioneer in one of the greatest of human causes, working in extraordinarily difficult circumstances to lead a people, in the face of prejudice, not only against her race but against her sex... . I think that what Mrs Maxeke has accomplished should encourage all men, especially those of African descent.[79]

A lot rested on the South African's shoulders. Du Bois believed that Maxeke possessed the capabilities to emerge as one of ten people destined to become race leaders in the world.[80] She more than lived up to the billing. Maxeke was classically trained, which was important given that White anthropologists who coined the term that Du Bois later elaborated on in his essay, The Black Talented Tenth in 1903, deemed that education fundamental for the roles they needed to carry out in their respective communities.[81] Maxeke incorporated a mixture of ideologies into her political and social arsenal. For example, Du Bois stoked her pan-Africanist leanings, but so did the African Methodist Episcopal Church (AME). The African Methodist Episcopal Church

> grew out of the Free African Society (FAS) which Richard Allen, Absalom Jones, and others established in Philadelphia in 1787. When officials at St. George's MEC pulled blacks off their knees while praying, FAS members discovered just how far American Methodists would go to enforce racial discrimination when they made plans to transform their mutual aid society into an African congregation and exclude American born Blacks.[82]

Weekly AME worship provided an important example of how Blacks could exercise independence and praise God at the same time.[83] When Maxeke decided to follow the path of Pan-Africanism, she had prominent examples from which to model. South Africa already had its hand in the Pan-Africanism cookie jar thanks to one of the country's early exponents, Alice Victoria Kinloch.

William and Sarah Alexander's second child was born when the ballistic American Civil War took off and spiraled into brutal battles, Texas Confederates recaptured Galveston, dwellers began occupying the first homestead in Beatrice, Nebraska, and in South Africa, Marthinus Wessel Pretorius resigned as State President of the Orange Free State (OFS) in 1863. In 1895, at thirty-two years of age, Kinloch crossed the European pond for England. David Killingray writes in his study of Black South Africans in Britain before 1912 the following:

> … her motives for coming, or the invitation that she received, has not yet been discovered. [Kinloch] appears to be the 'South African lady, resident in England' whom the editor of Fraternity, the London published journal of the Society for the Recognition of the Brotherhood of Man, described as 'our valued South African'.[84]

Kinloch soon rendered several talks at the invitation of the Aborigines Rights Protection Society (ARPS) and the Writers' Club in London (an association for progressive minded women) within a blink of an eye. Slated for early May 1897, Kinloch issued a harangue about the compound system in a talk entitled 'The Ill Treatment of Natives in South Africa', which addressed the situation in Kimberley and Rhodesia (present-day Zimbabwe and Zambia), the places where African laborers faced unrelenting oppression.[85] The speech: caused such an uproar that the Newcastle-Upon-Tyne intellectual gathering was inclined to call upon her Majesty's Government to take such action as shall effectually stop the cruel and violent measures by which the natives in South Africa and elsewhere are being deprived of their lands and liberty.[86]

In a similarly related topic, 'Are South African Diamonds Worth Their Cost?', Kinloch tears into big mining interests. Their avaricious and capitalist ways led to the poor working conditions under which her husband Edmund Kinloch, who came to London the year after her arrival in 1896, and others had endured to grease the wheels of affordable African labor. A copy of this historic nineteen-page document lies in the papers of British Christian missionary Harriet Colenso, the fifth child of John Colenso, the first Bishop of Natal, which can be found in the archives in Pietermaritzburg.[87] She authenticates her explosive diatribe with her maiden name and initials A. V. Alexander signed in her own hand to solidify and endorse her observations of African men going to work naked so that White mine owners could inspect their bodies and cavities for stolen diamonds or as she also declares, "the old sin of 'Sodom' is rampant in the De Beers Compound."[88]

When Kinloch put the mining enterprises' moral economies on trial, she temporarily took the weight off the backs of woefully paid, inhumanly mistreated, and constitutionally comprised African workers who by pains of the 1911 Mines and Works Act or the Colour Bar Act as it was colloquially known could only occupy unskilled positions unlike Whites and Coloureds who obtained more specialized jobs. Johannesburg's 'City of Gold' and Kimberley's 'Big Hole' gained extreme notoriety in Kinloch's condemnation, in fact, she hit the raw nerve that other South Africans also poked at, and intimately tied to land.[89] She took her activism to another level when she teamed up with Trinidadian Henry Sylvester Williams and Sierra Leonean Thomas John Thompson to bring African descendants to London for the first worldwide Pan Africanism Congress (PAC) "to protest [the] stealing of lands in the colonies, racial discrimination and [to] deal with all other issues of interest to blacks" when they met 23–25 July 1900 in London.[90] Kinloch failed to make the meeting's first proceedings. She and her husband had returned to South Africa by that time where they busied themselves with raising bees, poultry, and pigs on a farm called 'Nil Desperandum' at Verulam in Victoria County, Natal.[91]

The second PAC conference, which met in Paris, France, took place during the year that framers outlined the terms of the Treaty of Versailles that brought the First World War to an end in 1919. This was the same time that Maxeke began mustering up steam to combat the pass laws with her Bantu Women's League, a year after its official establishment. While she pursued social justice in South Africa, Du Bois and the National Association for the Advancement of Colored People (NAACP), a body formed in Niagara Falls in 1909, welcomed fifty-seven delegates (at least three of them women: Ida Gibbs Hunt, Charlotta Bass, and Addie Hunton) from Africa, the West Indies, and the United States. Attendants tried unsuccessfully to petition Germany to liberate its colonies (Togo, the Cameroons, German Southwest Africa, Ruanda, Burundi, and Tanganyika) which ended up being mandates of the Allied Powers as part of the country's punitive damages for the First World War.

The 1921 PAC conference continued the push for self-determination for African countries and those nations within its diaspora. Convenors had tapped Plaatje to deliver the all-important keynote address for this occasion, however because he was unable to attend, Du Bois ended up reading his words. Plaatje peppered his commentary with hard-hitting truths much like Kinloch's scathing critique against South Africa's mining interests. His compatriots Dr. John and Angeline Khumalo Dube along with a host of others heard these inciteful words:

> Mr. President and members of the Pan-African Congress, I bring to you the greetings of six million British [South African] subjects.... We have faithfully borne more than our share in the spread of British dominion in South Africa; for a mere pittance, we have built the beautiful railroads and magnificent cities and towns of the subcontinent; in return for a scant subsistence allowance and at frightful loss of life we have during the past quarter of a century produced for our masters more gold and diamonds than the rest of the world; we have paid all the government's taxes both affair and unfair, in addition to which we have given our sons and daughters in service to the most thankless taskmasters that ever controlled forced labour.[92]

Plaatje's speech acknowledges contributions that Africans made towards development, however, all this came with opportunity costs, which included the loss of precious life, and relatively consistent substandard pay. Reciprocity appeared non-existent. Its near absence represented a serious liability for nations failing to uphold labor standards. South Africa's dereliction in this regard spelled disaster and contributed to the growing Pan-African problem that had many African people turning towards America for solutions. The reason for this was simple, "... Black Americans ... provided an example ... of educated, emancipated black people."[93] Maxeke also drank from this same cup as her recognition of the AME church's push for self-determination motivated her to pursue this for her people.

An extensive tour of Southern Rhodesia (present-day Zimbabwe) and Bechuanaland (present-day Botswana) saw her issue a message contained in a scripture from Matthew V, verse 14, and Corinthians II, verse 3. She stood before women wearing multi-colored uniforms—the AME's black and white, the Dutch Reformed Church (DRC)'s blue, and black and the Wesleyan's red, white, and black. Maxeke reminded her audience of Black women's responsibility to the African race. "[They] are the light of the world," she said.[94] She manifested her profession for African unity in another way. Maxeke wrote three of the twelve musical compositions that she and her husband Marshall Maxeke, *Umteteli waBantu* editor, and activist, produced. Hymns 17, 89, and 111 are all endorsed with the initials CM at the end. Her most popular song was *Phakama Afrika* (Hymn 17).[95]

Phakama Afrika derives from an isiZulu, and isiXhosa word that means *Vukani Bantu!* or 'rise up Afrika'. A Natal newspaper first used the phrase *Vukani Bantu* in 1903, but because the government viewed the words as incendiary, the print medium closed its reporting doors. Things fared differently for Dr. John L. Dube who had issued the same call in his newspaper *Ilanga laseNatal* three years later when he skated by with only a threat to shut down his venture in 1906.[96] Failure to censure *Ilanga laseNatal* was a huge political mistake as the platform represented an early form of Black advocacy.[97] Its pages treated several issues like the franchise, identity politics, land ownership, and political organizations among other important subjects. Maxeke's music continued this trend of lobbying for Black solidarity. The first stanza of *Phakama Afrika* threads the chant of *Vukani Bantu* with its call for Africans to *sukuma* (stand up) for their rights:

Rise Africa	Wawexuliseka
Seek the (truth) Savior	Wanqul' izithixo
Run now come closer	Uhleli ngok' enyangweni
You are left out by other nations	O Afrika, buya[98]

The vocal piece blends all Maxeke's ideologies together: a religion, Christianity; an ideology, Pan-Africanism; and a concept, transnationalism. Another hymn with the same title but written by Isaiah Shembe who founded the Church of the Nazarene which became a large separatist order, and a prophetic healing institution, is in conversation with Maxeke and Mgqwetho. Composed between 1911 and 1926, the piece is a call for Africans to militantly respond as the first two out of a five-stanza poem illustrates:

> He who is beaten is not thrown away
> Let him not despise himself,
> Rise up, rise up
> Ye Africans.
>
> The form of the doorway
> Cause you to bend,
> Rise up, rise up
> Ye Africans[99]

Maxeke and Shembe both composed hymns that sought truth through the eyes of their respective Gods—for Shembe, Jehova, for Maxeke, Jesus. They also converse with Tshabalala who also believed that [Africans were] lost not worshipping any deity, instead they appeared alienated from the spiritual word.[100] Shembe substantiates this interpretation in another work, Hymn No. 24 in which the verse reads, "See he comes by way of the clouds He will come to call his people, even those who are asleep will wake up from the dust of the earth Amen Halelujah [sic] Praise ye all."[101] The separation between Africans and the earth is signaled in this verse in which Shembe is in intellectual harmony with Plaatje and Adelaide Charles Dube in their respective works.

During the segregation era, the AmaZulu the subject of Shembe's compositional pieces increasingly labored in the gold and copper mines thereby leaving families in Natal to live in government-constructed hostels on the Witwatersrand where they received food, healthcare, and bunks for several months at a time for a relatively cheap wage.[102] Laborers based in Natal and the Witwatersrand already had vociferous union to speak on its behalf, the Zulu Washermen's Guild, the AmaWasha, which existed well before the Union of South Africa formed in 1910, but that representation was not enough to stave off the flourishing rise of eroding rights and a government bent on entrenching its power through racial separation.[103]

The policy of segregation added exponentially to the feelings of alienation. Even leaders felt this sting.

Maxeke was no stranger to forlornness. Her pain reincarnated the reverberation of the Second Anglo-Boer War (South African War) that exposed South Africa's growing racial fault lines. Casely Hayford also felt estrangement but in her indigenous Africa. She was born a member of the Creole elite in West Africa's Sierra Leone. After spending forty-two years abroad in Europe (1872–1914), the United Kingdom-raised African felt more at home on the island reputed for its expansionary endeavors than the country established by freed African captives in the late eighteenth century. Both women turned to nostalgia to cope—Casely Hayford pined for the Diaspora, while Maxeke longed for the continent as the notes, chords, and clefts littered letters that charted the ebbs and flows of her volatile and sanguine moods. Cultural scholar Tsitsi Ella Jaji contends that these feelings were part of Maxeke's path towards defining her modernity as this quote illustrates, "Her signifying on remoteness and loneliness was complicated by the fact that her status as a distinctly modern subject had been ratified by her experiences as a foreigner in Britain, Canada, and the United States."[104]

In *Phakama Afrika*, Maxeke speaks of Africa's saddened state, "you are left out by other nations."[105] Adelaide Charles Dube and Plaatje discuss Africans as outcasts, but like Mgqwetho, Maxeke goes further when she labels the continent's ostracized position within the world not just within South Africa's borders. Maxeke and Mgqwetho align ideologically once again. In the stanza "Bow in surrender Trust the Lord He carried your sin for you to be saved", Maxeke calls upon Christianity for salvation whereas Mgqwetho strongly urges Africans to seek the assistance of traditional healers.[106] She writes, "Oh dear! Dear, oh dear! The shame and disgrace of it! We wither and perish for lack of a healer and Africa's forelegs sink deep in the quagmire: we repeatedly stab her year in and year out."[107] Cosmology is in conversation with theology in these cultural art forms. Salvation and solace are found in the earth, in religion, and in energy politics (a term coined and explicated by the author). Energy politics refers to the innate connections that people physically and spiritually had with each other but that they also expended through forms of corporeal solidarity and inter-connectivity.

Mgqwetho's body of poetry invokes different emotions and energies; on the one hand, anger emerges while, on the other, longing takes center stage. Reckoning and resurrection occupy juxtapositions in this dialectic of energy politics that her orality fuels between the past and the contemporary state. Maxeke and Tshabalala wanted this reclamation to happen between Africans and God. *Phakama Afrika*'s final verse states, "God has created for you a conviction himself receive it now and rise up Rise, O Africa. Amen."[108] Sibusisiwe Violet Makanya offered another form of speech; ethnography that she amplified throughout rural Natal and urban Johannesburg.

Sibusisiwe Violet Makanya

Sibusisiwe Violet Makanya (Fig. 4.2) arrived thirteen years after the Boers and the British, and their African and Coloured soldiers had participated in the first of a series of virulent wars in 1894. Myrtle Trowbridge captures the early years of Makanya's life in an unpublished biography that even while stopping abruptly in 1956 fills some of the major pieces of the activist's life, particularly her birth, rearing, education, and her philosophies.

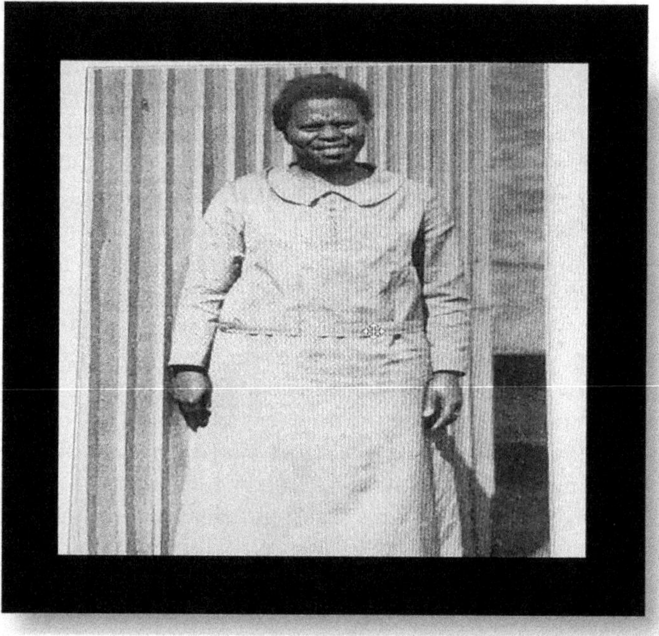

Fig. 4.2 Sibusisiwe Violet Makanya. Miss Makanya in Boston, *The Missionary Herald*, November 1927

Makanya was the first born and the pride and joy of parents Nxele and Nomagqoka Makanya. Her isiZulu name 'Sibusisiwe' meant "blessed from heaven", and the Scottish one 'Violet' symbolized the name of a bluish, purplish colored flower.[109] The Makanyas made their home in Imbumbulu, a rural area located on the South Coast of Natal bordered by Madundube on the north and Mid-Illovo on the south. This woman, who went on to render her 'blessings' upon South African society and America for a three-year spell, was inculcated within the tradition of Christianity, and the spirit of *Ubuntu*. Makanya proved to be a diligent worker whose soul only found rest when she was working as a *Bantu World* feature of this visionary describes.[110] She worked hard to save the nation by not forgetting about its rural component. Brigalia Bam spoke about the significance of Makanya's calling, "For those of us who've gone abroad to study, there is a tendency for us not to return to rural areas, but Sibusisiwe Makanya returned. She incorporated rural life into her programme. It was an aspiration to see her intensity to work and ground herself in the rural area. She chose to live and work in Imbumbulu and not in Durban."[111] Deep devotion to betterment, citizenship through Christ, and social programs guided Makanya's activism, her philanthropic efforts, and her leadership goals.

Makanya traversed the American South, the Middle West, and New England, and other parts of the Northeast all in the name of education, social immersion, and cultural exchange. The South African's three-year tenure (1927–1930) on American soil helped Makanya to hone her already adept skills at service-learning, and catering to the African community, something she carried out by inking an unwritten social contract with rural South Africa. Focusing on the country's unurbanized communities placed Makanya even further into a league of her own as her political ideology filled a large, cavernous hole. As South Africa's first rural sociologist, Makanya performed in much the same manner as the great African American intellectual Dr. W. E. B. Du Bois who in writing about *The Philadelphia Negro* diagnosed her African community and sutured it.[112]

The Bantu Youth League represented her engine for social change. In 1930, Makanya founded the body with these aims: "to nurture in Bantu youth the ideals of good citizenship as exemplified in the life of Christ; to encourage and cultivate in Bantu youth a love for and pride in their institutions and a desire to preserve the worthy ideals and customs of the Bantu people; to encourage cooperation among Bantu youth leaders; to break down sectarianism by encouraging cooperation of young people of different denominations; to cultivate appreciation of the culture of other races and to encourage inter-racial cooperation."[113] The BYL initially started in the United States when Makanya was studying at Columbia's Teachers College in New York City, the third American institution she had attended. She had spent some time at Booker T. Washington's Tuskegee before going on to the Schauffler Institute in Cleveland, Ohio. Makanya's principal advisor Mabel Carney recommended that the PSF support the South African's application to Columbia's Teachers College even when she initially had doubt about her study as this quote reveals:

> ... after [she] came to know her better, ...[she was] greatly surprised, in fact, almost amazed at her ability. The trouble in dealing with her [she was] now convinced is that [they had] considered her "a mere fowl" as Aggrey would say when in reality she [was] an "eagle" of innate vision and perspective.[114]

The first official meeting of the American Committee of the Bantu Youth League (ACBYL) of South Africa took place in New York City on 29 May 1930. Carney (secretary), John M. Phillips (Chairman), Philip C. Jones (Treasurer), Makanya (League Director), and several guests met to discuss several items: the committee's reorganization; the formation of an executive sub-committee, to hear the treasurer's report, to discuss the budget, to make a calendar for meetings, and to revise the booklet, laid out the League's purpose, and program.[115] The committee made one last request when it asked her to remain in touch. Makanya did exactly that.[116] She wrote several letters over the years that provided extensive detail on the activities of her body. Relations further developed when this ethnographer allowed overseas, South African, and other African national visitors to her home, and to the BYL's headquarters (Fig. 4.4). The BYL's post doubled as a command center but also as a meeting place for the local Sunday school, the community's Bantu Teachers' Association and interracial gathering where Makanya supplied guests with newspapers and magazines in a small reading room.[117] Visitors also learned about the activities that the BYL carried out like a night school for the youth, summer, and national conferences, traveling expeditions, and the formation of new clubs.

Immersion experiences represented both a curse and a blessing. Makanya's effort to bring visitors to Umbumbulu depicts the inherent difficulty. South Africa's policy of segregation failed to exempt rural communities from the throes of its restrictive measures. Most of Makanya's foreign White guests had to attain permission from the Magistrate in Natal in order to step foot in the designated African areas. Makanya found this requirement an indignity, and a waste of her time.[118] Despite this protestation, drives from the center of town to the more remote Umbumbulu provided a good contrast of the area's diverse landscapes. Makanya routinely stopped at a school where her sister and four other teachers taught six classes. A total of 160 pupils all learned daily in the same, poorly constructed one room where only iron rafts and walls supported the structure.[119] Makanya's home (Fig. 4.5), on the other hand, appeared sturdier. A concrete block foundation supported a five-roomed house without indoor plumbing. The lack of amenities failed to preclude Makanya from receiving and hosting guests in her spacious living room or housing them in the guest bedroom. Along with a master suite, she had a study and a kitchen, and in other buildings on the grounds, Makanya offered cookery and housewifery to young girls and adult women.[120]

Makanya initially got her feet wet in social work as one of the founders of the Bantu Purity League (BPL). She and her fellow Natal resident Nhlumba Bertha Mkhize established this organization to teach young girls about propriety and retaining their virginity until marriage. As the latter once said, "We talked to the girls and told them that a girl is just like an egg. Once a girl gets 'pahla' she's pahla'" (When she's broken, she's broken).[121] Makanya had several tricks up her conscience sleeve to uplift African youth, and women educationally, socially, and morally. The lady rumored to have sat on her stoop in a flowing dress accentuated by the shiny, red lipstick that adorned her lips, and the roughly worn shoes she wore maintained a rigorous traveling schedule throughout Natal, and parts of the former Transvaal on the BYL's behalf. Makanya acted like the solo African female preacher that historian Deborah Gaitskell describes when she carried out these 'sociological' rounds without the structure of an institution or regular pay.[122] Several chronicles of her trips describe the geographic terrain, mode of travel, established chapters, and the friendliness of the people she encountered. Makanya wrote this about one expedition she carried out in support of a BYL junior chapter:

> I spent in April three happy weeks visiting a few communities on the South Coast. I left Imbumbulu for Imfume on the 8th, stopped for a brief chat with Mqadi, Head-Teacher, Odidini. By the way, we have a Junior chapter here known by its local name as "ISIHLANTI." Those who have tried to go

> to Imfume by way of Odidini know that the descending of steep hills leading to the Illovo River does not make the trip enjoyable especially on horseback, however, one feels repaid when she reaches her destination and is the recipient of warm hospitality that "Vumandaba" always extends to her guests.[123]

Makanya loved being in the Kwela family home situated in Amahlongwa, another South Coast town. She mostly admired their home's cleanliness and their weed-free yard.[124] Makanya continued her praise by extending it to the couple's two sons. They were teachers of this community's BYL chapter, 'MLIL'OVUTAYO'. Smaller clubs focused on home improvement, agricultural work, and community life. Participants engaged in tree-planting, home ventilating, and road-making among other service activities.[125]

On another occasion, the South African accepted the invitation of the Oscarsberg Mission. This Swedish Lutheran Station lay forty miles north-east of the coal-mining town of Dundee situated in the valley of the Biggarsberg Mountains between Ladysmith and Newcastle. Makanya shared her excitement with contagion. She wrote this about the terrific experience, "what a rich joy it is to see different denominations beginning to realize that the success of Christs' progress among the Bantu people will largely depend upon native and white leaders thinking in terms of a Bantu Community and of the world at large."[126] When Makanya traveled throughout Natal and the Transvaal, she was on a mission to enhance the BYL's profile in rural South Africa. Makanya's mandate also entailed creating collaborations among other organizations, which, for example, she did by attending and speaking before a DOA meeting in *eThekwini* (Durban). She used the forum, which took place amid civic leaders, social workers, politicians, and educators, to discuss hygiene, domestic crafts, nutrition, and breastfeeding.[127] Makanya's quest to save the nation reversed the mission of the William J. Fulbright Scholars and the Peace Corps Programs by training indigenous people to carry out social work within their own countries rather than sending them outside to foreign ones.[128] Rural Natal represented the ideological and theoretical landscape that she believed was more important to carry out and to sustain practical needs within these respective communities where she conducted rounds.

Makanya's philosophy differed from her former Phelps-Stokes sponsor Dr. Charles T. Loram, who believed that the future of Africans lay in the countryside. She on the other hand questioned this viewpoint, "Why should the African be denied the right to grow his maximum and be able to earn an honest livelihood? In my time as a pupil, … we wrote the same exams as the Europeans and the results proved beyond doubt that we were more than equal to the task, considering that not only the language but the 'tests' were foreign to us."[129] Makanya kept education high on an agenda, and a mission fueled and injected by the financial donations from American or indigenous benefactors. Western Cape Paarl resident Mrs. Lucy Johnston, for example, gave Makanya £25 ($500) after an address to a Conference of Community Workers held at Imbumbulu.[130] In-kind gifts poured in to enhance Makanya's offerings. Living close to home had its benefits, her mother joined in the activism by planting extra vegetables; a cornucopia of potatoes, cabbage, beans, green mealies, and other harvested items, to feed the herd boys.[131] Such generosity afforded Makanya the opportunity to maintain "a demonstration garden, conduct Sunday School, organize and run a winter school for young girls and adult women, put on an annual leadership training conference for community workers, and to establish a night school for herder boys".[132]

Night schools mostly took place during the cold, winter months. "It was time when the harvesting [was] over and the rains which mark the beginning of the new plough season have not fallen and so women have little in their hands."[133] During the 1930s, government and mission schools educated 25% of school-aged children. Many Africans paid for schooling or failed to attend due to costs since education was not compulsory.[134] Matriculants operated under a system of flexibility. They worked during the day and studied at night; for instance, young boys herded sheep, goats, and cattle while adult women fetched water, worked in the fields, and washed clothes. All matriculants received up to three hours of free tuition to defray costs already subsidized by volunteer drivers like Isaac Dhlomo, an African bus operator, and an Indian man named Mr. Ram both of whom offered free conveyances to the night school. Sometimes they stayed throughout the week and returned to their respective homes on the weekends. Eager matriculants sat on "long benches with slates in their hands eager to learn by the dim light of a lantern or two to fathom the mysteries of reading, writing, and arithmetic":[135]

> Under the flickering light of a crude oil lamp swinging from the low roof the boys sit on three hard and narrow benches, each boy holding a slate in his hand and following the instructions of the teacher whose equipment consists only of a small blackboard. On one side of the floor are straw mats, to be unrolled later and spread on the ground when the boys go to sleep. For

> the youngsters spend the night there going back to their homes early in the morning… one evening we joined them as they sat around an open fire roasting meat… . They sang for us, haunting melodies, the words, and music having been composed by the boys themselves. Some day a collection of the herder boy's songs will make a distinct contribution to a story of African music.[136]

As much as Makanya championed her nation's development and growth, she also understood the importance of cultural retention. Her discussion of tribalism is glowing and introspective. While tribalism promoted indigenous customs, and fostered cooperation, Makanya argues for its modification in the Report of the Interdepartmental Commission on the Social, Health and Economic Conditions of Natives. When the proceedings took place in 1942, Makanya lived under the rule of an African chief at Imbumbulu whom everyone looked upon "as the center of their lives". Makanya criticizes these revered leaders for their shortsightedness in understanding that the community had to incorporate new ideas to promote growth rather than eschewing individualism and its role in development. "Their excuse is '*Ni si bizela abelungu*'"—when any progress is noticed or if there is talk of progress for the benefit of the community, they say "you are attracting white people into our centres".[137] Makanya's push to save the nation consisted of a proposal for the government to offer African leaders an incentive program:

> It would prove to be an incentive if the Government were to offer prizes to these chiefs who show an interest in progress and who are ambitious for their people to get ahead. Say for instance the chiefs showed an interest in education. Take for example the Maqadi district. If the Chief there would take an interest in education, and if perhaps once a year, or even say once in every three years, he would take a count of the number of children in school and show his interest in that way, it would act as a great incentive if some tangible reward were given to him for his efforts. Say for instance a count were taken of the number of children at school in this chief's district and that chief's district and the districts of some other chiefs and if a reward were offered to the chief in whose district the largest number of children went to school, I think it would answer well and act as a great incentive.[138]

Another resolution centered on tree planting. "If the chiefs could be induced to take an interest in cultivating the beauty of the landscape, it would help a lot. They should take an interest in these matters. And the chief who has the greatest number of trees planted in one or two years should receive some recognition. And roads too—or should I rather say paths? Roads which go to their kraals should be looked after; something should be done in an effort to inspire them in this regard."[139] This resolution highlighted development. The next one focuses on dispelling myths and promoting interracial cooperation and immersive learning.

Makanya appeared on a radio program entitled *Native Life in South Africa* possibly a play on Plaatje's ethnographic indictment against the country's segregationist laws. The program opens with an entreaty for Whites to visit Africans. She encourages tourists to move beyond Durban's white-sanded beaches to visit African homes amid the lush, verdant valleys where they stood. Makanya examines her people's diversity, but like Marks she bifurcates them into:

> "those who have accepted a higher standard of living through contact with the white man, and those who still live their tribal life-content to follow on the beaten paths of their ancestors".[140] Her possible condemnation of Western culture follows this depiction, she wrote, "Why should [we] discard some of [our] finest customs, which have made it possible for them to live, to love, and to laugh?"[141] The inquiry is anything but rhetorical. She answers her own question with this dioramic painting, "Here we are at dusk at Iqayimjangas Kraal… . Some of her pupils are tired—for the boys have been out all day tending the cattle and goats—the girls have all day long been carrying on their backs fat and thin babies."[142]

Participants sat in a circle and waited with bated breath to hear the scintillating stories of Ugogo (grandmother) that took place within the kraal where cattle typically resided, but in this case, its inside domain represented a site in which to carry out democracy, diversity, and gendered relations.

Wife of D. D. T. Jabavu Florence Thandiswa Jabavu spoke highly of traditional culture and its mores in a piece entitled 'Bantu Home Life' which appeared in *Christianity and the Natives of South Africa: A Yearbook of South African Mission* (1928). The essay makes a good case that rails against missionary education for the following reason. Lovedale College-trained Jabavu put her certificate in elementary teaching to good use when she argued that the African family life disintegrated under colonialism. In a viewpoint reminiscent of NND who proudly championed isiZulu culture, Jabavu points out that polygamy consisted of a structure that bred 'independence, industriousness, and collective supportiveness' (*Ubuntu, isivivane*) among African women.[143] Ugogo, who was part of this social and political network, preserved history, maintained genealogical knowledge, and passed down praise songs, historical narratives, and oral traditions whose social import lay in the fact that during this time:

> the Zulus having no books of their own, it may be said that their memory is the only library they possess and certainly some have very good ones. Here the westerner makes a grave mistake when he says that the loyalty of the African children to their parents is actuated by fear. The children having no books depend on their parents for the way, hence this saying: "Inyati I buzwa kwaba pambili" which translated would mean "If you would know the way watch those who gone the way."[144]

As one of the nation's revered custodians, this beloved and ardent supporter of African people 'knew the way'. Makanya lived for nearly eight decades, dying one year shy of this mark in 1971. Makanya's death signaled the burning of a library as an African proverb professes. At the end of her long life, European colonialism still held on tightly to a bevy of African nations: Zimbabwe, Namibia, Angola, Mozambique, and Guinea-Bissau among others which eventually attained independence in preceding and succeeding decades. Mpama/Palmer was still going strong politically when Makanya took her last earthly breath. Scholars Mia Roth and Robert R. Edgar document 'Aunty Jo's' colorful life behind the Kremlin's Wall.

Josie Mpama/Palmer

Mpama/Palmer (Fig. 4.3) began her public career during the ferocious campaigns mounted against the lodger's permits in Potchefstroom in the 1920s. She was the daughter of a Zulu man (Stephen Mpama) and a Coloured woman. Throughout her vibrant, political life, which spanned from 1903 to 1979, Mpama lived in Potchefstroom, Sophiatown, and eventually in Mzimhlophe, Soweto, where she assumed the Africanized surname, Mpama, instead of her given moniker Palmer. The former name provided her and her children privileges in Sophiatown which included better schools and other advantages.[145] Living in different parts of Johannesburg exposed Mpama/Palmer to many historical occurrences like Alexandra's bus boycotts, and the anti-pass campaign that she led along with African teacher David Bopape in the forties. She belonged to or held leadership positions in the DOA and the CPSA.

During the twenties and the thirties, the CPSA cemented its grip on Potchefstroom in the following successful way. When the municipality

Fig. 4.3 Josie Mpama/Palmer was an activist whose career spanned decades. As a member of the Bantu People's Theatre put on plays like Eugene O'Neill's *The Hairy Ape* and *the Plumes* in an effort to "reflect the true life, feelings, struggles and aspirations of the Bantu people" (*Drum Magazine*, June 8, 1975)[146]

charged T. W. Thibedi with "convening a meeting without a permit and inciting racial hostility", CPSA attorney Sidney Bunting got him off on the grounds of free speech.[147] Evidence of other successes added to the body's resume. CPSA leadership and members participated in Alexandra's bus boycotts and also in issues of transport in Brakpan, Port Elizabeth (PE), and Western Native Township. The body also supported dockworkers in Cape Town who protested in solidarity with Abyssinia (present-day

Ethiopia) and its quest to stave off colonization by Italy. Despite these accomplishments, the CPSA only garnered a membership of approximately 3000 constituents in the late twenties; however, it never captured the momentum of that growth thereafter; in fact by 1940 the numbers had shrunk to 280 dues-paying members.[148] Dismal tallies failed to stop Mpama/Palmer from rising within the CPSA's ranks.

Of the posts Mpama/Palmer held, she became the only African woman to serve on the Political Bureau's Central Committee (PBCC). Even with this lofty accomplishment, Mpama/Palmer lambasted the organization for this primary reason. "The Party in the early 1930s was something like a church organization, politically illiterate, but that its black members were nevertheless willing to fight when called upon by the Party to do so."[149] Mpama/Palmer believed that the CPSA needed to win over the masses and attract the poor so that they could fight for better conditions and become a mighty mass party. She had to admit to herself and openly with this statement, "We work in the village, for example, and all the time we worked there we carried on our struggle more on economic lines, and now that I have studied, I find my political mistakes. But how can I develop the masses on political lines when I myself am politically backward? We have mass activities and, in the factories, too, but only on economic lines. Even if we did work in the C. P. and based the struggle on political lines and had influence on the masses who looked upon us as leaders of the masses, as those who can defend and lead the masses, what happened? All the comrades were put in the centre and would become helpless creatures. I am ashamed to think of what was done for the two years I was in the district. It seems to be pretty bad where all become just the same… . I do not know all the European comrades, but I know the Natives and, as a matter of fact, I do not see four or five people who could take over the leadership."[150] Another problem was that the organization did little for women when as she proclaimed, they were "the most militant fighters".[151]

Mpama/Palmer also launched assaults against female leaders with an unrelenting wrath. She described the DOA as merely a tea party, which this book refutes on several grounds, but more specifically in the intellectualism that its founder and constituents espoused (Chap. 6).[152] Mpama/Palmer also believed that the NCAW's leadership was responsible for burying the political body.[153] North Carolinian Madie Hall Xuma (MHX), wife of ANC leader Dr. Alfred B. Xuma, and leader of the Zenzele Clubs, came under fierce fire when Mpama/Palmer accused her of being apolitical. The embattled leader who relocated to South Africa and lived there from 1940 to 1963 issued a rebuttal, "I decided to stay out [of politics] because this is a foreign country to me. I didn't want to get involved in controversial matters."[154] The need for female unity heightened. Given the political climate and Hertzog's amassing power, Mpama/Palmer issued several calls for women to organize as these headlines suggest, "An Appeal to African Women to Join the Struggle against Oppressive Laws" and "African Women Must Be Organised We Are Prepared to Move". These *Umsebenzi* and *Mochonono* editorials explain why Mpama urged African women to galvanize. Each submission laid out what she believed represented the necessary steps to save the nation: **accompaniment**, **waking up**, **moving forward** (phambili), and **mobilization**. Accompaniment highlighted gender when Mpama/Palmer addresses inferiority and non-exposure in 'Educating Our Bantu Women'. She writes:

> It is quite true as you say that some people say women are inferior to men, but in most cases those men who are politically advanced are to be blamed for the backwardness of their wives, sisters and daughters. For instance, most men will go out to either sports meetings etc. etc., and never have the slightest thought of taking their womenfolk with them.[155]

Mpama/Palmer offers criticism and a suggestion at the same time. She leans heavily on African men as the heads of households, while also blaming them for African women's inexperience in the political arena. This highly reputed activist sought this goal through the 'blended relationship' she proposed: "... Wives or women friends accompanying [men] to meetings to participate long term in the liberation struggle rather than just return home after the attainment of a victory like in the case of Potchefstroom, a town situated in the Northwest Province, where residents there successfully opposed the lodger's permits in the late twenties."[156] Lodger's permits were licenses that granted the municipality the authority to regulate the occupancy of dwellings. Children over the age of eighteen could no longer live rent-free with their parents.[157] Renters also suffered when they tendered lodger's fees for letted out rooms. A surge of arrests and assaults on women skyrocketed when the municipality enforced the lodger's permits.[158] Potchefstroom's economy took another hit when the ability to earn money lessened for African and Coloured women. On top of everything else, demographic changes soon struck the Northwest town. Migrants from neighboring areas flooded Potchefstroom and saturated its market so much so that demand for labor plummeted to deafening levels.[159] Evictions began to soar as did the court cases. Mpama/Palmer and other women met nightly to strategize.

As part of the **waking up process**, these militant dissenters sung in the streets. They moved throughout each artery until all women had been collected. Young boys carried out the summons for these gatherings with the blowing of bugles usually around 2 am.[160] Galvanization led to Potchefstroom's female populace's insistent challenge to authority. Not only did these protesters march throughout the town to return furniture and other household belongings to evictees, but they also supported their efforts to attain legal recourse. Mpama/Palmer turned the state's architectural layout on its head and to her constituencies' advantage when the policy of containment served as a major pawn in the defendants' chess game. Potchefstroom's corners served as holding stations. Mpama/Palmer orchestrated this intellectual feat brilliantly by only allowing witnesses to enter the courtroom at their designated times to avoid tampering.[161]

Mpama/Palmer experienced overwhelming success, however, she realized that in order for the women to move forward, they had to do the same and recognize their capabilities beyond their roles as mothers and wives. She asked, "Is this not the time for women to wake up and to say my place is no longer in the kitchen but on the political platform to demand my rights?"[162] For this to happen, African, Coloured, White, and Asian women needed to attain political education in order to stand with world leaders to demand freedom and equality for all.[163] Through accompaniment, waking up, moving forward, and mobilization, Mpama/Palmer addresses the question of womanhood by turning the gaze onto them so that they could see that:

> It is today or never! We do not expect to undergo worse than we have done in the past. No matter how effective a struggle our men put up it will prove fruitless without our help.[164]

Cecilia Lillian Tshabalala

Despite Tshabalala's reticence to discuss race in her own personal life, she freely elaborated on America's system of Jim Crow. She confronted race through the use of comparative history, firsthand experiences, and religion. Editorials clearly reveal her positionality as an insider/outsider who

Fig. 4.4 Cecilia Lillian Tshabalala. "The Message for the New Year", *Bantu World* 13 February 1938. Tshabalala used her insider/outsider status to reflect on the contemporary world in which she lived. As a member of the South African Diaspora, and as an African in the United States, Tshabalala learned first-hand about America's race relations. It is unfortunate that Tshabalala failed to share any comparisons between the United States and South Africa which could have offered fresh insight on two countries with similar systems of oppression

reflected on anti-blackness/otherness from the comfort of her South African home. Tshabalala (Fig. 4.4) witnessed the disconnect between America's international image which highlighted racial unity, and the domestic one which cultivated discriminatory practices within the United States, South Africa's segregationist doppelganger. In later years, legal expert Mary Dudziak makes this same contention. In *Cold War Civil*

Rights, Dudziak declares that America hid the domestic skeletons in its racial closet by projecting a positive international image.[165] America seemed to forget that people traveled. Tshabalala assumed the position of an oral historian during her time in the United States where she engaged in a negotiation with the reading public, the impacted subjects, and the interpretation she rendered to the historical record.

Tshabalala puts Christianity on trial and on the stakes with this sizzling commentary in an editorial appearing in the *Bantu World*'s 'Women Supplement', when she declared, "The Orient could not very well understand Christian workers coming from a country where human beings like NEGROES are still lynched and burnt at the stake."[166] Expulsed Indigenous Peoples and Japanese inhabitants attended the Chautauqua conferences where religion, camaraderie, and sisterhood stood as the centerpieces of this spiritual and intellectual gathering. This contrasted with the life they left behind. "Women … had been driven out of INDIA and JAPAN because of the prejudices exhibited to all races of colour in the Christian home whence come missionaries such as AMERICA, where those Indians and Japanese students are barred from entering aristocratic boarding houses and hotels."[167] But while this welcomed annual event drew in hundreds from across the world, its focus on Christianity led Tshabalala to question the faith. Brotherly love turned into a murderous affair especially when practitioners still lynched and burnt African Americans at the stake and kept their human cuts and joints as souvenirs.[168] Of the 4743 lynchings recorded from 1882 to 1968, 3446 (72.2%) were Black, while Whites rang the death toll 1297 times (27.3%).[169] Ida B. Wells-Barnett was a fierce critic and meticulous documentarian of these lawless murders carried out for alleged transgressions, to maintain control and to intimidate especially with African Americans gaining greater political liberties. Her pamphlet *A Red Record* provides statistics and other data during this horrific time in America's history.[170] Over seventy lynchings took place mostly in the southern states and the Midwest during Tshabalala's tenure on American soil.

Trees and ropes took the lives of African Americans. Sailors on the SS Mendi that Tshabalala alludes to died being consumed by crashing and thunderous waves when another vessel collided with the troopship. A shortage of laborers and a request by Great Britain for additional manpower led Prime Minister Louis Botha to answer the European nation's call by deploying the Native Labour Contingent to work behind the

French front lines. The SS Mendi came to life in Glasgow, Scotland, when the British African and Steam Navigation Company launched operations in 1905. The boat earned its initial use as a mail carrier, but during the First World War, its battalions began conveying delayed shipments of supplies along the combat zones. On 21 February 1917, 600 African soldiers lost their lives when the boat lowered into the depths of the sea near the Isle of Wright. Tshabalala's observations on lynchings and the SS Mendi also resonates with the inclusion of Abyssinia (present-day Ethiopia).[171]

Considered one of the world's darlings, Ethiopia (formerly Abyssinia) earned its reputation from several sources. The Bible vividly describes this land of kings and queens as place of welcome, as this quote illustrates from Psalms 68:31 "Princes shall come out of Egypt; Ethiopia shall soon stretch out her hands unto God."[172] Many centuries later, the country earned fame because Menelik II had militarily outmaneuvered Italy in the decisive Battle of Adowa in 1896. That historic victory further convinced Diasporic African descendants, particularly those espousing Rastafarianism, of Abyssinia's divine importance. Italy refused to let Abyssinia rest on its militant laurels. The boot-shaped country situated on a peninsula that juts into the Mediterranean Sea was content with licking its wounds until Fascist leader Benito Mussolini decided to compete with European juggernauts Great Britain and France to obtain overseas acquisitions. With Italy's interest in colonization renewed, Mussolini eyed its unrequited prize, Abyssinia, and challenged this Horn of Africa state once again when it intervened in its border dispute with its neighbor Somalia. Mussolini sent his forces, and for five years they occupied Abyssinia and disrupted the country's status as one of only two African nations not colonized by European powers from 1935 to 1941.[173] The other country having this distinction was West Africa's Liberia, which had strong ties to America, another one of the fourteen attendants at the Berlin Conference.[174]

Tshabalala drew from this historical background to issue a bold pronouncement about this nation. She wrote, "True, Abyssinia ... has been instantly wiped off the map of the world; and no angel nor missionary has told us why in spite of our prayer."[175] The DOA leader recognized that the birthrights of South Africa, Abyssinia, and other African countries faced the impending loom of their respective cultures and political systems being historically erased as various colonial powers continued to sink their political teeth deep into the soul of the African continent. Tshabalala's drawing on actual historical occurrences conjures up deprivation as a threaded book theme—the loss and the potentiality of human life; the finality and the infinity of their oral obituaries; and the issue of domination and subordination. "The prevalent view in Britain was an absolute belief in the superiority of the white man. So, although it was deemed necessary to conscript and recruit from the Caribbean, Africa and India, there was uneasiness at the prospect of putting weapons into the hands of colonial subjects."[176] Tshabalala addresses internationalism yet again, but this time she explores its quotidian practices. Instead of focusing on the subaltern, she turns to the everyday practices of domination within transnational settings like Abyssinia (present-day Ethiopia), the United States, Japan, and China. Her tenure within the Gold Coast from 1919 to 1922 is alluded to in American newspapers, but not within the editorials that she submitted to the *Bantu World.*

She went to the Gold Coast at a time when the British controlled the country just years shy of the Amalgamation of southern and northern Nigeria which united these regions in 1914.[177] Insights on missionary life, British colonialism, and ethnic relations proposed to bear additional interpretations and comparisons on the rule of dominant powers, on being another African national from another country, ethnicity, and linguistic tongue, and her position as a twenty-one-year-old single woman navigating a new terrain. Tshabalala's reticence to share her personal life and experiences is a continual theme threaded throughout her commentaries. Other African women fill in the missing blanks that her silence fails to amplify. Several things happened during African women's tenures and visits abroad: they gleaned ideas about nationhood; and they also witnessed similar systems of oppression. Jim Crow represented an eerie reminder of South Africa's articulation of segregation as a national policy.

Notes

1. Njabulo S. Ndebele, Forward, Sol T Plaatje and the 'power of all' in Janet Remmington, Brian Willan and Njabulo Ndebele, *Sol Plaatje's Native Life in South Africa: Past and Present* (Johannesburg: University of Witwatersrand Press, 2016): ix–xiv.
2. "Africans Resist White Control," https://www.facinghistory.org/confronting-apartheid/chapter-1/africans-resist-white-control, date accessed 16 April 2021 and M. J. Daymond, Dorothy Driver et al., *Women Writing Africa: The Southern Region* (New York: The Feminist Press 2003, 161–162.
3. Zubeida Jaffer, *Beauty of the Heart*, 100.

4. Solomon Tshekisho Plaatje, https://www.sahistory.org.za/people/solomon-tshekisho-plaatje, date accessed 28 November 2021. In 1901, Solomon Tshekisho Plaatje, who served as clerk, as an interpreter, and as a teacher among other titles, established *Koranta ea Becoana*, a Setswana-English weekly that he edited for at least six years. His other works included "*Mhudi, An Epic of South African Native Life a Hundred Years Ago* (1930), *The Mote and the Beam: An Epic on Sex-Relationship 'Twixt White and Black in British South Africa* (1921), and translations of four Shakespeare plays into Setswana".
5. Solomon T. Plaatje, *Native Life in South Africa: Before and Since the European War and the Boer Rebellion*, http://www.gutenberg.org/ebooks/1452, date accessed 6 June 2018 (hereafter Native Life in South Africa). See T. R. H. Davenport, *The Beginnings of Urban Segregation in South Africa: The Natives (Urban Areas) Act of 1923 and Its Background* (Grahamstown: Rhodes University, 1971).
6. A. B. Xuma: "Bridging the Gap between White and Black in South Africa" (1930) Commentary by Harvey Feinberg, Connecticut State Universityhttps://www.milestonedocuments.com/documents/view/a--b-xumas-bridging-the-gap-between-white-and-black-in-south-africa/ date accessed 11 November 2020.
7. Solomon T. Plaatje, *Native Life in South Africa: Before and Since the European War and the Boer Rebellion*, http://www.gutenberg.org/ebooks/1452, date accessed 6 June 2018 (hereafter Native Life in South Africa).
8. Native Life in South Africa online.
9. Ibid. See Kenneth J. Doka, *Disenfranchised Grief: Recognizing Hidden Sorrow* (Maryland: Lexington Books, 1989), 3.
10. Dawne Y. Curry, *Apartheid on a Black Isle: Removal and Resistance in Alexandra, South Africa* (New York: Palgrave Macmillan, 2012), Chapter 5: They Died Horribly, 101–115. See Dawne Y. Curry, "When Apartheid Interfered with Funerals: We Found Ways to Grieve in Alexandra, South Africa," *International Journal of Interdisciplinary Social Sciences*, 2, 2, (2007), 245–252. I coined the term oral obituary to discuss how narrators who stood before the Truth and Reconciliation Commission (TRC) explained how people died rather than how they lived. These tribunals, which were held in different cities and townships throughout South Africa, document the atrocities that occurred under apartheid from 1960 to 1994. When Irene Tukie March, Margaret Madlana, and others offered testimonies before the TRC, they discuss the daily routines, eating habits, pastimes, health conditions, and other mundane activities that their sons Philip March and Bongani Madlana carried out before they brutally passed away.

11. A. J. Christopher, Segregation and Cemeteries in Port Elizabeth, South Africa, *The Geographical Journal*, 161, 1 (March 1995): 38.
12. Siyinbinza iAfrika (We're Stabbing Africa!) *Umteteli waBantu*, August 2, 1924, 8; see also Jeff Opland, *The Nation's Bounty*, 178.
13. Ibid.
14. M. J. Daymond, Dorothy Driver et al, *Women Writing Africa*, 161.
15. Ibid.
16. See Elizabeth A. Eldredge, Sources of Conflict in Southern Africa, C. 1800–30: The 'Mfecane' Reconsidered, The *Journal of African History*, 33, 1 (1992): 1–35 and Julian Cobbing, The Mfecane As Alibi: Thoughts On Dithakong and Mbolompo, *Journal of African History*, 29 (1988): 487–519.
17. M. J. Daymond, Dorothy Driver et al., *Women Writing Africa*, 161.
18. Nontsizi Mgqwetho, *Umteteli waBantu*, December 8, 1923, 4.
19. M. J. Daymond, Dorothy Driver et al., *Women Writing Africa*, 161.
20. Nontsizi Mgqwetho, *Umteteli waBantu*, December 8, 1923, 4.
21. See Orlando Patterson, *Slavery and Social Death: A Comparative Study* (Cambridge: Harvard University Press, 2018).
22. Daymond, Dorothy Driver et al., *Women Writing Africa*, 161.
23. Ibid.
24. Ibid.
25. Ecclesiastes 3:20, https://biblehub.com/commentaries/ecclesiastes/3-20.htm, date accessed 29 May 2021.
26. Nancy J. Jacobs, *African History Through Sources: Colonial Contexts and Everyday Experiences, c. 1850–1946* (Cambridge: Cambridge University Press, 2014), 172.
27. Thembela Vokwana, A New Take on the Work of Caluza, https://www.newframe.com/a-new-take-on-the-work-of-caluza/#:~:text=Umteto%20we%20Land%20Act%20%28also%20known%20as%20Silusapo%2FiLand,Native%20National%20Congress%2C%20which%20later%20became%20the%20ANC, date accessed 26 November 2021.
28. Ntongela Masilela, *An Outline of the New African Movement in South Africa* (Trenton: Africa World Press, 2013), xii–xxv.
29. Nancy J. Jacobs, *African History Through Sources*, 173. See also Reuben Tholakele Caluza, "The Land Act Song (Umteto We Land Act)" (London: HMV Studio B, 1930).
30. Nontsizi Mgqwetho, Listen, Compatriots! In M. J. Daymond, Dorothy Driver et al (eds). *Women Writing South Africa*, 176–177.
31. Duncan Brown, My pen is the Tongue of a Skilful (sic) Poet: African-Christian Identity and the Poetry of Nontsizi Mgqwetho, *English in Africa*, 31, 1 (May 2004): 26.
32. Ibid.

33. Jeff Opland, *The Nation's Bounty: The Xhosa Poetry of Nontsizi Mgqwetho* (Johannesburg: University of Witwatersrand Press, 2007).
34. Duncan Brown, My pen is the Tongue, 26.
35. Ibid.
36. Ibid., and Nontsizi (Cizama, Imbongikazi yakwaCizama) Mgqwetho https://www.sahistory.org.za/people/nontsizi-cizama-imbongikazi-yakwacizama-mgqwetho, date accessed 28 December 2020.
37. Daymond, Dorothy Driver et al., *Women Writing Africa*, 176–177.
38. Duncan Brown, My pen is the Tongue of a Skilful Poet, 28.
39. Margaret McCord, *The Calling of Katie Makanya* (Cape Town: David Philip, 1995), 215, op. cited Brandy Thomas, "Give Them Their Due": Black Female Missionaries and The South African-American Nexus, 1920s-1930s, B. A. Thesis, The Ohio State University, Columbus, Ohio, 2011, 67–68.
40. Jeff Opland, *The Nation's Bounty*, 178.
41. M. J. Daymond, Dorothy Driver et al., *Women Writing Africa*, 161.
42. David Killingray, Significant Black South Africans in Britain before 1912: Pan-African Organisations and the Emergence of South Africa's First Black Lawyers, *South African Historical Journal*, 64, 3 (2012): 403–404. See *The New Age*, November 4, 1897, 79.
43. Michael Savage, "The Imposition of the Pass Laws on the African Population in South Africa, 1916–1984." *African Affairs* 85, 339 (April 1986): 181.
44. Ibid.
45. See Julia C. Wells, *We Now Demand! The History of Women's Resistance to Pass Laws* (Johannesburg: University of Witwatersrand Press, 1993).
46. Julia C. Wells, *We Now Demand!* 21–22, 48, 53–54. See Native and Coloured Women of the Province of the Orange Free State, 'Petition of the Native Coloured Women of the Province of the Orange Free State' in M. J. Daymond, Dorothy Driver et al., *Women Writing Africa*, 158–161.
47. Julia C. Wells, *We Now Demand!*, 40–43.
48. Ibid.
49. Zubeida Jaffer, *Beauty of the Heart: The Life and Times of Charlotte Mannya Maxeke* (Cape Town: ZJ Books, 2016), 117.
50. "Amadodakazi kwaZulu," *Ilanga laseNatal*, August 31, 1946, 9.
51. Jeff Opland, Nontsizi Mgqwetho, Listen Compatriots!, 176. Nontsizi (Cizama, Imbongikazi yakwaCizama) Mgqwetho https://www.sahistory.org.za/people/nontsizi-cizama-imbongikazi-yakwacizama-mgqwetho, 24 December 2020.
52. Ibid.
53. We're Stabbing Africa, *Umteteli waBantu*, August 2, 1924, 8. See also https://www.poetryinternational.org/pi/poem/11272/auto/0/0/

Nontsizi-Mgqwetho/Were-Stabbing-Africa/en/nocache, date accessed 28 December 2020.

54. Ibid.
55. See Leonard Thompson, *A History of South Africa* (New Haven: Yale University Press, 1990).
56. Thulani Sokombela, Looking Back and Looking Ahead: The Poetry of Nontsizi Mgqwetho http://www.ipedr.com/vol42/020-ICKCS2012-K10010.pdf date accessed 17 March 2021.
57. Yimbongikazi Nontsizi Mgqwetto, Mayibuye ! I Afrika ! Awu I. *Umteteli waBantu*, December 8, 1923, 4.
58. Ibid., and Duncan Brown, My Pen Is the Tongue of a Skilful Poet, 28–35.
59. Adu Boahen, *African Perspectives on Colonialism* (Baltimore: Johns Hopkins University, 1989), 10–25.
60. Augusta Welden Comstock, 'Africa in Spelman, Spelman in Africa,' Spelman Archives, *Missions*, 12, 1 (January 1921): 23.
61. Ruth Isabel Seabury, *Daughter of Africa*, 78.
62. Nombonisa Gasa (ed.), *Women in South Africa History* (Pretoria: Human Sciences Research Council, 2007).
63. Helen Bradford, Not a Nongqawuse Story: An Anti-heroine in Historical Perspective in Gasa (ed.), *Women in South Africa History*, 43–90.
64. Africa Information Service (ed.) *Return to the Source: Selected Speeches by Amilcar Cabral* (New York: New York University Press, 1973), https://www.jstor.org/stable/j.ctv12pnps, date accessed 1 January 2021.
65. Adu Boahen, *African Perspectives on Colonialism* (Baltimore: Johns Hopkins University, 1989), 10–25 and Robert O. Collins, *Historical Problems in Imperial Africa, Problems in African History* (Princeton: Markus Wiener Publishers, 2007), 29–35.
66. Yimbongikazi Nontsizi Mgqwetto, Mayibuye ! I Afrika! and Plaatje, *Native Life in South Africa.*
67. Lee Hirsch, Director, Amandla: A Revolution in Four Part Harmony, 2002.
68. Deborah Walker King, African Americans, and the Culture of Pain, https://www.upress.virginia.edu/title/4442 date accessed 7 April 2021.
69. 'Africa, My Native Land,' and Nontsizi Mgqwetho, Listen, Compatriots! in M. J. Daymond, Dorothy Driver et al. (eds.) *Women Writing South Africa*, 161–162, 176–177.
70. What they said about missionary school pioneer Dr Charlotte Maxeke, https://gatewaystoanewworld.wordpress.com/2016/01/29/what-they-said-about-dr-charlotte-maxeke/ date accessed 15 April 2021.
71. Tsitsi Ella Jaji, *Africa in Stereo*, 50–52.
72. Margaret McCord, *The Calling of Katie Makanya* (Cape Town: David Philip, 1995), 54.
73. "Women's Suffrage Bill," *Umteteli waBantu*, March 28, 1921, 3.

74. Zubeida Jaffer, *Beauty of the Heart*, 138–139.
75. Nombonisa Gasa, *Women in South African History*, 146–148.
76. *Nombonisa Gasa, Women in South African History*, 146–147.
77. Zubeida Jaffer, *Beauty of the Heart*, 125–126.
78. Ibid., 126.
79. Ibid., 64.
80. Ibid. and W. E. B. Dubois, The Talented Tenth Essay, 1903.
81. Du Bois, The Talented Tenth Essay and Summary, https://study.com/academy/lesson/web-du-bois-the-talented-tenth-essay-summary-theory.html, date accessed 8 August 2020.
82. African Methodist Episcopal Church Overview, https://www.learnreligions.com/african-methodist-episcopal-church-699933, date accessed 11 May 2021.
83. Zubeida Jaffer, *Beauty of the Heart*, 62–63.
84. David Killingray, Significant Black South Africans in Britain before 1912, 401–402.
85. Ibid., 402.
86. Post Slavery Feminist Thought and the Pan-African Struggle (1892–1927): From Anna J. Cooper to Addie W. Hunton, https://www.globalresearch.ca/post-slavery-feminist-thought-and-the-pan-african-struggle-1892-1927-from-anna-j-cooper-to-addie-w-hunton/5575039, date accessed 15 December 2020, Hakim Adi, *Pan-Africanism: A History* (London: Bloomsbury Academic, 2018), 20, Tembeka Ngcukaitabi, *The Land is Ours: South Africa's First Black Lawyer and the Birth of Constitutionalism* (Cape Town: Penguin Books, 2018), 43-47, 51, 55, 56, 273.
87. David Killingray, Significant Black South Africans in Britain before 1912, 403. See PMBAR, Harriette Colenso Papers, A204 Box 33, letter dd. 2 August 1899.
88. Ibid.
89. See Saul Dubow, *Illicit Union: Scientific Racism in Modern South Africa* (Cambridge/WUP African Studies) (Cambridge: Cambridge University Press, 1997), William Beinart and Saul Dubow, *Segregation and Apartheid in Twentieth Century South Africa* (New York: Routledge, 1995), and *Making A Voice: African Resistance To Segregation In South Africa* (African Modernization and Development Series) (New York: Westview Press, 1997).
90. David Killingray, Significant Black South Africans in Britain before 1912, 404.
91. Ibid.
92. Africans Resist White Control, Chapter 1, https://www.facinghistory.org/confronting-apartheid/chapter-1/africans-resist-white-control, date accessed 28 December 2020.
93. Zubeida Jaffer, *Beauty of the Heart*, 101.

94. Mrs. C. M. Maxeke's Extensive Tour, *Bantu World*, 12.
95. Zubeida Jaffer, *Beauty of the Heart*, 100.
96. Richard Ralston, Reviewed Work: *Vukani Bantu! The Beginnings of Black Protest Politics in South Africa to 1912* by André Odendaal, *Journal of Southern African Studies*, 13, 3 (April 1987): 441.
97. Ibid.
98. Zubeida Jaffer, *Beauty of the Heart*, 100.
99. Nkosinathi Sithole, Beyond African nationalism: Isaiah Shembe's hymns and African literature, *Literator*, 35, 1 (November 2014): 1–8, https://www.researchgate.net/publication/296185928_Beyond_African_nationalism_Isaiah_Shembe%27s_hymns_and_African_literature, date accessed 2 March 2020.
100. John A. Williams, *From the South African Past: Narratives, Documents and Debates* (New York: Houghton Mifflin Company, 1997), 235.
101. John A. Williams, *From the South African Past: Narratives, Documents and Debates*, 236.
102. "Amadodakazi eMfume M. S.," *Ilanga laseNatal*, February 5, 1944, 7–8.
103. See Keletso E. Atkins, Origins of the AmaWasha: the Zulu Washermen's Guild in Natal, 1850–1910, *Journal of African History*, 27, 1 (March 1986): 41–57 and Charles Van Onselen, *Studies in the Social and Economic History of the Witwatersrand, 1886–1914, Vol. 1: New Babylon* (Studies in the Social & Economic History of the Witwatersrand) (London: Longman Publishers, 1982).
104. Tsitsi Ella Jaji, *Africa in Stereo: Modernism, Music, and Pan-African Solidarity* (Oxford: Oxford University Press, 2014), 51.
105. Zubeida Jaffer, *Beauty of the Heart*, 100.
106. Ibid.
107. We're Stabbing Africa, Siyayibinza-I Afrika!!!, *Umteteli waBantu*, August 2, 1924, 8.
108. Zubeida Jaffer, *Beauty of the Heart*, 100.
109. Myrtle Trowbridge, Sibusiswe Makanya, unpublished biography, Sibusiswe Makanya Papers.
110. Violet Sibusisiwe Makanya, *Bantu World*, March 3, 1937, 10.
111. Umehani Khan, A Critical Study of the Life of Sibusisiwe Makanya and Her Work as Educator and Social Worker in the Umbumbulu District of Natal 1894–1971, 82, https://researchspace.ukzn.ac.za/xmlui/handle/10413/16962, date accessed 4 February 2021.
112. W. E. B. Du Bois, *The Philadelphia Negro* (Philadelphia: University of Pennsylvania Press, 1899).
113. Letter from Sibusisiwe Makanya to Agricultural Missions Foundation, Inc., From a Record of the Bantu Youth League Work, July 1930–July

1935, 1, Historical Papers, Cullen Library, University of Witwatersrand, AD843/RJ/Pb13, Organisations, Bantu Youth League, Box 251.

114. Letter from Mrs. Mabel Carney to Dr. Charles T. Loram, 13 June 1930, Historical Papers, Cullen Library, University of Witwatersrand, AD843/ RJ/Pb13, Organisations, Bantu Youth League, Box 251.
115. Letter from Sibusisiwe Makanya to Agricultural Missions Foundation, 1.
116. Ibid.
117. Umehani Khan, A Critical Study of the Life of Sibusisiwe Makanya, 97.
118. Lavinia Scott, General Letter, Adams, June 7, 1933, written by Lavinia Scott, 1907–1959, in American Board of Commissioners for Foreign Missions Papers, of Harvard University. Houghton Library (ABC 77.1 (Box 47; individual biography. Makanya, Violet S.—Makhanya, Mrs. Hamilton) (Cambridge, MA) (07 June 1933), 3 page(s) (hereafter Lavinia Scott letter).
119. Ibid.
120. Ibid.
121. Sibusisiwe Violet Makanya, https://live.fundza.mobi/home/library/non-fiction-books/against-the-wind-new-readers-publishers/sibusisiwe-violet-makhanya/ date accessed 3 January 2021.
122. Deborah Gaitskell, "Hot Meeting and Hard Kraals: African Biblewomen in Transvaal Methodism, 1924–60," *Journal of Religion in Africa*, XXX, 3 (2000): 279, and Pam Brooks, *Boycotts, Buses, and Passes: Black Women's Resistance in the U.S. South and South Africa* (Amherst: University of Massachusetts Press, 2008), 90.
123. Sibusisiwe Makanya, For Mr. Lovall's Circular Minutes, The Bantu Youth League Papers, Natal, Historical Papers, Cullen Library, University of Witwatersrand, Organisations, Bantu Youth League, Box 251, AD843/ RJ/Pb13.
124. Ibid.
125. Ibid.
126. Sibusisiwe Makanya, For Mr. Lovall's Circular Minutes.
127. Amadodakazi aseAfrika: Ukuqalwa Kwawo-The Formation, *Ilanga laseNatal*, April 9, 1938, 13.
128. W. E. B. Du Bois, *The Philadelphia Negro: A Social Study* (Philadelphia: University of Pennsylvania Press, 1995).
129. Glimpses of Native Life in South Africa, Radio Talk by Sibusisiwe Makanya, Durban, Natal, South Africa, Historical Papers, Cullen Library, University of Witwatersrand, Organisations, Bantu Youth League, Box 251, AD843/RJ/Pb13, 1.
130. Umehani Khan, A Critical Study of the Life of Sibusisiwe Makanya, 87.
131. Ibid.
132. Lavinia Scott Letter, 1.

133. Ibid., 2.
134. Umehani Khan, A Critical Study of the Life of Sibusisiwe Makanya, 84.
135. Ibid., 85.
136. Lavinia Scott Letter, 2.
137. University of South Africa (UNISA), Department of Native Affairs: Report of the Interdepartmental Commission on the Social, Health, and Economic Conditions of Urban Natives, 1942, Mondelinge Getuienis Voor Die Natarelle Kommissre/Minutes of Verbatim Evidence, V. 9, 6304.
138. Ibid., 6304–6305.
139. Ibid., 6305.
140. Umehani Khan, A Critical Study of the Life of Sibusisiwe Makanya, 85–86.
141. Ibid.
142. Sibusisiwe Violet Makanya, Glimpses of Native Life in South Africa, 1.
143. V. M. Sisi Magaqi, Florence Thandiswa Jabavu, Bantu Home Life, in Daymond, Dorothy Driver et al., *Women Writing Africa*, 189.
144. Sibusisiwe Violet Makanya, Glimpses of Native Life in South Africa, 1.
145. Ibid., 55.
146. Robert R. Edgar, *Josie Mpama/Palmer*, 102.
147. Sibusisiwe Violet Makanya, Glimpses of Native Life in South Africa, 55.
148. Dominic Fortescue, The Communist Party of South Africa, and the African Working Class in the 1940s, *The International Journal of African Historical Studies*, 24, 3 (1991): 482.
149. Ibid., 482, 484, 490, 492.
150. Robert R. Edgar, *Josie Mpama/Palmer*, 21, 103, and Apollon Davidson, Irina Filatova et al. (eds.) *South Africa and the Communist International: A Documentary History, Volume II Bolshevik Footsoldiers to Victims of Bolshevisation 1931–1939* (London: Frank Cass, 2003), 194–195.
151. Josie Mpama, Address of J. Mpama to Sixth National Conference, CPSA, September 1936 (Extract from Conference Minutes), in Apollon Davidson, Irina Filatova et al, *South Africa and the Communist International: A Documentary History, Volume 11 Bolshevik Footsoldiers to Victims of Bolshevisation 1931–1939* (London: Frank Cass, 2003), 215–216.
152. Josie Palmer Papers, Institute for Commonwealth Studies, London, England.
153. Cherryl Walker, *Women and Resistance in South Africa* (New York: Monthly Review Press, 1982), 80.
154. Pamela Brooks, Boycotts, *Buses, and Passes: Black Women's Resistance in the United States and South Africa* (Amherst: University of Massachusetts Press, 2008), 173.
155. "Educating Our Bantu Women", *Mochonono* 22, November 1933 op. cited Robert R. Edgar, *Josie Mpama/Palmer*, 174.

156. Robert R. Edgar, *Josie Mpama/Palmer*, 41–51, 58, 64, 65, 67.
157. Ibid., 41.
158. Julia C. Wells, *We Now Demand! The History of Women's Resistance to Pass Laws in South Africa*, (Johannesburg: University of Witwatersrand Press, 1993), 66.
159. Ibid., 67.
160. Julia C. Wells, Josie Mpama interview, Potchefstroom, 1977.
161. Julia C. Wells, *We Now Demand*, 66–72.
162. Robert R. Edgar, *Josie Mpama/Palmer*, 174.
163. Ibid., 175.
164. Ibid., 179.
165. See Mary Dudziak, *Cold War Civil Rights* (Princeton: Princeton University Press, 2002).
166. Cecilia Lillian Tshabalala, "Miss C. L. Tshabalala's Address" *Bantu World*, January 15, 1938, 11.
167. Ibid.
168. Ibid.
169. "History of Lynchings," https://www.naacp.org/history-of-lynchings/ date accessed 2 May 2021.
170. See Ida B. Wells Barnett, *The Red Record Tabulated Statistics and Alleged Causes of Lynching in the United States* (Alpha Editions, 2018), Michelle Duster, *Ida B. the Queen: The Extraordinary Life and Legacy of Ida B. Wells* (Atria/One Signal Publishers, 2021), Alfred M. Duster et al., *Crusade for Justice: The Autobiography of Ida B. Wells*, Second Edition (Chicago: University of Chicago Press, 2020), and Paula J. Giddings, *Ida: A Sword Among Lions: Ida B. Wells and the Campaign Against Lynching* (New York: Amistad, 2009).
171. SS Mendi, https://www.sahistory.org.za/article/ss-mendi, date accessed 4 May 2021.
172. Bible, Psalms 68:31.
173. See Harold G. Marcus, *A History of Ethiopia* (Los Angeles: University of California Press, 2002).
174. Other countries that participated were Sweden, Norway, Great Britain, France, Austria-Hungary, Germany, and Portugal among other nations.
175. Cecilia Lillian Tshabalala, "Miss C. L. Tshabalala's Address."
176. Baroness Lola Young, The hidden history of the sinking of the SS Mendi, https://www.britishcouncil.org/voices-magazine/hidden-history-sinking-ss-mend, date accessed 4 May 2021.
177. See Toyin Falola and Matthew M. Heaton (ed.) *History of Nigeria* (Cambridge: Cambridge University Press, 2008).

CHAPTER 5

Travel Narratives of Globetrotting African Women

On a beautiful Sunday morning accentuated by blue skies and voluminous sunshine, the Union Castle rang its bell to alert passengers of high noon tea. Like others onboard, South Africa's Rilda Matta ignored the call and its incessant urgency to enjoy the revelry all around her. A raft of sea lions frolicked in and out of the water in a move that Matta defined as an act that praise God. Flying fish also gained her rapt attention. Matta's visual pallet was filled yet again when the sun rose and set like a fiery ball before it vanished into the depths of the water and the expanse of the horizon. Sometimes, Matta and fellow passengers [saw] nothing else but the periwinkle ocean below and the cerulean sky above. In a travel narrative that notes geography, meteorology, animal life, race relations, and American culture, Matta witnessed the market town of Kenilworth, the Portuguese archipelago of the Madeira islands, and other land masses on this inaugural trip at sea.[1] Matta's American tour started at Cape Town's heavy trafficked harbor before passing through the Cape of Good Hope and headed northbound the same year that Tshabalala founded the Daughters of Africa in 1932.

Magnificent views and a swanky ship, the size of a huge mansion, more than made up for the incessant and eruptive seasickness that this first-time adventurist experienced.[2] Eslanda Robeson describes her motion sickness as beginning when the boat she traveled on to South Africa on her African journey neared the treacherous Cape Rollers.[3] Matta only speaks briefly

D. Y. Curry, *Social Justice at Apartheid's Dawn*, African Histories and Modernities, https://doi.org/10.1007/978-3-030-85404-1_5

about the seas' rapid pace rather than dwell on the subject. Instead, she concentrates on the stops along the voyage. The crew stocked up on its waning supply of meat and filled the ship's nearly empty galley with several fattened boars during one call to port. Residents also capitalized on the passengers' consumer purchasing power when they peddled baskets, linen, clothing, and other items that their transient clientele possibly needed.[4] Following purchases, the vessel continued to round the western side of the African continent where they skirted pass the peripheries of several countries: Angola, Congo, Gabon, Nigeria, Togo, Ghana, Benin, the Gambia, Guinea, Senegal, and Mauritania. They inched even closer to Mediterranean-straddled Morocco once they passed by the Madeira Islands. When the boat reached this destination, the captain and his passengers routed another archipelago, the Canary Islands situated sixty-two miles away.

Based on a map, and the few sites that Matta mentions, the boat continued northerly and circumnavigated the Iberian Peninsula, chartered the English Channel, and three weeks later finally docked at Southampton. Matta imbibed the seaside village and took in all of its splendor, and its demography, and was surprised to see only two Black men from the West Indies during the entire five-day layover. The apparent lack of racial diversity failed to color Matta's opinion of Great Britain. If anything, the Britons' etiquette won her over. They referred to Africans as ladies and gentlemen rather than as the diminutive boy and girl or the contrived names of 'Annie', 'Jane', 'Martha', 'Jim', or John that South African Whites used to demean them.[5] Katie Makanya witnessed British hospitality and etiquette forty-four years before Matta had the experience. When she and her sister arrived in Southampton, White men raced to take the entourage's numerous pieces of luggage.[6] These South Africans had until this moment equated whiteness with brusque behavior rather than the genteel demeanor that they had encountered on Southampton's and London's streets. America, on the other hand, offered Matta a different reality and a brand new set of rules.

Many visiting nationals received their first branding while on Ellis Island's hallowed grounds. Authorities added to the officialdom by documenting their nationalities, occupations, ages, and marital statuses on official forms. Newly arrived Africans and those transplanted for a while also ran the risk of facing prejudices that defined and stereotyped them.

Before Entry: Ellis Island and the Politics of Welcome

Situated between New Jersey and New York and on approximately twenty-eight acres of reclaimed land, Ellis Island has served as a celebratory center for newly freed African captives; as a naval magazine; and as a detention center. From 1892 to 1954, at least twelve million immigrants were processed from Italy, France, Austria-Hungary, Canada, and other nations. Some prospective immigrants enjoyed stepping foot on America's welcome mat, while others faced refusal right at the country's door. "For the vast majority of immigrants, Ellis Island was truly an 'Island of Hope'—the first stop on their way to new opportunities and experiences in America, [but] For the rest, like Matta, and Emma Delaney Mason and countless others it became the 'Island of Tears'—a place where families were separated, and individuals were denied entry into the United States."[7] Contained in the biography of Adelaide Casely Hayford, this statement corroborates the officialdom that visitors faced. "Landing was… a formidable procedure. Officials investigated passports, pockets, and every detail of proposed visits."[8]

Unlike Casely Hayford who entered the country relatively easy, Matta, who registered as passenger #9012024532494, faced detention and almost deportation. Mason spent her first twenty-five days at Ellis Island until the Brandons posted a $500 bond and became her sponsors. The Liberian lived with the couple for a month before she carried on with her impending journey.[9] When the Hansa bullishly steamed towards Ellis Island, and Fatima Massaquoi witnessed the Statue of Liberty in proximate view, the Liberian native finally saw her 'promise land'. *The Autobiography of an African Princess* captures Massaquoi's colorful and eventful life in Africa, Europe, and North America. Massaquoi's editors animate this compelling narrative with an array of accounts: her attendance at German Nazi rallies, her Fisk University days, and her Liberian homecoming. The book, which serves as the fulfillment of Massaquoi's dying wish carried out by her daughter Vivian Seton, allows another African woman to speak during the inter-war period.[10]

Matta's and Massaquoi's narratives encapsulate experiences of select African women who trotted the globe and traversed the continent. Matta wanted to learn cosmetology; Tshabalala went for missionary training; Soga helped to spread Christianity and to share her Madras, India, experience; Casely Hayford and her niece Kathleen Easmon sought financial support for an all-girls school; Mpama was a delegate to the Comintern; Frieda Matthews accompanied her husband, an ANC leader, and a professor, to London and others like Flora Zeto grew up in Atlanta, Georgia. These fearless daredevils landed on the continents of Africa, Asia, North America, and Europe where they visited or lived in Southern Rhodesia (Zimbabwe), Uganda, and the Gold Coast (Ghana), India, the United States, Canada, the Netherlands, and England among other global and continental sites.

They sailed the high seas, crossed the rails, and journeyed the roads to set the world on fire, to amplify Africa in stereo, and to form threads of solidarity on different continents, in various states, and in multiple cities throughout the world. As scholar Athambile Masola writes, "the theme of travelling [was] part of the nexus of class and education [that highlighted] the 'micropolitics of everyday life' … since it is largely a practical part of life."[11] Travel allowed them to bolster their careers, to profess their belief in God, to obtain education, to solicit financial assistance, and to form collegial networks. These adventurers and others like them took part in this educational, professional, financial, and personal migration that swept the continent before, during, and after the inter-war period.[12] Newspapers captured their movements and moments by branding them with reports that seared their flesh with the presses' hot irons.

In 1846, renowned orator, former enslaved captive, and anti-slavery abolitionist Frederick Douglass stood before an erudite audience in England and explained branding. He stated, "A person [being] tied to a post, and his back, [palms, shoulders, cheeks or buttocks] … was branded, laid bare; the iron was then delivered red hot, and applied to the quivering flesh, imprinting upon it the name of the monster who claimed the slave."[13] Newspaper columns represented the modern posts and searing that Douglass describes. Instead of hand-held artifacts, figurines, or other glass-contained objects, imagery, and prose visualized exhibits in the newspapers' version of curated, proto-digitized museums. Journalists engaged in several methods to 'introduce' South Africans, Liberians, Malawians, and other African representatives to their subscribers. 'Othering' represented one of the more blatant examples correspondents employed to reposition the dominant/subordinate narrative.

African and African American men and women by contrast were not above using strategic essentialism to subvert or to disrupt the dominant power structure. Postcolonial theorist Gayatri Chakravarty Spivak contends, "Strategic essentialism occurs anytime a minoritized group or member of a minoritized group takes on or 'owns' derogatory stereotypes and then applies them in acts of strategic resistance against systemic power."[14] For example, from 1811 to 1815, Sara Baartman, derisively called 'the Hottentot Venus', performed before audiences in costume. A tortoise shell adorned her neck, animal skins draped her half-clad body, face painting appeared under her eyes and on her cheeks, and stockings covered her shapely legs.[15] Baartman's accoutrements, while acknowledging longings of home, fueled myths about a primitive, hypersexual, and exotic Africa. Reified depictions led many Africans of various persuasions and nationalities to dress in traditional clothing, sing in vernacular languages, and tell romanticized, stereotyped, or essentialized versions of African history. They were not the only ones to engage in this strategy. African Americans also followed suit to either curry favor, to accrue revenue, or to play subaltern politics.[16]

Itinerants engaged in another power move when they often reversed the gaze and allowed Africa to critique or glorify America, Europe, or Asia. Nokutela Ndima Dube praised her Zulu homeland and its cultural import, but like Katie Makanya saw the value in some of Western culture; Soga appreciated the cooperative fusion of people from other ethnicities and races, Tshabalala called America on its hypocrisy; Matthews' comments underscored the social construction of race; Makanya learned the nuts and bolts of service learning and how to level the playing field for underprivileged Africans; and others like Maxeke gained great insight on how to be a political entrepreneur for social justice. Most subjects provided 'field' reports of their experiences.

Dispatches with and from an African Point of View

Charlotte Maxeke and Katie Mannya Descend on England

Excited sisters Charlotte Mannya Maxeke and Katie Makanya nee Mannya ran all the way home through Kimberley's darkened streets, where they eventually crashed through the gate in front of the family home and rushed into the dining room for the older one to sing, "we're going to England." That vocal followed with additional singing, stomping, and dancing in a tiny space between the table and the wall. Before everyone knew the entire family had become involved in the revelry. The father started to clasp his hands while the mother initially reluctant joined in the celebration with a bellowing laugh and heightened foot tap on the wooden floor.[17] When the day came for the sisters to depart, they left with an entourage. Paul Xiniwe, owner of the Temperance Hotel in King William's Town, a Lovedale graduate, and a primary school teacher, led the diverse group of singers who comprised the African Choir during its four-year European tour from 1890 to 1894. Paul Xiniwe's wife Eleanor Xiniwe, their two nephews, and a chaperone, Miss Clark, a music teacher from Cape Town, accompanied other vocalists who landed with the sisters at Southampton's docks.[18] The entourage saw the expanse of the city from sea to inland.

Katie Makanya's life's experience reached indelible print with the assistance of Margaret McCord. McCord was the daughter of a medical doctor. Katie Makanya worked for her father. In fact, a room at the McCord Hospital bears her name. McCord began documenting her subject's incredible story in 1954.[19] Apartheid was in its sixth year, but by that time, the government had already created major legislative measures that curtailed collaborations like the one that occurred between this White and African woman. The memoirist provides extensive detail on the landscape that Katie Makanya witnessed. Of particular interest was London's unkempt environment. Manure was piled up so high on the streets of the country's commercial and tourist hub, Piccadilly. Bird droppings encrusted a statue in Trafalgar Square where some of the city's main attractions lie. Makanya took in these sites and made this observation, "the white people here are a puzzle—here in England, they did not seem to notice the dirt and grime, yet in Port Elizabeth Mrs. Hutchinson was always asking, 'won't you kaffirs ever learn to keep things properly clean?'"[20]

Sightseeing continued throughout the city with the entire crew eventually ending up at the Macready House, a charming, lovely building situated on Henrietta Street in the heart of downtown London. A male host only identified by his last name Howell welcomed them and went over the itinerary. When Howell finished all the pleasantries, he informed them of the choir's name change. The ensemble went from being the African Choir to the Kaffir Choir.[21] Howell believed that the new moniker helped Europeans to better digest the idea of an all African entourage. Protestations emerged from the sixteen-member choral group because they wanted to honor Orpheus McAdoo and his Jubilee Singers.[22] They all believed that Howell and other Europeans had spit on their guests as the isiXhosa word 'kafula' translates in English. The unilateral decision reinforced the prevailing dogma that had repeatedly stereotyped, infantilized, and denigrated them as Africans.[23]

Even when they performed at some of the finest halls like Holly Lodge where approximately 28,000 people filled the audience seats or smaller events held in schools, churches, or private receptions, the group addressed the largest elephant in the performing room, their blackness.[24] Chorists carefully chose their song selections. They also made sure to don traditional clothing. Beaded robes fully covered the women's breasts while carved wooden combs added a glamorous addition to their naturally styled hair. Anklets of seed pods further accentuated the elegance they already exhibited and illuminated. Their wardrobe choices were juxtaposed against European ladies wearing gowns that matched their parasols and European men who dressed in tall grey hats and frock coats.[25] Notions of whiteness emerged even further through the site's location. Holly Lodge was set on grounds adorned by clumps of yellow and purple chrysanthemums, nicely, manicured lawns, and cherry-red rose blossoms.[26]

Food added to this visual splendor. Meats, jellies, sandwiches, hard-boiled eggs, cakes, cheeses, trifles, nuts, sweets, and huge platters of fruit flanked both sides of the stage where a small brass band stood.[27] The South African entourage got both their tastes and their ocular palates whet amid nature which added another touch to the setting's alluring ambience. The environment branded the notion of gentility and superiority save one exception, the intrusion of a group of Africans onto the sacred space of Whiteness. Maxeke, Makanya, and their colleagues participated in their own ascriptions when they reified traditional, African dress, and perpetuated ideas of a 'Dark Continent' full of primitivism, which pleased Europeans who brought into Social Darwinism, race science, and the 'Civilizing Mission'. They carried over this image with their song selections.

Many compositions addressed hunting, traveling, weddings, or cultural beliefs. The African Choir performed two different sets that featured solos and group harmonies. Two of the tunes drew on the isiXhosa tradition of choral music. They featured the compositions of the prolific exponents, Reverend Tiyo Soga, and John Knox Bokwe. Soga's 'Lizalis' idinga lakho' is a call to arms for Africans to fulfill their God-given promise, a message similarly expressed in Bokwe's 'Vuka Deborah' (see Chap. 6).[28] These tunes and other similarly related ones allowed its conveyors to access the beauty of their language. Indigenous tongues bellowed out clicks and intonations that rose and lowered with each crescendo. Crowds often roared when the troupe combined its diverse, entertaining talents. Paul and Eleanor Xiniwe's nephews danced and sang the isiXhosa composition *Singamwele* which dealt with the issue of twinhood. Twins are viewed as a blessing/fortune, and as a curse/misfortune in many African societies.[29] This song signaled positive connotations as its purveyors combined singing with rhythmic moves.

Their most resplendent attendant, Queen Victoria, wore a modest black dress with a white lace bonnet, and fingers laced with rings that patted the chair's arm with the flat of her hand in syncopation to the tunes, 'Merry Peasant', 'the Dawn of Day', and on the 'Mountain'. A rendition of the 'Lord's Prayer' ended the festivities. When all was said and done, the Queen greeted the South Africans with these words, "I am pleased to see you here and I admire your singing very much."[30] The mood lowered to a somber decibel when the Queen's blonde-haired granddaughter made this remark, "Granny, granny come away, I don't like these darkies—hush Alice you must not be afraid, these are Granny's people."[31] This statement, which reeked of condensation, was a back-handed compliment bestowed by this grand dame who ruled a nation that had pillaged and had colonized countries into pseudo submissions as the many revolts, rebellions, and independence movements suggest. The Queen's comment did, however, carry significant weight, and this was not lost on Katie Makanya who made it a point to highlight this encounter to a captivated McCord. Her remarks were also very telling and clearly indicated the psychological hold that colonizers had placed upon Africans' identities, and their lack of belief in themselves.

Daughter of renowned composer John Knox Bokwe, and the wife of highly esteemed professor and ANC activist, Z. K. Matthews addressed her piece, 'Mrs. F. Matthews on Her Thrilling Experiences in London', to "her dear country women". She penned her observations to appear in the *Bantu World* even while she basked in being in the land of Big Ben, the London Bridge, Westminster Abbey, and the Buckingham Palace. Matthews expressed her excitement about the progress of African women in every sphere of life. But "as an African woman with a love for pretty gay wear, I felt quite disgusted with the dull browns, greys, and greens that I saw around me day in and day out".[32] Like Matta, technology also captured her imagination, "I don't think any newcomer could fail to be most highly impressed at the ingenuity of man when he comes for the first time into contact with the underground service of trains. It is just marvelous to be in one of these tubes."[33] She then turned from development to race. A large concentration of African descended people marveled Matthews. London alone had a sizeable amount of diversity with its population of nearly 600 Africans and 5000 Indians added to the city's overall numbers.[34] Matthews ultimately transported her understanding of race from the South African context to England. She ended up lumping everyone together based on South Africa's definition of Coloureds as people of mixed ancestry. When Matthews witnessed London's American Negroes, Chinese, and West Indians, she automatically conferred the label of Coloured onto these different groups.[35] Race hit her in another way during a visit to Elstree.

Filming had begun for a highly controversial motion picture that featured the old days of slavery in this village (Elstree) situated in Hertfordshire, fifteen miles of southwest of London. At the time, widely known actor and vocalist Paul Robeson was starring as an African chief in this silver screen depiction.[36] Matthews went beyond this village to meet several West Africans. A series of conversations led Matthews to understand the tremendous progress that many African females had made as professionals. Matthews admired their sense of duty. One of the young women credentialed with an LLB vowed to return to Sierra Leone, the West African nation established by Black British loyalists in 1787, to start a legal practice there. Others went into midwifery or nursing.[37]

Compliments soon turned to criticism when she openly wrote about the toll that foreigners experienced trying to acclimatize to host countries.[38] Matthews was not ashamed to share the longings for home that swelled up inside of her. Alienation, assimilation, and acculturation represented the trifecta that many like Matthews experienced or used as a coping strategy. Emotion colored or enhanced travel experiences, in fact, such a sensation conjures up whether the yearning was part of a nation's welcomes or its goodbyes. Matthews' testimony and Maxeke's American tenure affirm both possibilities. Their inner struggles capture different examples of energy politics that expose the tensions between acquiescence on the one hand and resistance on the other one. The body and the 'self' ultimately refracted and mirrored each other in the analysis of micropolitics. Mpama/Palmer presents another narrative constructed by an international experience. She only disrobes herself through a short biography that focuses upon her childhood, and her estranged parents. Official documents and popular culture offer other lens into her life as a leader of the CPSA or barely through a 1978 *Drum Magazine* article which raised more questions than the interviewee answered.[39]

Josie Palmer/Mpama and the Russian Travelution

Despite all the complaints that Mpama/Palmer (Fig. 5.1) levied against the CPSA, they did not preclude her from accessing the advantages that came with her alliance to the communistic ideals spewing out of the Red Mecca. The body tapped her for an important, educational mission the same year that South Africa's White minority held a general election that resulted in the Nationalist Party under Herzog winning the most seats in 1933. Even with all going on in the country, and the constant regulation of African mobility, Mpama/Palmer trained at the Communist International's (Comintern) headquarters in Moscow. Several stories abound about how she ultimately landed in the Soviet Union. Roth traces her circuitous itinerary in the following way—Sophiatown—Cape Town-German Southwest Africa—(Ovamboland, Walvis Bay)—Angola—Marseilles-Paris—Soviet Union.

Her highly dangerous and exciting journey began in full steam in Cape Town, an urban area framed by the iconic Table Mountain and the icy cold waters of the Atlantic. Mpama/Palmer concocted an elaborate ruse.

Fig. 5.1 Josie Mpama/Palmer (https://www.sahistory.org.za/people/josie-palmer, date accessed 26 November 2020. Josie Mpama/Palmer risked the constraints and legalities of South Africa's policy of segregation to journey to the Soviet Union. No one really knows how she reentered South Africa. A photograph within Robert R. Edgar's work on this subject provides the only clue of her possibly completing this task by entering the country through Mozambique.)

The highly reputed Reverend F. W. Gouw was on her financial radar. He represented an important key in her elaborate plan which was nothing short of an Oscar-worthy performance. Mpama/Palmer pretended to be a Zulu girl in need of money to support her medical studies. Her ingenious charade worked like a charm. The South African succeeded in convincing the monetarily flushed Gouw to sign an indemnity which allowed her to attain a passport. The document reached her hands with the name Albertina Alexander Palmer emblazoned on its pages.[40] Roth's version of the story does not end there; in fact, it is just the beginning. A detour to Ovamboland in Southwest Africa (present-day Namibia, a former German colony that South Africa took over following that country's loss in the First World War) had the South African spending significant time in this prohibited area controlled by a prominent African chief. Ovamboland was a former homeland (Bantustan) that the South African government created for exclusive African occupation (something it replicated in South Africa with the 1970 Black Homelands Citizenship Act which succeeded in establishing ten ethno-linguistic homelands that skirted the country). Evidence from Department of Native Affairs' (NAD) official documents placed Mpama/Palmer there in May 1934. Roth's account continues.

Mpama/Palmer allegedly followed that visit with a trip to Walvis Bay, the second largest city in Namibia, formerly German Southwest Africa (GSWA). She had wanted to board a ship there to reach Europe, but her plans fell by the wayside when politics entered the conversation. Nazism was on the insipient rise in Europe. Its racist tone, temper, and tenor touched other shores like the African continent where a divided South Africa supported Germany, and the other side, the British. Instead of allowing Mpama/Palmer to set sail on one of its ocean liners, the German company refused her passage. Roth shares that Mpama/Palmer who felt as if she was left with no other solution traveled further north to reach the former Portuguese colony of Angola which flanks the Atlantic Ocean on the continent's western side.[41] A few days, or weeks, led to months before she attained the passport that gave her carte blanche to travel throughout the European continent. Possession came with another important perk. She could apply for travel funds from the South African government. Mpama/Palmer's indirect route eventually took her from South Africa to Southwest Africa to Angola and then to Marseilles and Paris, France, and finally onto the Soviet Union.[42] Roth weaves an interesting account, but it is here where historian Robert R. Edgar questions the itinerary and the dots that she geographically connects. In Edgar's narrative all roads led to ardent Communist followers Matilda and Julius First, and their mattress business in Edgar's narrative.

The idea of Africans traveling to the Soviet Union has a history that began long before Mpama/Palmer's quest to visit the nation straddled by Europe and Asia. Africans began trekking to the Soviet Union for stints up to two years beginning in the 1930s. Africans masqueraded as cargo workers or as stowaways on the ships of prominent White business owners who owned fleets of steamers, and fishing boats; used other Africans' passports—Doyle Modiakgotla, for instance, boarded an ocean liner posing as a member of a singing group that traveled to London to make records; or employed organizational bodies that acted as tools of deception.[43] Mpama/Palmer's machination developed in the following way.

First spun a tale that had the CPSA awarding her an all-expense-paid trip to the resort city of Yalta on the Crimean Peninsula. But instead of going there to relax, and unwind, First would feign illness to sign into Yalta's sanitorium for medical assistance with Mpama/Palmer acting as a nurse.[44] A major problem developed. On the day she and her cohort were set to launch their mission, a yell from one of First's employees that seemed to be heard around the world halted everything. The boisterous laborer had exposed Mpama/Palmer's intentions to travel to the Communist Red Mecca, the Soviet Union. That outburst immediately foiled the ensuing plot and put the business, which had served as the meeting and departure point for the upcoming European trip, under scrutiny by the South African Police (SAP).[45] Hard to believe, but the mission took a different turn following this derailment. Instead of an abortion, the plot continued with Roth maintaining that Mpama/Palmer lived in the Soviet Union as Albertina Alexandra Palmer, which Edgar refutes, and so does the subject with her own hand.

Comintern officials required all participants to write an autobiographical essay. Mpama/Palmer shared personal details and the aliases she used in Moscow—Beatrice Henderson, Josephina Mofutsanyana, and Winifred Palmer.[46] "When Mpama/Palmer traveled to the Soviet Union for a year of party training in mid-1935, the CPSA's internal squabbles drew her into a life-and-death showdown between rival factions as dictator Joseph Stalin was preparing to launch the 'Great Terror'—arresting and executing hundreds of 'enemies of the state' and shipping over a million more to prison camps."[47] Mpama/Palmer set her sights on the University of the Toilers of the East (KUTV) amid this turmoil and deadly horror.

On 21 April 1921, Moscow's Communist International (Comintern) established the KUTV with the goal of training cadres from all over the colonized world. The curriculum consisted of the Marxist Doctrine and courses in English, Math, and geography that supplemented and complemented specialized classes on the political economy, history of the revolutionary, propaganda agitation, public speaking, journalism, historical materialism, Leninism, military, party, and trade union building.[48] The KUTV divided its participants into two groups. Ethnic minorities who inhabited the Soviet Union made up the inner circle, while the outer ring consisted of colonized nations like South Africa, and other parts of Africa, in addition to those countries in South America, Australia, Europe, and Asia. The Comintern issued its own regulations.[49] The body forbade KUTV students from taking photographs, issuing public pronouncements, or carrying out random conversations with anyone outside of the body while on Muscovite soil. They all had to surrender their passports and any other travel documents and only received them back upon their departure from the Soviet Union. Authorities prevented students from using their real names, so pseudonyms were prevalent.[50]

Activism complemented and supplemented Mpama/Palmer's studies. She participated in the Comintern's Seventh World Congress. Former Russian politician, revolutionary, and leader Vladimir Lenin created the Comintern, two years after the Bolshevik Revolution resulted in an armed insurrection in Petrograd, two years later in 1919. The Seventh Comintern, which met in Moscow from 25 July to 20 August 1935, opened in the Hall of Pillars in the House of Unions. The meeting marked a significant departure from the conference held several years before. It went against the rising tide of fascism that was sweeping Europe at a frenetic speed when participants cast their support to the Popular Front and its broad-based constituency that worked to attain objectives like the Communist Party even though both were ideologically opposites. Over 500 delegates comprising sixty-five parties attended. Three hundred of them had full voting privileges. Amid the shows of collaboration, and solidarity, a major conceptual battle spilled over from the meeting halls in South Africa to the Comintern stage in Moscow. Problems began not long after the Sixth Comintern endorsed the slogan, the 'Native Republic' in 1928. Adopted to address the South African Question, which pertained to the racial and class tensions that tore apart the nation at its volatile seams, the concept drew both support and consternation.[51] When all the in-fighting and outside refereeing were done, the party split right down the middle. Mpama/

Palmer's testimony before the Executive Committee of the Comintern (ECCI) broke the stalemate but failed to quell the volcanic tensions that mounted.

Mpama/Palmer faced an exceedingly difficult quandary, who would she support, the lover and father of her son Dennis, Moses Mauane Kotane, or her common-law husband Mofutsanyana and his pick, Lazar Bach, a committed trade unionist, and editor-contributor of *Umsebenzi*, one of the CPSA's three mouthpieces. Bach was the son of a factory owner, who emigrated from his native Latvia at the beginning of the twentieth century's third decade where he landed in Johannesburg. Of Jewish origin, and possessing fluency in Russian, Bach immediately embraced labor politics as a leather worker and joined its union. Organizational politics also led him to the CPSA. He moved up the ranks as an elected member of the Central Committee (1930). Bach eventually held the most prominent position as the body's chair (1933).[52] The rest of his life was not as rosy. The Soviet Union considered Bach an immediate threat. Things became so intense for Bach that the Comintern launched an investigation. Proceedings determined that Bach represented a Trotskyite, an adherent of a Marxist ideology based on permanent revolution. He was summarily sent to the gulags, the forced labor camps created by Stalin, situated along the Kolyma River where he died from natural causes.

Bach's ideological nemesis grew up in Tamposstad, an area located in the Rustenburg District not far away from Zeerust, the rural community that led an impressive anti-pass campaign in 1957. Kotane had belonged to the ANC, but his disappointment with this body forced him to leave. He returned to his Communist roots. Kotane capped this move with a trip to Moscow. He trained for a year at the Lenin School that the great revolutionary and theorist founded. The school, which ran from 1926 to 1938, offered courses that prepared participants in political work. Trained militants ultimately engaged in radical activism throughout the world.[53]

Bach's and Kotane's loggerhead over the 'Native Republic' concept deepened when the British-South African politician Sidney Bunting stirred the pot with his interpretation of the 'Native Republic' to mean "that the class struggle and the achievement of socialism under the leadership of the Communist Party [would rest on] the achievement of national liberation and the ending of all forms of national and race discrimination and oppression".[54] When the dust finally settled, Bach cast his vote with Bunting leaving Kotane hanging out to dry. A motion to present this case before the Comintern initially passed but was later withdrawn when tensions began to accelerate, and morale continuously soured. Things eventually imploded and landed on Moscow's doorstep, and on a subpoenaed Mpama/Palmer who was already participating at the KUTV. A lot was at stake. The CPSA's eroding foundation neared dissolution. Also not helping matters was the strained and tepid relationship that the body had with Moscow's Central Communist Party.[55]

Fragile interactions faced another test when Bach and Kotane gave Mpama/Palmer a prepared speech. She was literally and figuratively in hot water when the activist threw caution to the wind, and her own inclination to discuss gender to read the proverbial script. Bach and Kotane layered and textured the speech with dashes of incendiary fire. "Mpama/Palmer gave a speech implying that the popular front strategy, newly championed by the Comintern, should be merely the means to achieve an independent republic led by black South Africans."[56] Big Red Brother felt this sting's hot peppering and made Mpama/Palmer pay for it. She defended her honor and dignity before the Marty Commission that began with intensive hearings in late November 1935. Mpama/Palmer escaped serious retribution on Muscovite soil, however, the South African had officially stabbed her common-law husband in the back when she chose her lover Kotane in this seismic dispute.

A stressful time behind the Kremlin Wall soon came to an end, but not without concern. Mpama/Palmer sensed that the Russian and South African states had her under surveillance for quite some time. Red flags waved wildly before her. The most obvious and startling one came from her assigned Comintern representative. He planned to send her belongings to the Union Mattress Company, the same business that participated in her foiled travel plot. Shipped items to that location potentially presented all kinds of problems like her complicity in foreign and local escapades against South Africa's segregationist government.[57] Secrecy was so premium that a photograph taken in Mozambique provides the only suggestion as to how Mpama/Palmer possibly reentered South Africa.[58] Even an interview for *Drum Magazine* failed to clear anything up; instead, it adds more mysterious lore to her story. This self-proclaimed do-it-yourself social worker, nurse, and general advice bureau dug in and responded in this fashion when asked about Russia, "you understand I can't go into too many details about this, but I am to tell you that in 1927, for the first time, I became actively involved in politics."[59] Her reticence ended there. She inadvertently chronicles her inability to withstand Moscow's frigid frost which took a toll on her body as evidenced by—bronchitis and acute appendicitis—sicknesses that landed her in the hospital nine times. One of those visits included a major operation.[60]

While Mpama/Palmer left her return to South Africa for conjecture, she more than stamped her imprint on the country's history. She boycotted Alexandra's buses and continued pushing for civil rights. Along with activists Lillian Ngoyi, Helen Joseph, and others, she helped to establish the Federation of South African Women (FSAW) in 1955. She even shifted her dogma during the last decades of her life when she went from the Marxist ideals of Communism to the monotheistic religion of Christianity.[61] In 1979, at the age of seventy-six, South Africa lost this liberation stalwart who began her humbling beginnings in Potchefstroom but ended her life in the densely populated Sowetan township, Mzimhlophe.

America, the Not So Beautiful

Africans from different parts of the continent arrived in an America heavily embroiled in deep-seated racial tensions. Jim Crow segregation, ironically, governed the melting pot and defied the diversity it so passionately championed. Public buildings, schools, and transportation conveyances contained strict stipulations to enforce separate but unequal facilities. Stringent divisions and disparities carried over to water fountains, restrooms, theaters, hotels, restaurants, and other spaces that catered to consumers. America's reputation fell several decibels down when news of lynchings and murders stunned and devastated affected populations. The nation spiraled even further when it turned its newspapers into 'printed' museums to curate caricatures that entrenched the 'Dark Continent' motif, notions of race science—measurements of noses and other observation of other body parts to connote inferiority, and the Sambo (happy-go-lucky slave) and Savage (the childlike cannibal) images the media perpetuated. Race science practitioners played large roles in how newspapers immortalized Africans and their descendants around the globe.

Europeans, Americans, and other nationalities who invoked Social Darwinism participated in the scientific measuring of heads and noses with Western instruments and imposed a system of racial hierarchies with Whites resting on the apex and Africans on the bottom.[62] In Baartman's well-known account, European scientist George Cuvier wanted to prove two main hypotheses with the remains of her body: that Africans were closer to nature or beasts rather than the evolved man; and that the genitalia contained an extended labium that he referred to as the 'Hottentot

Apron'.[63] 'Scientific experiments' along with adjectival descriptions further put Africa on trial in the court of public opinion where its inhabitants ended up being dissected, prodded, and displayed as specimens for a prying, an insatiable, and a subjective White gaze.

Nokutela Ndima Dube

A family of Christian converts welcomed Nokutela Ndima Dube (Fig. 5.2) into their household in 1873. That was twenty years after the Inanda Seminary the institution that she graduated from was founded by missionaries Daniel and Lucy Lindley. Marriage to the most widely

Fig. 5.2 Nokutela Ndima Dube (As one of the architects of the Ohlange Institute, Nokutela Ndima Dube served as an influential teacher, as a dressmaker, and as a composer. With her husband Dr. John L. Dube, she wrote *Amagama Abantu* (*A Zulu Song Book*) which chronicles the development of Zulu choral music. Published in 1911, this work serves as an attempt to retain isiZulu culture amid British penetration and settlement going back to when these Europeans began to colonize Port Natal in 1840. Photo courtesy of Cherif Keita)

recognized African statesman Dr. John L. Dube had its perks. Travel featured prominently in her life. The Dubes journeyed to America several times to raise money for their venture, which they succeeded in acquiring funds, equipment, and material. Founded in 1900, the school was originally called the Zulu Christian Industrial School before it became the Ohlange Institute, a year later in 1901. Dube aptly chose the school's name as Ohlange, an isiZulu word that means "the point of new growth in a plant or an ancestor for a descended family". Ohlange served as a pipeline or ancestral root for African students seeking educational and professional training abroad. Many Ohlange graduates attended historically Black colleges and universities (HBCUs).[64] Nokutela Ndima Dube capitalized on her extensive experiences. When her husband enrolled at the Union Missionary Institute for theology, she followed suite and ended up majoring in Music and Home Economics.

During her forty-four years on earth, this prominent educator and political activist crusaded for the betterment of African people. Her death from a kidney infection during the year that Russia's Bolshevik Revolution erupted in 1917 did not spell the end of her interesting narrative, if anything, it gained increasing momentum. Nokutela Ndima Dube was not a media darling, but she did cause a sensation for reasons of race science, physiology, and Social Darwinism. Several correspondents used their columns to focus on her complexion, physical features, and civilized attributes. Journalists engaged in branding with descriptions like her blazing black eyes, smooth brown skin, and handsome regular features. At least two newspapers, the *Nebraska State Journal* and the *Edinburgh Daily Courier*, describe Makanya with this iterated title 'This Zulu No Savage: Comes to America to Study Our Way', while the *Los Angeles Times* referred to her as 'Brilliant Zulu Girl'. Body shape, comportment, and clothing become part of an ongoing narrative that fetishized and denigrated African descended peoples. Makanya and Nokutela Ndima Dube experienced similar coverage. One article characterized Makanya as plump, amiable, dainty, and smartly dressed. The author could not leave well enough alone. He went beyond Makanya's outerwear to include comments about her pink silk underclothes. Makanya becomes disrobed, and her alleged 'savagery' gets exposed. The mammy figure also arises with this statement, "this genuine article who comes straight from the kraal of the clan of Makanya to study in America, might be mistaken for your Aunt Sarah—except she is some shades darker than the smartest sun tan."[65]

Reporters also put Nokutela Ndima Dube's intelligence on the table when they included the opinion of missionaries who had reduced the isi-Zulu language to a mere writing code, as if to insinuate that Nokutela Ndima Dube's mother tongue, isiZulu, which consisted of over twenty euphonious clicks was easy to decipher or could be reduced to a simple cryptograph.[66] This was also a back handed way of denouncing Dube's intelligence and placing emphasis on her ability to learn arithmetic, geography, and history until she mastered these subjects. The same *Kansas City Journal* piece that features her husband, his accomplishments, and his American education turns around and stereotypes Nokutela Ndima Dube as the "dark brown sweetheart that was waiting for him in Zululand" as if she represented that society's version of Tammy Wynette's subject in her song, 'Stand By Your Man'.[67] She defied gender conscripted norms at every important historical turn. Nokutela Ndima Dube and her husband established the first isiZulu newspaper in Natal (1903), *Ilanga laseNatal*, which is still in print today. They both represented pioneers in the field of education. Even with this huge accomplishment, it was evident that reporters consistently failed to see the forests for the trees about Nokutela Ndima Dube. Instead, they issued comments like:

> she knows in herself what it is to be a Christian, but she is not quite sure yet. She is in her civilized state now, but she is homesick for Zululand. NND turns the table on her interviewer when she says, O, no, I want not to be a barbarian again, but I like not all civilized customs. Americans are too extreme, and they are not happy for it.[68]

Determined to illuminate Nokutela Ndima Dube's life, Malian scholar Cherif Keita rescued the South African from historical obscurity with a project simply titled, but complexly driven called *Ukukhumbula uNokutela* (Remembering Nokutela Ndima Dube) (Fig. 5.2).[69] Keita mined several archives to trace Dube's resting place to a Brixton, Johannesburg, cemetery where she laid in an unmarked pauper's grave. Keita's action represented several feats: it rendered NND audible again, and visible in today's society; and it enabled her, like Baartman, with whom she shared a similar fate, to experience repatriation.[70,71]

How Dube's and Baartman's repatriation entered the public record years later is important for understanding the role that print mediums played in eulogizing not only the deceased but also the living. Burial and excavation occurred in several ways. When journalists concealed their subjects by objectifying and racializing them, they also took away their personhood and, in an unexpected way, lumped them all together rather than tease out their differences. NND, Makanya, and other African subjects experienced a baptism, but instead of being bathed in Holy water, they underwent a trial by fire in the coverages that bore their names, and the narratives that skewed their stories. But NND struck back against the empire with this interesting reflection:

> I do not like your women. They are very busy—very engage but they do no work as my Zulu women do. They must be taken care of too well or else they complain. They hurt their bodies with their clothes, and they will not bother with children. They are no use in the house kraal and they have too many clothes. American women are always busy—everyday they go shopping always for something to wear. Never do they wear anything until it is gone. That is not better than my savage people who wear none. I do not wish the Zulus to become like that. It would make many unhappy kraals there. Our great work is to teach the uncivilized how to live, to teach them how to use tools for cultivating their land, to build houses, and to clothe themselves. It is only the useful of the civilization that we want them to know. The school we will open will be for that. It is not a denominational school. Zulus do not understand denominations, but we only want to help them. But civilization is not all. I like my country better. I like to go there this minute.[72]

Richard V. Selope Thema was a staunch ANC advocate and leader. He formed part of the delegation that went to England to speak on behalf of South African soldiers, many of whom were Black. His comments mirror Nokutela Ndima Dube:

> We shall have to do what the American Negroes have done—adapt ourselves to our new environment. That is to say, we should assimilate so far as possible the good things of western civilization and discard those that are bad.[73]

Sibusisiwe Violet Makanya's Cross-Country American Rounds

The long arduous journey for Makanya to the North American continent began auspiciously. Makanya left the idyllic setting of rural Imbumbulu to travel to a country that her uncle Dr. John L. Dube spoke about frequently. Makanya was ferried on a boat originally built for the White Star and Dominion Lines in 1911. Regarded as the fateful Titanic's sister, the Olympic which had been a First World War troop vessel transported Makanya and 2763 other passengers across the high seas to the seemingly inviting shores of America.[74] Taken in 1927, this trip constituted Makanya's maiden voyage and perhaps her last one overseas. It coursed the waters from Southampton, one of the United Kingdom's largest ports to the American homeland and Ellis Island, where the Statute of Liberty loomed nearby in New York. Passenger records branded Makanya as an African, a teacher, a literate English speaker, and a numbered traveler #901726665300. Her country of origin (South Africa) appeared alongside her last permanent address (Southampton, England) and her birthdate (1895) while the South African's marital status was blank.[75]

She was not alone. Another South African Amelia Njongwana accompanied her on this maiden voyage.[76] At the behest of Dr. Charles T. Loram who sat on the Phelps-Stokes Commissions and the largesse of Caroline Phelps, who set up the foundation with this proviso, "… that a portion of her money be used for educational purposes in the education of Negroes both in Africa, and the United States, Native American Indians, and deserving White students", the philanthropic organization decided to finance both of their educations.[77] Loram became highly interested in 'Native' education when he served as the Assistant Inspector of Schools (1906–1917). His passion eventually landed him in a doctoral program at Columbia University in New York. Loram's time in the United States coincided with the heyday of Booker T. Washington and his intellectual rivalry with Dr. W. E. B. Du Bois. An exchange of correspondence between Loram and 'The Wizard of Tuskegee' ultimately led to a visit to the famed institution. Loram followed up this tour with ones at other historically Black colleges and universities (HBCUs) like Penn, Hampton, and Virginia Union. Loram ended up writing a dissertation that he turned into a book entitled *The Education of the South African Native*.[78]

Loram firmly believed, which was in stark contrast to Makanya, that Africans' future lay in the countryside. Phelps-Stokes, the Jeanes School, and the Penn School focused on turning Africans into farmers, carpenters, dyers, tool makers, cooks, and seamstresses rather than preparing them for the transition from rural to urban life (see Chap. 3).[79] Acceptance of the foundation's offer led Makanya and Njongwana on the high seas where seasickness entered and colored their travel experience aboard the Cunard Liner. All that went by the wayside when she and her traveling companion witnessed the iconic Statue of Liberty, the welcome they anxiously awaited.

A group of Americans, who were part of Penn's Industrial School, whisked them immediately away from New York harbor's welcome mat.[80]

Revelry soon turned to disbelief and disenchantment. The two spent a summer at Tuskegee, the epicenter of a widening interest in industrial education, where they received training on how to establish rural-based community centers in South Africa. Tenure in rural Alabama coincided with the critical contributions to land cultivation and crop rotation by Diamond, Missouri native, and agricultural scientist George Washington Carver. Despite Tuskegee's reputation, and their instruction, the South Africans felt educationally constrained. Tuskegee failed on all fronts to provide examples that took their home country's urban centers into consideration. Makanya wanted greater control over the classes she selected. Seeing the erupting volcano with Makanya and Njongwana, Phelps-Stokes offered a proposal that the former spurned and the latter accepted. Njongwana went on to enroll at the Atlanta School of Social Work (present-day Spelman College) on the PSF's dime, while Makanya, on the other hand, stood steadfast in her convictions, and severed ties with the body even at the expense of her own financial welfare.

Makanya's public rebuke of her sponsor not only raised eyebrows but also set the parameters for Africans' engagement with philanthropic institutions. Makanya continued to dot her historical itinerary on American soil by attending different institutions. She was already the product of the Adams Mission School, and the Inanda Seminary; in fact, she taught at the latter institution from 1916 to 1927. Makanya's departure from Tuskegee led her from Alabama and the Deep South to Ohio, and the Mid-West. The Schauffler Training Institute, and ultimately the Teachers' College, Columbia University, welcomed the South African as one of their studies. Her program for Winter Session 1929–1930 consisted of Social Work, Health Care for Infants, Student Advisement, Rural Sociology, and Education focused on Boys and Girls Clubs. Village Schools in Foreign Lands, Social Religious Work, Rural Education and Country Life, Rural Sociology, the Village and Its Relation to Farm and City, Work with Young People, and Field Work in Rural Education rounded off the Spring Session's course selections.[81]

Scholarships awaited Makanya, however, they failed to defray all of the expenses that she incurred.[82] Financing came from other sources. She cleaned bathrooms and toilets. Makanya also made invaluable church connections that ultimately led to paid speaking engagements. Various church and women's groups financed Makanya's travel by rail. Different families hosted her in each city. Chicago, Illinois, Davenport, Iowa, Omaha, Nebraska, Des Moines, Iowa, Salt Lake City, Utah, and San Francisco, California, connected the dots from one coast to another. Makanya engaged in 'staging' which consisted of costuming, dioramas, and politics.[83] Rendered at the World's Sunday School convention, this dioramic setting reinforced stereotypes of Africans, but she did disabuse them of one thought. Her fluency in English indicated that she and other Africans like her had a well-developed acumen. One of her chroniclers, Umbeki Khan, makes an important intervention with her study, but also with the documentation of these stops. A summation of the experience is contained here.

Immigration officers initially ridiculed Makanya because of her mother tongue, and the beautiful intonations of the clicks that she pronounced when she uttered her mother's name. Dehumanization continued and met Makanya in another important way. In Los Angeles, California, and Dayton, Ohio, Makanya told her audiences that "black men had a soul worthy of saving just as much as his white brother". American audiences quenched Makanya's African thirst so much that missionaries dedicated the year 1928–1929 solely to African themes. A Poughkeepsie, New York, newspaper correspondent described Makanya's costume as a 'witchdoctor's' outfit (Fig. 5.3). Her choice of fashion reified the myths and stereotypes of 'Darkest Africa' rather than the 'Brightest One'. She further set the dioramic scene with tales about her grandfathers who had seven wives, occasionally dined on human flesh.[84] Ironically, Makanya was quite surprised by the Mormons and their propension for polygamy given her grandfathers' own practicing of this belief. Salt Lake City introduced Makanya to the famed Mormon leader Brigham Young, but his narrative added more bewilderment for the South African who made it clear that their explanations fell far short in providing the evidence to support the argument for multiple wives.[85] America's landscape emerged as a recurring theme. For instance, the ice-capped mountains in Colorado's capital city of Denver impressed the BYL founder. The view pleasantly reminded her of the impressive Drakensburg Mountains that form a border between KwaZulu/Natal and the Kingdom of Lesotho that South Africa completely surrounds as a perforated state.

Finally, after three years in the United States (1927–1930), Makanya began the journey home on board the same vessel with Tshabalala in 1930. She left American soil with a degree from the Teachers' College, Columbia University. Makanya also made important connections with

Fig. 5.3 Sibusisiwe Violet Makanya (https://live.fundza.mobi/home/library/non-fiction-books/against-the-wind-new-readers-publishers/sibusisiwe-violet-makhanya/ date accessed 26 November 2021. This photo of Sibusisiwe Violet Makanya was taken when she was in the United States. Makanya traversed the American South, the Middle West, and New England, and other parts of the Northeast all in the name of education, social immersion, and cultural exchange. The South African's three-year tenure (1927–1930) on American soil helped Makanya to hone her already adept skills at service-learning and catering to the African community, something she carried out by inking an unwritten social contract with rural South Africa.)

White and African American members of the American Committee of the Bantu Youth League (ACBYL; see Chap. 3). Tshabalala by contrast broke down barriers between Africans and African Americans by serving in prominent leadership positions within Black churches. Social gospel and activism went hand in hand for Tshabalala who after returning to South Africa began her quest to save the nation. Tshabalala started the Daughters of Africa, wrote newspaper editorials, and formed the Women's Brigade in Alexandra Township while Makanya put important things on the table by appearing before Native Economic Commission and journeying around the country doing 'rounds'. She was among several people who called for the state to establish worker recreation sites, for the construction of black villages as opposed to mine compounds, for evening schools, and for women's social centers—some of the things that she championed as the BYL's leader. Her own ICU enthusiastically endorsed the African miners' strike which erupted when feuding parties failed to reach a deal that landed them in a violent protest over inadequate wages and unsafe laboring conditions two years before apartheid seized the political stage in 1946. Makanya and Tshabalala left America's climate of lynching African Americans to face South Africa's inhumanity where the country's labor and segregation laws metaphorically and figuratively left their people impotent.

Matta, Hayford, and Massaquoi Take a Bite Out of the Big Apple

Poverty and deplorable housing conditions of New York City's indigenous peoples shocked Matta. But, instead of making a comparison between South Africa and America's indigenous peoples, Matta likens them to the Indians on the subcontinent and sees race in biological and complexional terms. She wrote, "The Red Indians (possibly the Delaware, the Seneca, the Oneida, the Iroquois, the Erie, and the Mohawk) look something like the Indians of India, but they are reddish in colour."[86] Matta also missed the opportunity to connect America's indigenous people with her own, the Khoisan, a conglomeration of groups that include the Namaqua that formed part of the southernly Bantu migration into Namibia where they settled and dispersed. As First Peoples, they shared similar histories: removal, near extinction, political disenfranchisement, encounters with alien peoples, and rapid rises in mortality due to smallpox, and other airborne and communicable diseases. Reflection on these themes could have really shared significant light on the empirical and theoretical ways that the histories of the United States and South Africa intersect. Matta's immersive experience continued her learning in another profound way.

The sightseer paid close attention to the towering, skyscraping buildings that littered New York's impressive and inundated skyline. Many of her observations appeared gendered, and racial, in fact, she viewed the city in masculine terms with her emphasis on architecture, crime, and a Chinese underworld. She seems to insinuate that New York was a highly volatile world inhabited by mostly male participants and ethnically profiled Asians. Matta's visual stroll further feasted on the city's many structural feats. New York's subway and its rapidly paced trains out-ran the snail-like carriages that ferried Capetonians to and from an urban center colored by its history of enslavement and its amalgamation of different ethnicities. Matta's interest in the trains led her to comment on the city's roaring channel underneath the Hudson River that connected New Jersey, the 'Garden State', to New York, 'The Empire State'. "Many times, I have gone by an automobile through the channel, and heard the waters of the Hudson River running above. When I was there for the first few months, I felt that I was a stranger in a strange land."[87]

Technology also captured Mina Tembeka Soga's attention when she toured the United States following the religious conference held in Madras, India. Seabury, who recounts Soga's exploits, recalls the time when the South African went to the Automat, one of the city's finest restaurants, and she kept dropping nickels in the slots and opening the glass doors. Her interest piqued even further when she witnessed the glass knobs at Pennsylvania Station where curiosity got the best of the educator. Soga wanted to know how the glass knobs magically opened the doors because she wanted to tell her students back home.[88] New York also came to life for Casely Hayford and her niece Kathleen Easmon, who visited this vibrant and active metropolis, during a tour that took them to thirty-six American cities from 1920 to 1922. Born in 1868, the same year that Hampton University became an educational institution, Casely Hayford lived a colorful life that spanned ninety-two years. She died just when African nations attained the highest number of countries liberated from colonialism (seventeen), the increasing momentum of the Civil Rights Movement, and the rise of an alternative form of resistance, Black Power, in 1960.

From 1872 to 1894, Casely Hayford immersed herself in European culture. She resided in Axim, one of the United Kingdom's thriving suburbs in England before going to Germany. Casely Hayford's interest in music led her to the Stuttgart Conservatory where she trained for three years at the famed German institution. Exposure to two different European countries made Casely Hayford worldly; however, it failed to compensate for the alienation she felt and experienced on the African continent. Both the Gold Coast, where her husband originated, and Sierra Leone, where this member of the Creole elite was born, had rejected her. During one visit home residents frowned upon her barren state. Casely Hayford faced another rebuke from the United Negro Improvement Association (UNIA), a body founded by Marcus Josiah Garvey that originated in Jamaica but had branches throughout the world that emerged on the political scene in 1921. UNIA leadership ultimately cut ties with her over a financial dispute.[89] The lady dubbed an African Victorian feminist by her biographer Adelaide Cromwell also ruffled feathers when she pursued the development of all girls' school which the UNIA believed treaded closely to the body's own objectives. An embattled Casely Hayford stepped down from her position amid a cloud of swirling controversy of whether or not she funneled UNIA funds to support her educational endeavor.[90] When the financial wells dried up in Sierra Leone and the Gold Coast, respectively, Casely Hayford, and her niece, turned to the United States to tap its citizens for a much-needed monetary injection.

Casely Hayford and Easmon did more than witness New York's underbelly. They lived in Harlem, one of the metropolis' distinctly African American neighborhoods. The Sierra Leoneans came when 'Harlem was in Vogue'. A thriving literary and artistic movement exploded and evolved within Harlem's urban and culturally diverse bosom. Poets penned legendary verses, and novelists gripped readers with alarming introspections into race, and sexuality, and other topics of social import during this cultural renaissance.[91] Harlem represented a cultural haven and a multigenerational community that by the First World War had clearly defined itself as a Black residential enclave within Manhattan, and on the 'Main Stem', the artery that represented 125th Street. Latinos, Italians, and other ethnic groups have in recent years moved to different parts of Harlem.[92] A significant number of African Americans relocated to the Bronx and Brooklyn. Some remained there.[93] When the Sierra Leoneans checked in at the Harlem boarding house, their presence caught the rapt eye of curious onlookers. The pair became instant celebrities; in fact, they were so popular that a Harlem filmmaker wanted to document their 'Big Apple' experience.[94]

As the ship sailed along the Hudson River, Massaquoi gazed at the iconic Statue of Liberty. The Liberian Princess thought about the monument's importance. France bestowed America this gift the same year that

Cecil John Rhodes had discovered gold, and ignited a frenzied rush for this precious, elusive metal on South Africa's minerally endowed Witwatersrand in 1886. More concerned with the Statue's representation rather than its historical roots, Massaquoi took into consideration the intersecting themes of gender, liberty, and justice. Even while acknowledging the various forms of power that iconic statue captured, Massaquoi still thought that it represented 'the weaker sex' whose main purpose was to protect those who lived in her house (Ellis Island).[95] The 'Mother of Exiles' controlled the country's welcome mat on a metaphorical home that she guarded, and surveilled. Massaquoi's paradoxical depiction diminishes and elevates the Statue of Liberty even while conceding that it "evokes the desire of being a light and guide to those entering her hall, leading to the walls of her home, with torch in hand".[96] Massaquoi further discounts her social import as a transnational figure who stood on global ground. Travel formed part of her genetic and social makeup. She lived on at least three different continents: Europe, Asia, and North America.

Despite this incredible feat, Massaquoi busied herself with understanding gender through simplistic terms that downplayed the importance of women like her who trotted the globe. Ellen Pumla Ngozwana, a University of Fort Hare graduate, daughter of Methodist ministers and the future wife of a Ugandan Prince, fell prey to the same interpretation when she focused on African women's professional advancement in 'The Emancipation of Women' and excludes travel as part of their social climb. Found within the *Bantu World*, 'The Bantu Women on the Move' series more than compensates for Massaquoi's and Ngozwana's omissions, and their obliviousness to travel being a political act. Annette K. Joseph-Gabriel corroborates Masola's original assertion when she points out how Eslanda Robeson "resisted the nostalgia of the diasporic homecoming story [to craft] instead a nuanced narrative of black women's mobility as resistance in the interconnected struggles of imperialism in Africa, Europe, and the United States".[97]

For those residing on the continent, and journeying to other parts of it, they blended together two different stories. One was based on fictive and extended kin while the other reinforced Tshabalala's and Lembede's concept of one-ness. When Mrs. William Dube and others crossed transnational boundaries, they connected landmasses and geographies. Her two sightseeing tours to Mafeking (capital city of the Northwest Province), Tete (largest city on the Zambezi River), Blantyre (Malawi's center of commerce and finance), Rhodesia (present-day Zimbabwe/Zambia),

Nyasaland (present-day Malawi), and Portuguese East Africa (Tanzania, Kenya, Mozambique) represented an anti-colonial assault because Africans interacted with each other on the ground.[98] Because Ngozwana only viewed mobility through one lens, she misses the opportunity to further theorize and to deconstruct this term. Travel constituted as much as an African concept as a Western one. In *Reversing the Sail*, historian Michael Gomez examines African descendants from antiquity to more contemporary times. He argues that Africans physically, emotionally, intellectually, and geographically engaged in a migratory movement across the pond and within the continent.[99] Different from African captives who came to America against their will, African women made a conscious choice to reverse the sail and to leave their places of origin for different host sites.

Matta originally came to America with a short, coiffed Afro, but after observing and admiring the pressed locks of African American females, she began to question her femininity, and maybe perhaps her Africanness. Not wanting to appear boyish, Matta turned to the pressed, curled locks to feminize her appearance (Fig. 5.4).[100] Photographs depict Matta's look upon arrival to the United States and upon departure to South Africa. Chemically relaxed hair also made a resounding political statement. This happened years before the era of the Black Power, 'Black is Beautiful' Movement, or the rise of Steve Biko's Black Consciousness Movement (BCM) of the sixties and the seventies. Hair indicated acceptance of whiteness or blackness, however, Matta appeared to view locks in terms of gender rather than race. Matta emulated African Americans at a time when they themselves struggled with their own identities regarding the politics that surrounded hair. It could be said that Matta and some African Americans viewed their heads as subjects of decolonization. Instead of African descended peoples wearing overalls, printed African fabrics, and other examples of liberated threads, Matta's hair symbolized a transformative change in fashion, and her insurgent push towards 'freedom'.[101] Western standards of beauty appeared to trump African ideals.

Matta's acceptance and imposition of straightened hair offer a different form of the 'self' as an analytical category within the experience of travel. The South African soaked up her 'new-found' identity. Photographs, which served as a form of celebration for Matta, immortalized this new image. Matta accentuated her straightened hair by wearing flowing dresses embellished by dangling earrings and a scarf draping her right shoulder. Photographers used a tool of the dominant to revert the power structure and display an African woman in her 'own' words or if you will, her 'own'

Fig. 5.4 Rilda Marta(sic), Trip to the United States Full of Excitement, *Bantu World*, June 29, 1935, 12 (Matta's cultural revival also came with the jettisoning of her long-term decision to travel to the United States to pursue medicine, and law, for a career in hairstyling which she pursued.)

conception of African Black womanhood. A cultural awakening occurred on one hand and, on the other, a metaphorical death took place when she privileged the West over the Global South and engaged albeit maybe reluctantly in a battle between natural curls and straightened hair. The South African took a huge bite out of the 'Big Apple' and left in cosmetological flair with a new coiffure and a professional certificate in hairstyling.

Mina Tembeka Soga: India and the Twenty-Four American City Tour

Soga's American visit came on the heels of her debut as the first African female delegate to speak before her host the International Missionary Council (IMC) in Madras, India (1938). The IMC began four years after the Bolshevik Revolution (1917), and the same year that the CPSA hit the political scene in 1921. Forty years later in 1961, the IMC merged with the World Council of Churches (WCC), the same year that the Peace

Corps became a reality, and South Africa severed its ties with the British Commonwealth and became a Republic. Chief Albert Luthuli was another South African sent on this heralded mission to Asia. His autobiography *Let My People Go!* mentions this world-wind trip. Luthuli's selection to this auspicious occasion came from his involvement in the Christian Council, an interracial body that operated in Natal. He served as both a delegate and a member of the Executive Committee until the South African government served him his first banning order and he resigned under strenuous circumstances. Luthuli devotes several pages to this journey to India; however, there is no mention of his countryperson Soga nor the names of other Africans like Thomas Samakange from Southern Rhodesia (present-day Zimbabwe) who shared his rarefied air. Instead, Luthuli refers to Africans collectively when he chronicles their second-class status aboard a ship where their European counterparts experienced first-class luxury.

When the ship left South Africa in its wake, racism reared its head on the very first Sunday out at sea. They all highly anticipated Sunday service; however, plans fell through. A member of the White delegation extinguished their excitement with this terse statement, "well, gentlemen, the white passengers might object if you were to come to the first class to worship there. Would you make your own arrangements here?"[102] Luthuli's contingent complied with the request, but another member of a White delegation had other ideas especially after noticing their conspicuous absence. An invitation was thereafter extended to integrate, and they all readily accepted. An impromptu workshop in this previously forbidden first-class lounge where Blacks and Whites shared the same nautical and religious space resulted in a beautiful, denominational collaboration that did not cause the boat to sink into the depths of hell as Luthuli quips in his autobiography.[103]

Other impressions captured Luthuli's gratitude and his spiritual awakening. Robust and vigorous debate earned his immense appreciation as did "the thrill of seeing world-wide Christianity in miniature, [which allowed him to see] for the first time the result of the command, 'Go ye into the world and preach the Gospel'".[104] In Luthuli's eyes, the vague had now become precise. Attendants worked hard to grapple with the problems that Christianity faced—poverty, agricultural projects, church organization of home industries, and social services, something Luthuli writes that South Africa needed to change.[105] His scathing critique continued long after he returned from Madras, in fact, it intensified so much that he began pursuing equality as a local induna and as an ANC president.

Ruth Isabel Seabury also left her imprint. Seabury was an academic who originated from Boston, Massachusetts. As Educational Secretary of the American Board of Commissioners of Foreign Missions (ABCFM), Seabury went overseas every five years for the thirty years that she "was on the road". This esteemed member of the scholarly community represented one of forty-nine American and Canadian delegates selected for the same World Church Conference in Madras, India, that Soga and Luthuli also attended. Seabury took copious notes during this adventure which resulted in the publication of *Daughter of Africa* in 1945. Its pinkish cover (Fig. 5.5) advertises the insider's account that Seabury provides of Soga—a Black woman and her travels before and after the Second World War. Seabury compliments and supplements Luthuli's rendition. This titillating account opens with a praise poem written by Samuel Mqhayi, a prominent twentieth-century Xhosa intellectual who commemorates Soga's voyage. Mqhayi's creative piece is both a homage and a prayer that recognize the sea's overwhelming power and at the same time its unwavering mercy. As a measure of precaution, the ode calls upon the forces of Mother Nature to bless her journey as these lines indicate[106]:

Fig. 5.5 *Daughter of Africa* Book Cover (Photo from Ebay. Ruth Isabel Seabury's pocket sized book is chock full of important and personal details of Mina Tembeka Soga's journey to Asia, North America, and Europe. The work captures Soga's triumphs, disappoints, and tragedy, but mostly this narrative displays the subject's fortitude and growth.)

Let the seas be calm
And let the oceans still their rolling,
For our Princess is on her way
To the great world conference in Madras.[107]

Soga's fellow African Samakange issued a request for a prayer in his feature in the Zimbabwean newspaper, the *Bantu Mirror*. "I need their prayers and good wishes. I feel I am not worthy of the trust and very important position I have been called upon to fill.... But I trust in Him who has led His servants to ask me to take the wishes and words from the Christian Community of this country."[108] The *Mirror* carried his first letter which described his second-class rail passage through Rhodesia where friends greeted him at all the stops with gifts of money.[109]

"In July 1938, a short five months before the publication of Mqhayi's poem, a solemn committee of churchmen, English, Dutch and American, were meeting in Johannesburg when a charming American woman threw a bombshell into their deliberations—or, to put it better, a monkey-wrench into the machinery. For the first time South Africa was to send delegates to a world conference of churches. In all previous international gatherings of that kind two or three missionaries and possibly one African had represented the continent. This time they were to send seven South Africans, who would join five other Bantu representatives coming from other sections of the continent, to attend the great meeting of the International Missionary Council in Madras. In addition, there were to be five delegates from the white churches of South Africa. The delegates were to be chosen by Africa's own new National Christian Council. Now the nominating committee had met to make the final choice. The meeting was tense, for the job was especially important and already there were many candidates. Each denomination was hoping to have a representative, though everyone knew that would not be possible with the delegates."[110] Clara Bridgman of Johannesburg was the only female delegate who demanded, "There should be one woman, don't you think?" Politely but emphatically, they began to batter her down with arguments. The leaders of all denominations had been carefully selected—none of these could possibly be omitted. "You mustn't take two from any one church," they said. But though gracious and dignified, she stuck to her point. At least she said, "I think it should be an Africa woman, a Bantu." There was a long and heavy silence. A Bantu woman to take one of those places! To be the only woman on the entire delegation! But what woman was there who could hold her own among all these experienced men? ... "I want to suggest Miss Mina Soga," said Bridgman.[111]

Soga rose to the top of Bridgman's list. She boasted an impressive pedigree, which consisted of immersive experiences in the Presbyterian Church, the Scottish Mission, the Anglican Church, and a mix of denominations, Methodists, Reformed Church, and Anglican adherents. Deliberations led to the body formalizing their selection with a letter of invitation to Soga. The news surprised her so much that she questioned why the Council chose her for this coveted honor. Soga's humility blinded her. The future NCAW leader failed to see that she possessed the necessary credentials and the right temperament for this heralded mission.[112] She also benefited from Bridgman laying it on thick when she talked effusively about the candidate's alluring personality, and her charming demeanor—attributes she believed befitted an ambassador for the Madras conference.[113] Preparation for this auspicious journey called on Soga to select proper attire. Samakange had spent five pounds on two black suits, and two silk vests for his European trip.[114] Soga's journey, by contrast, epitomized the teachings of *Ubuntu*. Her father purchased the first-time traveler a portmanteau to hold her belongings while her mother made clothes and accessories. Soga ended up taking an ensemble of traditional outfits, beads, anklets, headbands, belts, dresses, different doeks, and other African accessories to line her bag. Soga then began mapping her itinerary.[115]

Seabury describes the journey "as if they had gone from New York to Norfolk, Virginia, by way of Pittsburgh and Washington, or from San Francisco to Los Angeles with a detour via Boulder Dam".[116] Soga's mission began when she left Queenstown en route to Bloemfontein, the city famed for the inaugural meetings of the ANC, the AAC, and the NCAW. The trip registered as approximately 195 miles or almost six hours of railroad travel plus or minus the stops along the way. Friends warmly greeted Soga in Bloemfontein.[117] She traveled further to Durban than Luthuli who lived in Grouteville and had the shortest distance to undertake. Fellow West, Central, Southern and East Africans came from Sierra Leone, Liberia, Nigeria, the Gold Coast (Ghana), French West Africa (Mauritania, Senegal), French Soudan (Mali), French Guinea (Guinea), Upper Volta (Burkina Faso), Dahomey (Benin) and Niger, French Equatorial Africa (Chad, The Republic of the Congo, The Central African Republic, and Gabon), the Belgian Congo, Angola, South-West Africa (Namibia), South Africa, Southern Rhodesia (Zimbabwe), Northern Rhodesia (Zambia), Portuguese East Africa (Mozambique), Nyasaland (Malawi), Tanganyika (Tanzania), Uganda, Kenya, Egypt, and Abyssinia. Everyone arrived ahead of schedule, so they used that time to get acquainted and to review the syllabus.

Tambaran, which hosted this international event, lay situated near Madras in the southern portion of Chennai, India. This suburb possesses a storied history that goes back to colonialism, state-building, and mercantilism. The British East India Company (BEIC) once used Tambaran as a camp during the Carnatic Wars that took place between the British, the French, the Marathas, and the Mysore in the eighteenth century. These dueling factions wanted control of the coastal strip in eastern India that ran from the north of Madras to Nellore, and southward to Tamil country. Today, the eastern and western sides divide the city. When the ship finally docked at Madras, and neared the iconic lore of the area, Africans and other passengers onboard the vessel witnessed India's winter season, two of the country's coldest months that ran from January to February. They put the plummeting temperatures to bed and began drinking from the magnificent view witnessed. Palm trees lined the crowded, bustling streets, and colorful arrays of flowers further beautified the landscape. Four large quadrangles (quad)s arranged in a campus style housed the guests.[118] Dining rooms, reception rooms, and dormitory wings made up the quads.

Throughout the eighteen days of spiritual upliftment, personal growth, and tragedy, Indian, Chinese, Japanese, American, European, African, and other nationals wore extremely colorful, gay garments. Japanese attendants, for example, dressed in eye-popping, flowing kimonos, while Indian women donned saris—the traditional garment wrapped around the waist with the other end draping the shoulder to produce a partially exposed midriff—Burmese participants adorned their tresses with beautiful headdresses, and Mahatma Gandhi's disciples dressed in stark white robes.[119] They all gathered in South Asia for eighteen intense and invigorating days of religious worship and Christian fellowship in India. Proceedings began with an initial retreat where Soga and her contemporaries worked hard to develop concrete and practical plans to carry out the Church's mission around the world.[120] Plenary sessions lasted for three consecutive days while worship occurred daily.

Hosts broke up 400 plus participants into smaller sized discussion groups. Conversations focused on Christianity's worldwide impact and the adherents' ability to create and maintain a Christian home, and the sanctity of the church's vibrant inner life. Problems laid at their intellectual tables too. One of the most immediate challenges was how to bring all races, creeds, and colors together on a continual basis.[121] Madras organizers succeeded in bringing together "Christians of the East, and the West of Older and Younger Churches in roughly equal numbers … that represented more than symbolism but that was actualized in the life and work of the Conference".[122] The Tambaran meeting delved deeply into examining how the church lives through theological and fundamental principles. It also addressed the nature and function of the Church, the relation of the Christian witness to the non-Christian religions and cultures; the place of the church in the work of evangelism along with the place of the church as a social, political, medical, and educational institution; and lastly, the church's position with the social and world order; and the subject of cooperation and unity among Christian adherents.[123]

Amid the gravity of the moment, participants faced real life challenges. A Chinese husband's wife remained at large for several weeks, a Japanese male paid a personal cost when he refused to accept nationalism, and a Muslim faced persecution for eighteen days because he refused to renounce Christianity and embrace Islam.

> Tragedy came to … Mina, too, while [they] were at Madras. … Soga received a cable at tea time, when the group typically received mail, that announced the death of her beloved mother. Wave after wave of homesick longing swept over her along with her grief. But even in sorrow she came to know the 'sustaining fellowship' of [their] Christian community, for as the word made its way from one to another, hundreds gave expression to their sympathy.… Color was not between [them] in that moment of sorrow.[124]

At one point during the proceedings, Soga got up and rendered an extemporaneous speech that did not leave any dried eyes. Soga poured out her wounded soul when she let it be known that her heart was heavy. When the future NCAW President spoke, she laid down her burdens, 'down by the riverside' as one African American hymn intimates. She matched emotion with methodological content through an argument that included a lesson in history. Sounding like a minister possessed with carrying out the gospel, Soga stated, "Behold me in this awkward dress of the West. It doesn't become me particularly, or go with me, yet the white man led us to believe when he came to Africa that everything African was heathen, and without intending to do so he confused us. We began to believe that everything Western—even the things of the white man—was Christian."[125] Soga made it known that Africans had professed a religion long before Europeans from various countries began arriving on the continent in the fifteenth century.

Soga complemented her critique with a list of possible resolutions. Reconciliation ranked high on her list. She uses the imagery of the heart as a metaphor for healing:

> If we wore clothes just like his, we would be more civilized—and perhaps more Christian. If we could speak the language of the white man so as never to make a mistake, we would be more civilized—and perhaps more Christian. So, millions of my people have assumed that by changing their dress they could take on Christianity. They have changed the exterior, but the heart is not changed. Christianity must be based on a changed heart. And for that the African must be at home with his God.[126]

The Queenstown native later contradicted herself. When Soga stood before American audiences, she contended that Africans "needed Christianity more than civilization". She doubled down on this assertion in another post-Madras meeting chronicled by Ohio's newspaper the *Newark Advocate* where she proclaimed, "The Christian religion is the only hope of my people. It is illimitable going on and on giving us room to grow."[127] Tshabalala echoed this constant message of a bereft African continent. One of her talks resulted in an audience member quipping, "Her Christian character and her presentation of … the needs of Africa in the twentieth century has won the love and sympathies of the American people."[128] Christianity trumped indigeneity in their eyes. This position differed from Nokutela Ndima Dube who praised and celebrated her Zulu heritage. She even critiqued American culture to an appalled correspondent who viewed the 'civilized' United States as far superior to any place on the African continent.[129] Soga solidified and modified her views as a post-Madras member.

The South African's American journey began with torrents of rain, and torpedoing pellets of sleet exacerbated by punishing and threatening gusts of winds. Soga immediately wrapped herself up in a swath of blankets to ward off the impending cold air. Mother Nature forced Soga to protect herself, but it also offered a cleansing in this meteorological welcome package that included shadowy views of the Statue of Liberty. The National Committee arranged the group's itinerary. Church officials and a throng of reporters welcomed the group at a luncheon. Cameramen feasted their eyes on Soga and wanted to put her on film because as one photographer put it, "She [was] a photographer's dream, a natural!"[130] They capitalized on the success of this inaugural meeting with a second scheduled event that consisted of a church dedication service. Seabury and Soga touched down in twenty-four American cities and several of the fifty states. Lincoln, Nebraska, Des Moines, Iowa, Boston, Massachusetts, Columbus, Ohio, and Kansas City, Missouri, represented a few of the cities and states they crossed.[131]

Experiences in different locales varied, however, her skin color mattered to those professing beliefs of exclusion or fear. Seabury does not name the cities where the transgressions occurred, but she does give a good idea about how Americans treated Soga. An assistant manager at one hotel asked Soga if she planned on wearing her colorful African doek to dinner. Soga threw back her head, laughed, and stated, "your American people like it, don't they?" The hotel employee wanted to honor the sacred White dining room space, and American social mores. He played on Soga's difference by accentuating her fashion piece to placate potential dissenters and to satisfy his own fear of reprisals. Soga's nationality, exoticness, and othering always trumped race. A manager of the prestigious Abraham Lincoln Hotel, presumably in Springfield, Illinois, placed the guests in a suite as his unregistered occupants so that he could conceal his African guest away from prying eyes.[132]

Seabury's hometown of Boston represents one of the few cities that she names in this adventure in Christian fellowship and lesson in American race relations. A hostess at one of Beantown's oldest and most distinguished hotels greeted them with a beautiful handwritten note inscribed on heavy vellum paper. Niceties continued to rain down on the delegation when staff offered their guests accommodations in the Green Room for their dining pleasure. They also possessed the option of inviting guests from different races for tea and meals.[133] With this gesture, segregation lived to see another day. When their travels took them to the Midwest, and the Lake Erie city of Cleveland, Ohio, Soga stated, "Ruthie, before we go anywhere in this hotel, I want you to find out whether I am welcome. For instance, would they rather I stayed away from the dining room?" The answer was "Just what do you mean? Where did you get such an idea? There is no place in this hotel where our African guest would not be welcome."[134]

Etiquette failed to define the next episodes in Soga's American tour. In one unidentified city, Soga and Seabury enjoyed entertainment while the men of the party went to the hotel. A problem emerged after they got off the 12:45 train in search of food and found that the Y. W. C. A. closed its dining hall on Saturdays, so the two of them left to procure food at a nearby hamburger joint. "Before [they] had so much as sat down at the counter, the female proprietor said belligerently, 'I don't serve niggers.'[135] [They] returned to the Y. W. C. A. hastily where Seabury made a dozen phone calls layered with all the trimmings—a princess from Africa, guest of the churches in the United States, speaker at mass meetings in their city the next day—conjured up the same result, no service. Seabury called the ministers in the city when she was left without any other recourse. The duo finally ate at 4 am, "But the hurt went very deep; all the apologies and regret of the city could not quite take away that scar from Miss Soga's heart."[136]

The nation's capital opened a different world for the South African. Tours of the city ultimately led to a visit to George Washington's Mount Vernon home in northern Virginia. Manicured lawns accentuated by magnificent views stimulated the visiting onlookers who marveled in all the beauty, and majesty, but ugliness, however, soon gripped them. Their driver told Seabury about the beautiful tearoom on the grounds, but the establishment's staff exercised their 'privilege' to treat the entourage discourteously. Seabury spoke to the proprietor in another example of America's version of exclusion. The owner inquired about Seabury's guest, and bluntly asked, "Is she black?" The academic responded by saying, "Yes, ... 'but,' hopefully, 'she wears a doek.' He shook his head and stated, 'It is against the law of the State of Virginia,' for me to serve a black person in the same public dining room as whites."[137] He directed them to another establishment located further back up the road. The place had no seating, but they could purchase sandwiches and lunch on the verdant lawn. They went on to experience this:

> The boy behind the counter looked at me as if about to protest, but I said firmly, We would like three ham sandwiches and three cups of coffee. He hesitated just a minute. Presently he put a ham sandwich on a plate in front of Dr. Yuasa, a ham sandwich on a plate in front of me—and before Miss Soga a ham sandwich on a paper napkin. I quickly shifted them. Dr. Yuasa saw the point, picked up the two plates, and said, "Come on, Mina, let's go out on the lawn while Ruth gets the coffee." I then turned to the boy and said pleasantly but firmly, "I would like a plate, please." "That wasn't meant for you, lady," he said. "I know—it was meant for my distinguished guest." "We ain't allowed to serve dishes to niggers," he said. "I would like a plate, please," I persisted. He went away and came back with the plate. "Now", I said politely, "I would like three cups of coffee—and not one of them in a paper cup," I said. I took them out to my friends on the lawn. "I guess he

> thought I was your maid, didn't he?" Said Mina with a twinkle in her eye. Later when I returned the dishes to the counter the boy ostentatiously broke the cups, undoubtedly on orders.[138]

Richmond, Virginia, was seeped in southern hospitality, and Seabury's delegation soaked up its warm and inviting reception. The Dean of Women of an unidentified university greeted the delegation at the train station. She then whisked them off to their campus accommodations. The former capital of the American Confederacy defied all the rules that typically governed race in Richmond. Blacks and Whites attended all the meetings, the luncheons, and the dinners together. The Interracial Fellowship orchestrated this staged engagement where races crossed the imaginary and real color line. When Seabury questioned the motives behind the affair and the arrangement, an official conceded, "The members of our Interracial Fellowship are conscious every minute. For many of the white folk this is a first experience and a memorable one in Christian brotherhood."[139] Richmond created a blueprint for race relations while Northern Virginia held on tightly to the reins of discrimination. Performative displays of hate differed from the love that Richmond manufactured. Mount Vernon employees refused to entertain notions of racial solidarity opting instead to exhibit their revulsion to patrons of color. Soga's entourage ate food near George Washington's home only for the server to destroy the plates when they finished their meals.[140]

When the exciting, multi-lingual, and ethnically diverse post-Madras panel came to Lincoln, Nebraska (Fig. 5.6), one of forty conferences held in the United States, it consisted of five delegates—from Japan (Dr. Hachiro Yuasa), India (Dr. Rajah Manikam), South Africa (Mina Soga), and the United States (Dr. Ruth Isabel Seabury). Attendants assembled at Grace Methodist Church, a religious institution established by Quakers and freed African American men in 1872. The sanctuary's basement, which traditionally had operated as a vocational school, probably was the setting for this convention. The delegation engaged in supper seminars that centered on three wide-reaching themes: 'The Church's Faith', 'The Church's Life', and 'World Peace'. [141] Soga discussed a well-rehearsed topic: African people needed Christianity; civilization was secondary. Africans she argued were content satisfying their spiritual needs by worshiping in the open air whereas the trappings of expensive churches captured westerners.[142] Student seminars followed individual presentations.

"Madras Comes to Lincoln;" All Nebraska to Be Represented at Conference in Lincoln This Week

A Japanese, an Indian, a South African and two Americans will form the nucleus of the post-Madras conference Thurday and Friday at Grace Methodist church.

Miss Mina Soga. Dr. Rajah Manikam.

This conference is one of about 40 being held in the United States, and the only one which will take place in Nebraska. The purpose of the conferences is to bring the people of this country in contact with men and women who were delegates to the world missionary conference at Madras, India, last December.

Dr. Hachiro Yuasa.

The speakers coming to Lincoln are Miss Mina Soga of South Africa, Dr. Rajah Manikam of India, Dr. Hachiro Yuasa of Japan and Miss Ruth Seabury and Dr. Earle Collins of the United States. The foreign delegates are pictured.

A highlight of the program Thursday will be supper seminars, open to men, women and young people, on three themes, "The Church's Faith," "The Church's Life," and "World Peace." These seminars begin at 6:30. Thursday afternoon from 2:30 to 4 there will be a meeting for women. The three seminars are to be concluded Friday morning, and at noon Friday there will be various denominational luncheons.

Admission by Ticket.

Friday afternoon, the five delegates will go to the Student Union building at the University of Nebraska to address students. At 6:30 Friday, there will be a laymen's supper, on which occasion Dr. Manikam and Dr. Collins will speak. The closing general meeting, to be addressed by the three foreign delegates, will begin at 8. Because the conference is statewide, those in charge explain, only those with tickets will be admitted. Proceeds of the tickets will be used to finance the conference.

The three foreign delegates are all recognized as leaders in their native lands. Miss Soga, a Bantu African woman, has been particularly successful in explaining Christianity in terms her people can readily understand. Dr. Yuasa was born in Tokyo, but he holds a doctor's degree from the University of Illinois, and since 1935 he has been president of Doshish university in Kyoto, the largest and most influential Christian college in Japan.

Dr. Manikam is one of the outstanding Christian leaders in India. Among other things, he is secretary of the Federation of Evangelical Lutheran churches in India and secretary of the National Christian council. He has done leading work as an author and educator.

Fig. 5.6 Madras Comes to Lincoln (*Nebraska State Journal*, 5 March 1939, 27. During this ticket-only meeting, South African Mina Tembeka Soga and two other post-Madras colleagues discuss the impact of Christianity upon herself and her people. While Soga concluded that Africans needed this faith rather than civilization, it appears that she advocated for this religion as the path towards modernity.)

The day's festivities concluded with a formal dinner and a meeting. Tours in other cities continued, and before Soga knew it, she was leaving the United States out of New York harbor for Europe. "This astonishing year!…(1938-1939) First I met Africa. Then I met the world and became a part of it. Then I was swept into the hope represented in this Western civilization in your country. And now tomorrow's world. I must try to bring young Africa into the world of tomorrow."[143]

Stories of these African women's encounters and engagements with Black internationalism focused on several different articulations. Historian Keshia N. Blain contends that Black internationalism is about "political struggle that centers on visions of freedom and liberation movements that emerged in response to the narratives about slavery, colonialism, and white imperialism".[144] This macroscopic interpretation needs to be flipped to incorporate the micropolitics of the 'self'. Biographies, oral histories, self-authored works, and travel narratives and other intimate texts embody artifacts of transnationalism. Literary media and women's and gender studies scholar Pumla Dineo Gqola explains why this is the case, she writes that "[those] who deal with everyday lived experience disentangle the daily struggles around which African feminism needs to be articulated".[145] Historian Robin D. G. Kelley further substantiates Gqola's assertion with this remark, "politics is not separate from lived experience or the imaginary world of what is possible; to the contrary politics is about these things."[146] Feminist studies scholar Maria Tamboukou's examination of historian Shula Marks' work *Not Even an Experimental Doll* exemplifies what the aforementioned academics articulate.

Marks compiles and analyzes letters between a triumvirate: fifteen-year-old Xhosa student Lily Moya, elderly White academic Mabel Palmer, and African social worker Sibusisiwe Makanya.[147] This exchange, which Moya's pleas initiated, is an exercise in the confluence of race, age, professional status, and geographical space. Marks argues that Makanya and Palmer failed Moya on emotional grounds, Tamboukou however begs to differ. Tamboukou analyzes power, desire, and emotion to "explore their effects … in producing realities and subjectivities within education".[148] Tamboukou further demonstrates that these letters provide a genealogy of feminist writing that concentrates on the 'self' as an inscribed construction of society.[149] African women's thoughts are part of the decolonialized artifacts that they left behind. They act as their blueprints for overcoming or at least tackling imperialism and other hegemonic forms of power during South Africa's segregation era and beyond. To best understand how reciprocity and dissidence interface, we need to reimagine cross-country cooperation to further explore the 'self' as a permeable commodity of Black internationalism. The African women who crossed the high seas took their training back home and implemented it. Their actions as activist intellectuals demonstrated how much the study and the unearthing of the 'self' is a personal and a political movement whose angst, joy, and pain are embodied in the cultural and political artifacts they left behind. Pumla

Dineo Gqola's *Agenda* piece further supports this substantiation.[150] How they disentangled those struggles follows.

Notes

1. Rilda Marta (sic), Trip to the United States Full of Excitement, *Bantu World*, June 29, 1935, 12.
2. Ibid.
3. Eslanda Robeson, *African Journey*, 30.
4. Rilda Marta (sic), Trip to the United States.
5. Ibid.
6. Zubeida Jaffer, *Beauty of the Heart*, 46.
7. History and Culture, https://www.nps.gov/elis/learn/historyculture/index.htm.
8. Adelaide Cromwell, *An African Victorian Feminist: The Life and Times of Adelaide Smith Casely Hayford 1848-1960* (New York: Routledge, 1986), 107.
9. "Miss Mason to Speak at Pine Street Church," *The Scrantonian*, December 15, 1946, 20.
10. Vivian Seton, et al. *The Autobiography of an African Princess: Fatima Massaquoi* (New York: Palgrave Macmillan, 2013).
11. Athambile Masola, "Bantu women on the move": Black women and the politics of mobility in The Bantu World, *Historia*, 63,1 (May 2018): 93-111.
12. Ibid., 93-100.
13. Brutal Act Used for Identification Purposes and Severe Punishment, https://blackthen.com/branding-of-slaves-brutal-act-used-for-identification-purposes-and-severe-punishment/ date accessed 17 January 2020.
14. Strategic Essentialism, https://newdiscourses.com/tftw-strategic-essentialism/#:~:text=Strategic%20essentialism%20is%20a%20concept%20that%20originated%20with,subvert%20the%20dominance%20that%20oppresses%20or%20marginalizes%20it, date accessed 21 April 2021.
15. Crais and Pamela Scully, *Sara Baartman, and the Hottentot Venus*. 70–76. See also Natasha Gordon-Chipembere, *Representation and Black Womanhood: The Legacy of Sarah Baartman* (New York: Palgrave Macmillan, 2014), Rachel Holmes, The Hottentot Venus: The Life and Death of Sarah Baartman (London: Bloomsbury, 2007), Bernth Lindfors, Early African Entertainments Abroad: From the Hottentot Venus to

Africa's First Olympians (Africa and the Diaspora: History, Politics, Culture) (Madison: University of Wisconsin, 2014).

16. Robert Trent Vinson and Robert R. Edgar, Zulus Abroad: Cultural Representations and Educational Experiences of Zulus in America, 1880-1945, *Journal of Southern African Studies*, 33, 1 (March 2001): 43-62.
17. Zubeida Jaffer, *Beauty of the Heart*, 42.
18. Margaret McCord, *The Calling of Katie Makanya* (Cape Town: David Philip, 1995), 33.
19. Ibid.
20. Ibid., 32.
21. Ibid., 33.
22. Ibid.
23. Ibid., 32.
24. Ibid., 35.
25. Ibid., 41.
26. Ibid.
27. Ibid.
28. Zubeida Jaffer, *Beauty of the Heart*, 48.
29. Ibid., 49.
30. Ibid.
31. Ibid.
32. "Mrs. Frieda Matthews Writes on Her Thrilling Experiences in London," Bantu World, March 9, 1935, 11. Letter to Mr. Kerr dated August 20, 1934, 2 pages, ZK Matthews: A1 Yale University, Institutional Repository, University of South Africa (UNISA). A letter written by her husband Z. K. Matthews to a Mr. Kerr of Yale University in New Haven, Connecticut, about his proposal to study under Malinowski in London. He also addresses other issues like his family, his post at Adams, and the pending financial obligations that lay ahead.
33. Ibid.
34. Ibid.
35. Ibid.
36. Ibid.
37. Ibid.
38. Ibid.
39. Robert R. Edgar, *Josie Mpama/Palmer*, 93.
40. Mia Roth, *The Communist Party in South Africa: Racism, Eurocentricity and Moscow, 1921-1950* (Johannesburg: Partridge Publishing: 2016), 187.
41. Ibid., 188.
42. Ibid., 189.

43. Brian Percy Bunting, *Moses Kotane, South African Revolutionary: A Political Biography* (London: Inkululeko Publications, 1975), 35.
44. Robert R. Edgar, *Josie Mpama/Palmer*, 84, Mia Roth, *The Communist Party*, 188.
45. Ibid.
46. Apollon Davidson, Irina Filatova, Valentin Gorodnov, and Sheridan Johns, *South Africa and the Communist International: A Documentary History, Volume II: Bolshevik Footsoldiers to Victims of Bolshevisation 1931-1939*, Document 57.
47. Robert R. Edgar, *Josie Mpama/Palmer*, 75.
48. Brian Percy Bunting, *Moses Kotane*, 58 and Robert R. Edgar, *Josie Mpama/Palmer*, 80. See Rossen, Djagalov, University for Toilers of the East (KUTV) https://globalsouthstudies.as.virginia.edu/key-moments/communist-university-toilers-east-kutv, date accessed 2 April 2021, Mia Roth, *The Communist Party*, 56-57.
49. Mia Roth, *The Communist Party*, 56-57.
50. Brian Percy Bunting, *Moses Kotane*, 20-22.
51. Mia Roth, *The Communist Party*, 32-34.
52. Ibid, 110.
53. Ibid., 176-180.
54. Mia Roth, *The Communist Party*, 32-34.
55. Robert R. Edgar, *Josie Mpama/Palmer*, 78-80.
56. Lazar Bach, https://www.wikizero.com/en/Lazar_Bach date accessed 23 March 2021.
57. Robert R. Edgar, *Josie Mpama/Palmer*, 91-92.
58. Ibid.
59. "Comfort in Moscow for Josie," *Drum Magazine*, June 8, 1975, 18-20.
60. Ibid.
61. Robert R. Edgar, *Josie Mpama/Palmer*, 152-167.
62. See Saul Dubow, *Scientific Racism in Modern South Africa* (Cambridge: Cambridge University Press, 1995).
63. Clifton Crais and Pamela Scully, *Sara Baartman*, 70-76.
64. Hampton University (formerly Hampton Institute) ranked high as an educational destination. It taught the likes of Fanny Mabuda, Madikane Qandiyane Cele (Dube's nephew), Cecilia Lillian Tshabalala, and Reuben Tholakele Caluza among others. Ohlange created a pipeline that played a profound role in the formation of early black internationalism. The Jeanes School, the Phelps-Stokes Fund, and the Penn School supported immersion experiences for Africans to study, to live in the country, and to learn practical theory later applied in their respective African nations. Service-learning opportunities like these capture the proto-formation of the American government's offering of the Fulbright and Peace Corps Programs that had their beginnings in the 1940s and the 1960s respectively.

65. This Zulu No Savage, The *Edinburgh Daily Courier*, September 21, 1929, and *Nebraska State Journal*, September 19, 1929, 8.
66. "A Zulu Young Woman," *Evangelical Visitor*, April 15, 1900, 16.
67. Remembering Nokutela Ndima Dube: time to implement the Freedom photo of tombstone Cherif Keita Chartehttps://www.iol.co.za/news/opinion/remembering-nokutela-dube-time-to-implement-the-freedom-charter-ccba8fd4-7748-44c0-a068-39931c422ae6 date accessed 3 March 2021.
68. "Ideas of a Zula Woman," *The Anaconda Standard*, January 8, 1899, 18.
69. Photographs provided by Cherif Keita for the author.
70. Remembering Nokutela Ndima Dube: time to implement the Freedom photo of tombstone Cherif Keita Chartehttps://www.iol.co.za/news/opinion/remembering-nokutela-dube-time-to-implement-the-freedom-charter-ccba8fd4-7748-44c0-a068-39931c422ae6 date accessed 3 March 2021.
71. Tsitsi Ella Jaji, *Africa in Stereo: Modernism, Music, and Pan African Solidarity* (Oxford: Oxford University Press, 2014), 32.
72. "A Zulu Young Woman," 16, and "Zulu Young Woman in Syracuse-Nokutela Did Not Want to be Interviewed-Does not like Americans," *The Buffalo Courier*, February 12, 1899, 2.
73. Brandy S. Thomas, "Give Them Their Due," 107.
74. Sibusisiwe Violet Makanya, Ellis Island Passenger Search, https://heritage.statueofliberty.org/passenger, date accessed 12 November 2020.
75. Ibid.
76. See Miss Amelia Njongwana Talks Again on Africa, *The Campus Mirror*, 5, 2 (November 15, 1928), front page Spelman Archives.
77. Umehani Khan, A Critical Study of the Life of Sibusisiwe Makanya, 39.
78. Friedrich (Freddy) Omo Kustaa, *Booker T. Washington and John L. Dube's Promotion of American Industrial Education Policies in the US South and South Africa, 1868-1946* (Seattle: Amazon Kindle Publishing, 2017), 151.
79. Umehani Khan, A Critical Study of the Life of Sibusisiwe Makanya, 39.
80. Ibid.
81. Bantu Youth League Papers, Historical Papers, Cullen Library, University of Witwatersrand, Organisations, Bantu Youth League, Box 251, AD843/RJ/Pb13.
82. See James T. Campbell, *Songs of Zion: The American Methodist Episcopal Church in the United States* (Chapel Hill: University of North Carolina, 1998).
83. Umehani Khan, A Critical Study of the Life of Sibusisiwe Makanya, 64. See also Nemata Amelia Ibitayo Blyden, *African Americans & Africa* (New Haven: Yale, 2019).
84. "Miss Mkanya's (sic) Charm, Intelligence and Flair," *Duncannon Record*, June 26, 1930, 5.
85. Umehani Khan, A Critical Study of the Life of Sibusisiwe Makanya, 64.

86. Rilda Marta, "Trip to the United States."
87. Ibid.
88. Ruth Isabel Seabury, *Daughter of Africa*, 94.
89. Adelaide Cromwell, *Adelaide Casely Hayford*, 107-110.
90. Ibid., 110-111.
91. Africans, Haitians, and other continental and diasporic peoples created their own literary and intellectual movement called Negritude which Senegal's former leader Leopold Senghor, French Guinan Leon Damas, and Martinican Aimee Cesaire developed to promote the positive attributes of blackness in the 1930s.
92. Harlem, https://www.britannica.com/place/Harlem-New-York, date accessed 2 February 2019.
93. Ibid.
94. Adelaide Cromwell, *Adelaide Casely Hayford*, 108-109.
95. Vivian Seton et al., *The Autobiography of an African Princess: Fatima Massaquoi* (New York: Palgrave Macmillan, 2013), 216-217.
96. Ibid.
97. Annette K. Joseph-Gabriel, Feminist Networks and Diasporic Practices: Eslanda Robeson's Travels in Africa in Keshia N. Blain and Tiffany M. Gill (eds.) *To Turn the Whole World Over: Black Women and Internationalism* (Chicago: University of Illinois Press, 2018), 39-40, Athambile Masola, "Bantu women on the move": Black women and the politics of mobility in The Bantu World, *Historia*, 63,1 (May 2018): 93-111
98. Mrs. William Dube, 'Bantu Women on the Move,' *Bantu World*, February 9, 1935, 10.
99. Michael A. Gomez, *Reversing the Sail: A History of the African Diaspora* (Cambridge: Cambridge University Press, 2014), 162-192.
100. "Miss Rilda Marta's Trip to the US Full of Excitement," *Bantu World*, June 29, 1935, 2.
101. Tanisha C. Ford, *Liberated Threads: Black Women, Style, and The Global Politics of Soul* (Chapel Hill: University of North Carolina Press, 2015), 1-11.
102. Albert Luthuli, Let My People Go: *The Autobiography of Albert Luthuli* (Kwela: Cape Town, 2006), 68.
103. Ibid.
104. Ibid., 79.
105. Ibid.
106. https://www.ebay.com/itm/BOOK-1945-DAUGHTER-OF-AFRICA-BY-RUTH-ISABEL-SEABURY/362938623965, date accessed 26 November 2021.
107. Ruth Isabel Seabury, *Daughter of Africa*, 56.

108. Terrence Ranger, Thompson Samakange: Tambaram and Beyond, *Journal of Religion in Africa*, 23, 4 (1993): 324.
109. Ibid.
110. Ruth Isabel Seabury, *Daughter of Africa*, 56-57.
111. Ibid., 57.
112. Ibid., 58.
113. Ibid.
114. Terrence Ranger, Thompson Samakange, 324. Thomas Samkange helped to establish the Southern Rhodesian Missionary Conference in 1928.
115. Ruth Isabel Seabury, *Daughter of Africa*, 59.
116. Ibid., 72-73.
117. Ibid., 84.
118. Ibid., 73.
119. Ibid., 73-74.
120. Ibid., 73.
121. Ibid., 76.
122. International Missionary Conference, The World Mission of the Church: Findings and Recommendations of the Meeting of the International Missionary Council, 4th Meeting, Madras, 1938 (London: International Missionary Council, 1938), 8-9.
123. Ibid.
124. Ruth Isabel Seabury, *Daughter of Africa*, 82.
125. Ibid., 78.
126. Ibid.
127. Christianity Seen as a Test of Other Faiths, *Newark Advocate*, May 24, 1939, 1.
128. "Miss Tshabalala Becomes a Missionary," *Ilanga laseNatal*, October 26, 1917, 5.
129. "A Zulu Young Woman," *Evangelical Visitor*, April 15, 1900, 6.
130. Ruth Isabel Seabury, *Daughter of Africa*, 94.
131. Other cities included Springfield, St. Louis, Champaign, Indianapolis, Cleveland, Pittsburgh, Buffalo, Washington, Grand Rapids, Detroit, and Richmond.
132. Ruth Isabel Seabury, *Daughter of Africa*, 102-103.
133. Ibid.
134. Ibid., 105.
135. Ibid., 104-105.
136. Ibid.
137. Ibid., 106-107.
138. Ibid.
139. Ibid., 108-109.
140. Ibid., 106-107.

141. "Madras Comes to Lincoln," *Nebraska State Journal*, March 5, 1939, 27.
142. "Christianity Needed for African Peoples, *Evening State Journal*, Lincoln, March 10, 1939, 2. "Madras Comes to Lincoln"; All Nebraska to Be Represented at Conference in Lincoln This Week, *Journal Star*, March 10, 1939, 2.
143. Ruth Isabel Seabury, *Daughter of Africa*, 113-114.
144. Keshia N. Blain, Teaching Black Internationalism and Amerikanah, https://ir.uiowa.edu/cgi/viewcontent.cgi?article=1029&context=history_pubs, date accessed 20 April 2021.
145. Desiree Lewis, Introduction: African Feminisms, Agenda: Empowering Women for Gender Equity, 50, African Feminisms One (2001): 7.
146. Robin D. G. Kelley, *Race Rebels: Culture, Politics and the Black Working Class* (New York: Free Press, 1994), 9 op. cited Brandy Thomas, "Give Them Their Due," 7.
147. Shula Marks, *Not Either an Experimental Doll: The Separate Worlds of Three South African Women* (Bloomington: Indiana University Press, 1987), 2-12.
148. Maria Tamboukou, Power, Desire and Emotions in Education: Revisiting the Epistolary Narratives of Three Women in Apartheid South Africa, *Gender and Education*, 18, 3 (2006): 3.
149. Ibid.
150. Desiree Lewis, Introduction: African Feminisms, *Agenda: Empowering Women for Gender Equity*, African Feminisms, 1, 50, (2001): 7.

CHAPTER 6

Oral and Written Resolutions to Segregation and Transport

Before an imagined Alexandran meeting that took place on the eve of the township's 1943 bus boycott, "... [RG (Richard Granville Baloyi)] addresses the body with a polite salutation, 'Mr. Chairman, ladies and gentlemen, I speak this morning as your representative in the Native Representatives Council (NRC) as well as being a bus-owner and a stand-owner.'"[1] These words canonized Baloyi in cultural form.[2] His chronicler Modikwe Dikobe offers his interpretation of Alexandra in his short story, 'We Shall Walk'. Dikobe's experience as a foot soldier, as an entrepreneur, as a trade unionist, as a hawker, and as a newspaper vendor put him in a unique position to untangle the plight of the subordinate class that he represented. After living a varied and highly mobile migrant life in several slum yards throughout Johannesburg, the literary author eventually settled in Alexandra where its people, landscape, and protests served as the backdrop for his poetry, short stories, and other creative works. Dikobe portrays the transport strike from all angles. He records the bus owners', the community's leaders', and the traveling patronage's capitalist, consumerist, and gentlemanly voices. Dissent also came from real sources.

The Alexandra Women's League (AWL), the ANC, the Alexandra Health Committee (AHC), and the Fourth International (FI) submitted memorandums to the Beardmore Commission of Enquiry (hereafter Beardmore Commission) formed by the government to investigate bus conditions in Witwatersrand, Vereeniging, and Pretoria.[3] Found in

D. Y. Curry, *Social Justice at Apartheid's Dawn*, African Histories and Modernities, https://doi.org/10.1007/978-3-030-85404-1_6

Dr. Alfred B. Xuma's personal papers, these memorandums like Dikobe's short narrative frame Africans' dispossession within the moral economy that defined them. Respondents call for a national minimum wage, a change in employment practices (Xuma), a women's only bus (AWL), a coupon system (AHC), and flats near places of employment (Fourth International). They also interrogate the impact of segregation through Alexandrans' consumer purchasing power (the Women's Brigade); analyze gender in travel (AWL); advocate for self-determination (ANC); compare conditions of other townships with Alexandra (AHC); and lastly, they entertain a socialist resolution (Fourth International).

One of the first serious analyses of Alexandra's bus boycotts appeared in Eddie Roux's seminal study, *Time Longer than Rope*. Roux was one of the founding members of the Young Communist League, and a full-fledged CPSA adherent. This son of an Afrikaner father and an English mother began his meteoric rise as a *Trek* reporter and as an editor of *Umsebenzi* (*The Worker*). In *Time Longer than Rope*, Roux writes erroneously (first transit boycott was in 1917, with 1940 being the first of that decade) that "the first Alexandra bus strike (1943) was a spontaneous mass movement, unprepared and owing little or nothing to political leadership", while the second one (1944) "was well prepared and had the support of a large committee representing numerous African and pro-African organisations".[4] In a very large way, their responses to increasing transport costs evolved into larger platforms for social justice. For example, CPSA and Non-European Unity Front (NEU) man Yusef Dadoo linked the bus issue to expropriation. At a meeting held at Alexandra's famed Number 2 Square, Dadoo declared:

> there [was] a bigger stake here than the bus fares. The future of Alexandra had not been decided. If [we] are beaten here today, it will be easy for people who want to expropriate [us] to beat [us] again. We must walk for months to save the township.[5]

"Africans and Coloureds provided the city with labor [that] saved the Johannesburg ratepayer the expense of laying out and maintaining a location to house the inhabitants of a [town that represented one of the largest in the union]…."[6] An increasing need for a cheap, pliable African workforce heightened tensions between the employer and the employed, the bus owners, and its fare-paying consumers, and the state and township residents, and their inability to afford transport. Alexandra's bus cartel and

Africans' employers had a vested interest in fueling the transport system. Some Africans offered ferrying services while for others "… a penny on the bus fares, the common precipitant of boycotts inflicted a direct and serious injury on urban communities located far from places of employment".[7] Alexandra paralleled other townships. The Fourth International contended as much as this statement corroborates, "The Alexandra boycott[s] not only [mirrored] the conditions of the residents of the township itself; it also [reflected] the economic and social conditions of all African townships skirting or far removed from the larger industrial centres in this country … as these affected not only the Bantu, but also the Indian and the Coloured people."[8] Over time, the buses of Alexandra came to symbolize developing tensions of the wider society: for Africans they represented the vehicle of White oppression, injustice, and exploitation; for Whites, the bus owners, and Johannesburg employers, they supported the wheels of affordable African labor.

Each strike (1940, 1942, 1943, and 1944) restored the original fare structure; however, the government ended up implementing some surprising transformative changes. Officials dissolved the ABOA, established a public utility corporation (PUTCO), and created an Employer Travel Subsidy, suggestions that the ANC, the AWL, the AHC, the Fourth International, and Dikobe recommended in their respective memorandums and short story. Different from previous scholarship, this examination offers a comparison between and among African women's organizations and male bodies that used their memorandums as oral texts to critique the policy of segregation while they offered resolutions.

The Alexandra Health Committee

In 1905, Alexandra began its iconic history as a Whites-only area. Alexandra sat northeast of Johannesburg where gold's discovery created a bustling mining town that required sufficient African labor beginning in 1886.[9] Kempton Park flanked its eastern corridor, Inanda, its western border, Bramley, its southern periphery, and Buccleuth, its northern quadrant. Disappointingly low prospects by White buyers, the township's hilly terrain, and its distance from Johannesburg's urban area forced its owner, Herbert Papenfus, a trained lawyer and dairy farmer, to convert the land reportedly named for his lover, his betrothed partner, or King Edward VI's wife into a Freehold in 1912.[10] Freehold status meant Africans and Coloureds lived within the peripheries of urban areas where they could own land, or rent houses or rooms like other Newclare, Martindale, and Sophiatown and other Freeholds that remained exempt from the racial sequestration mandated by the 1913 Natives Land Act (see Chap. 3).[11] Alexandra's immunity allowed for the development of a diverse racial and ethnic culture (AmaZulu, AmaXhosa, Basotho, Motswana) to emerge within the confines of a thriving and rapidly growing Johannesburg.[12] In later years, Alexandra expanded from its square-one mile to welcome the East Bank, Tutsomani, the River Park Project, and other areas in its geographical orbit.

The first political body to govern the township was the Village Association. Established by Alex Fortuin, the Village Association operated under his chairmanship beginning in 1912. The body met at the Don, which had a triple function as an administrative site, as a reception hall for weddings, and as a movie theater where patrons screened American westerns.[13] Within four years, the Village Association disbanded, and the Alexandra Health Committee replaced this governmental structure and ran the township for the next thirty-nine years from 1916 to 1955. An interracially mixed and mostly male African and Coloured ensemble met frequently at the AHC's headquarters on Second Avenue where it had a bird's eye view of the Pan African Square. Pink paint lathered the building further accentuated by red lettering highlighted the AHC's establishment in 1916. Officials had originally envisioned the Health Committee becoming a town council and/or municipality after developing from a nominated body to a partly elected one.[14]

As Alexandra's population mushroomed from its original forty inhabitants, an influx of new residents flooded into the township from rural South Africa, and from the overcrowded slum yards of Doornfontein and other sites around Johannesburg. By the time this migration had ended, Alexandra boasted an estimated population between 40,000 and 50,000 residents.[15] New and old inhabitants competed for the same financial resources and social services. The saturation put intensive pressure on the AHC's shoulders. Money problems consumed the body. Extremely limited funding came from taxation. Dog licenses, property holdings, business certificates, water, bicycles, ambulances, and refuse removal helped to pay for a very primitive sanitation system which consisted of nightsoil workers who picked up buckets of human excrements.[16] Limited economic windfalls also supported a modest clinic. A skeleton staff of a part-time doctor, a full-time nurse, several ambulance drivers, nightsoil workers, tippers, and a resident Health Inspector comprised the extent of the employees. The AHC barely afforded immunizations even with the staff's assistance in injecting patients with needed serums.

Alexandra's status as a 'Nobody's Baby' free from municipal control exacerbated problems. Everything fell upon the AHC to supply the township's social services. The AHC refused to sit idle. Members took advantage of the opportunities to explain their position on how segregation impacted Alexandrans. They zeroed in on transport which had other respondents chiming in on this important issue. The AHC's memorandum issues two proposals that use Orlando as an example to push for change within Alexandra around the tariff paying structure.

As one of Soweto's sprawling complex of townships, Orlando is situated in southwest Johannesburg. Orlando earned its name from Johannesburg's Mayor Edwin Orlando Leake. The township is divided into Orlando East and Orlando West. This directionally divided community swelled in the forties when James 'Sofasonke' Mpanza launched a squatters' movement that spilled over into other places like Alexandra and Benoni on the East Rand. The soaring demand for commuting services reigned high, thus precipitating the need to assist travelers in defraying their heavy economic burdens. Authorities opted to offset patrons' costs by offering a coupon sentence from the bowels of Soweto to the bosom of Johannesburg. Riders tendered 1.1s 9d ($5.43) for a three-month period. Alexandrans, by contrast, doled out 18s 9d ($4.68) per month.[17] A coupon scheme looked lucratively and conveniently attractive. Consumers could either pay a one-time fee for several rides or absorb the expenses daily. Although this proposal made sense economically for passengers, the ABOA rejected it and their patrons' ability to save potentially $1.81 per ninety days. Members of the Beardmore Commission ultimately sided with the ABOA. They made this decision even with the stunning information presented by sociologist Miriam Janisch who provided evidence of 978 families living well below the poverty line.[18]

With the AHC's second proposal, it theoretically joined with Alexandra Workers Union (AWU) and print shop owner Alfred Eddy P. Fisch, in the calling for the ABOA's dissolution.[19] They wanted a community-run transit service to replace the monopoly. This suggestion, however, went beyond ownership. Revenue generated by bus tariffs had the possibility of replenishing the township's coffers, which already stood in the red, and was inadequately prepared monetarily to address infrastructure issues. For many years, the ABOA resorted to fixing pot-holed ridden streets but often offset its costs by transferring those expenses onto its fare-paying consumers.[20] The AHC even donated £300 ($60) at one time, but the ABOA continued its relentless push to hike up the bus prices in order to generate profits. These surges still failed to conceal the fact that the badly needed financial injections proposed to raise Alexandra's standard of living and possibly put it on par with sister townships like Soweto.

The Women's Brigade

An array of African and White-owned newspapers devoted substantial coverage to the township's perennial transport issue. Even the lesser known but extraordinarily successful 1940 bus strike garnered attention in the *Bantu World*. The paper had a 'Women's Section'; however, news of the bus boycott and the females it features does not appear within Reginald R. R. Dhlomo's male-edited space. Instead, columnist Walter M. B. Nhlapo announced the protest in his 'Spotlight on Social Events' under the heading, 'Well Done Alexandra Township'. Nhlapo continues his congratulatory prose with this pronouncement, "The women are the amazons; they've sent an ultimatum to the bus owners asking for a reduction in the fare."[21] Nhlapo's very brief article leaves readers unaware of these protesters' overall mission; for instance, was fare reduction a short-term goal with no futuristic aims or part of a larger move to tackle and topple segregation? Nhlapo's piece also omits identifying details. Scholarly works rectify this situation when they repeatedly cite one fierce, impressionable woman, Cecilia Lillian Tshabalala who carried the baton of Alexandra's early female activists.

Former Johannesburg Senator and activist Hyman Basner wrote several things about Tshabalala in his memoir, *Am I an African?* Basner earned the township's support when the police arrested him for protesting the poll tax. Already a champion in their eyes and one of the prime instigators of the Emergency Transport Committee formed during the 1943 bus boycott, Basner became very acquainted with Tshabalala that he issued this intimate description of the DOA founder, and Women's Brigade leader, Tshabalala, "... liv[ed] in a filthy yard in a room she scrubbed clean with the same ferocity as she attacked anyone daring to cross the picket line".[22] The other image Basner bequeathed is Tshabalala as a revolutionary. Basner witnessed the Natal native parading throughout Alexandra's earthen streets wearing a tight-fitting black beret.[23] This accessory transformed the elegantly photographed Tshabalala into a militant readied for battle. Even Dikobe's protagonist Radebe urged his followers to "keep [their] drums beating to rally [their] force".[24]

This idea of gearing up for war echoed an earlier proto-nationalist form of resistance carried out by Igbo women in southeastern Nigeria called 'sitting on a man'. The circulation of a rumor that the British planned to tax African women signaled the beginning of a two-month war. Women initiated battle by wearing an armory comprising heads wreathed with ferns, faces smeared with ash or charcoal, bodies adorned with loin cloths, and hands clasped with sticks swathed in palms.[25] African women came from various hamlets to converge and to 'sit' on the colonial seats of officialdom—the warrant chiefs' homes and the Native Court by dancing and singing until their targets repented.[26] The Women's Brigade employed the Igbo's women's resistance strategy and 'sat on its man', the ABOA, in two principal ways: by forming a human shield of solidarity and by beginning a silent, symbolic palm reading of their clasped hands.

Having begun in the populous continent of Asia, palmistry dates back over 3000 years, and its metaphorical application in the bus boycotts is needed to explain how the different lines registered with these bus protests and the participants involved. For example, Alexandra's green and yellow-colored motorcoaches represented their 'lifelines' to meagre earnings in White suburban homes, the mineral-rich mines, and the industrial factories. Despite the dependence on public transport, Alexandrans faced a 'life or death struggle' to put food on their empty or sometimes poorly satiated tables. They tempted their fate lines daily. The overcrowded and poorly maintained buses coupled with erratic schedules interfered with Alexandrans' ability to arrive at work early or on time. Excessive waits also mortgaged precious, family time and interfered with the passengers' ability to plan their travel. The terminals presented another problem. Inadequately staffed bus ranks led to aggressive patrons pushing and shoving their way to the front of the lines. The unruliness inconvenienced other fare-paying consumers.[27] Tshabalala and her mobilized troops took all of these issues into consideration and ultimately turned the tables on the ABOA. They hit the cartel in its most vulnerable place. Newspapers flooded their pages with these types of headlines, 'Latest Move in the Bus Boycott: Cordon Drawn Across Road', or 'Cordon Stops Buses Trying to Enter Alexandra Township'.

Alexandran women also used their bodies to "…utter outrage at both public injustice and male viciousness'. In many African cultures, the sight of women's naked bodies insults their male counterparts, as this action serves to emasculate them.[28] All over Africa, and most vividly captured in South Africa (2001) during Liberia's Second Civil War (1997–2003), and most recently in the Central African Republic (CAR) (2014), nudity has been employed as a major weapon of the subaltern. Its use emerged in Alexandra when the Women's Brigade metaphorically took off their clothes. The defiant group formed a shield and allowed the sight of their rebelling vaginas to cast a disparaging spell on the male-dominated body whose barrel of the economic gun they stared down. Amid this symbolic 'nudity', Alexandran women delivered an oral proclamation that the AWL's memorandum reinforced and endorsed with its indelible ink.

The Alexandra Women's League

In 1943, Alexandrans kicked off the township's third bus boycott of the forties, by conducting a nine-mile procession. They marched from Alexandra's periphery along Louis Botha Avenue to Corlett Drive which stretched into the encircling northern White suburbs they congested. Fisch led this triumphant display of defiance with outstretched arms. During an interview with the widely circulated *Johannesburg Star*, he countered the bus company claims with his own concern about his people, "living costs had also increased so, why should we have to pay another 1s ($.25) a week for transport when we cannot even get mealie meal for our families?"[29] Housewives, washerwomen, domestics, and factory workers that formed the Alexandra Women's League addressed Fisch's question in a reply that features female commuters who made up more than 20% of the traveling patronage.[30]

"Ever since the bus riots, women have started their own society to form coalitions with other organizations within Alexandra."[31] This quote taken from the Communist organ *Inkululeko* (*Freedom*) and the memorandum possibly serve as the only extant material on this important Alexandran body. Different from the article, the memorandum, on the other hand, does more than introduce the body; it highlights the AWL's dissatisfaction, the composition of its group, the graphic descriptions of bus riding, bus terminal experiences, and its critique of the monopoly that segregationist and entitlement policies supported. The AWL set the tone and temper with this four-lined introduction: "In most cases women are of less importance than men in nearly all spheres of life, but we are not sure what the consideration that places us in this position is well-founded. We, therefore, herein present our difficulties in connection with transport services."[32]

A galvanized female citizenry issued their grievances with pronouncements that only identified their laboring category: "We are factory workers, when we leave our homes to go to work, we are just in a hurry to get there as anybody else; 'we are washerwomen,' 'and we must keep to it,' we are housekeepers ... we must be early to our jobs. But under the circumstance one cannot be early because the inadequacy of the bus service. ... 'one lives in constant apprehension unless one loses her job,' 'we are housewives and we want to go to town during the peak hours, we find it impossible to get conveyance' or ... one cannot be early because of the inadequacy of the bus service has created a position where in only the fastest and the strong get the privilege and unfortunately for us we are neither fast nor strong."[33]

Alexandran women complained about the bus company for several overarching reasons. Weekday commutes cost passengers 4d ($.08) per ride. Rates doubled on the weekends when they reached 6d ($.12). Germiston in southern Johannesburg, Rosebank in the city's north, Wynberg, and the Union Grounds represent some of the routes offered.[34] Operations typically began daily at 4 am with a full complement of thirty-seven buses; however, four hours later, the monopoly reduced the number of double-deckers to twenty-nine. Around 5 pm when commuter traffic was at its heaviest only a skeleton of eight buses accommodated late-returning Alexandrans. This operational procedure was not anything new.[35]

As early as 1934, Alexandra resident and trade unionist Daniel Koza had criticized the bus company for only operating thirteen buses to accommodate 15,000 patrons.[36] The Alexandra Women's League wrote of a similar disparity when the body proclaimed that the number of buses covering routes only averaged forty-five people per trip which meant that each bus had to do eighteen double trips a day even when drivers endangered commuters and 'doubled up' patrons.[37] On some days as many as seventy or up to a hundred people boarded buses legally registered to carry fifty-six patrons.[38] Five people often occupied seats originally constructed to accommodate three people. Xuma documented eighty-seven instances when the ABOA cavalierly violated the law and glaringly exceeded capacity limits. Xuma observed bus operations for four consecutive days from

Table 6.1 Evidence of Overcrowding

Bus No.	*Date*	*Total Trips*	*Per Trip Average Passengers*
T. J.25777	26th August 1943	56 (all buses)	77
T.J. 53632	same as above		70

26 to 30 August 1943 (Table 6.1). Below are examples of infractions that he documented in his personal papers:[39]

Other evidence comes from the documentation on the waybills which were divided into two sections, 'On' and 'Off'.

Waybills served as record of the number of passengers traveling daily by bus. Drivers were responsible for logging in passenger numbers at each scheduled bus stop; however, they only complied when they thought that a White inspector would board the vehicles for inspection.[40] When company supervisors examined the waybills, they cross-checked them with the numbers that the drivers verbally recited before they initialed the paper and recorded those counts in their own notebooks. The tallying was done so sporadically that drivers repeatedly exceeded the buses' capacity without being officially noticed; on some days as many as seventy people boarded fifty-two passenger buses.[41] Bus drivers violated governmental law under these conditions: when they doubled-up commuters, and failed to leave at least three seats vacant, or provide standing room for four additional persons.

As a bus conductor for ten years and as a dispatcher for another five, Max offers another example of unsafe boarding practices. He witnessed several unsafe practices during his periods of employment. Commuters often jumped in the buses through the windows before they stopped at the downtown terminus on Noord Street. Passengers either fell during the process, were pushed off during their near-death boarding attempts, or died when the drivers ran over their defeated bodies.[42] Max shared:

> There is almost always a struggle to get on the bus and many accidents occur from people falling and sometimes even being run over by the bus. This is worse on Monday mornings because there are more passengers on these days due to the fact that many workers who live at their places of work spend the weekends or Sunday nights in the township. No attempt is made by the bus companies or their servants to prevent the public crowding on the buses in this unorganized way while the bus is still in motion. There is no traffic controller to see that the passengers queue up and take their turn to board

> the bus in an orderly way. There is only one Despatcher for whom it is impossible to do this job adequately....The rush is so great that passengers even get into the windows of the buses. This disorganization at the terminuses causes a major delay in the filling of the bus. The buses would be filled and would move very much faster if the matter were properly ordered.[43]

A minority of bus conductors passed by male passengers in order to pick up female patrons. Fear of job loss possibly prevented this courtesy from becoming a practice, but the AWL soldiered forward and made its demands for a woman's only bus known.[44] Other problems mounted up because only one dispatcher manned operations, so it precluded the employees' ability to prevent incidents like these instead, the situation resulted in the "...fastest and the strongest ... passengers ... [enjoying] the privilege of being conveyed by the buses. Imagine then, [the AWL questions] the position of a woman."[45]

Dr. Alfred B. Xuma on Behalf of the African National Congress

Xuma was the seventh child of two fervent Wesleyans Abraham Mangali Xuma and Elizabeth Cupase Xuma. The family lived in Manzana; a town situated within the Ngcobo District in the Eastern Cape. His parents sent him to Clarkebury, one of the country's most prominent Wesleyan mission schools. Xuma took courses in Latin, and teacher training, and for extra-curricular activity, he participated in the chorus. His stay at Clarkebury represented a prelude of the political activist that he ultimately became.[46] In 1911, the year that the government established a color bar in the mining industry, Cape officials busied themselves differentiating between the teacher certificates that Whites earned versus the teacher training courses that Africans took.[47] Students responded in a move that preluded the school walk out that ignited the 1976 Soweto Uprising, when they voted with their feet only to return to classes a few days later.

Xuma got expelled from Clarkebury for his part in the protest, however, the institution readmitted him. He qualified to teach at the primary level, which the future ANC president did for two years beginning in 1912.[48] When the United States appeared as an option to advance his educational career, Xuma worked several jobs to pay his tuition and for room and board. His prospects initially looked dim. Xuma found a job at the eleventh hour with the American Cast Iron Pipeline, an outfit out of

Birmingham, Alabama, that injected the financial revenue he needed.[49] When all was said and done and following a short setback at the University of Minnesota, Xuma soldiered on, and left Minneapolis for Evanston, Illinois.

Xuma united in holy matrimony twice during his nearly seven decades on earth (1893–1962). His first wife Amanda Mason hailed from the West African nation of Liberia, a land settled by freed Black American captives brought to the continent by "the love of liberty". Three years into the marriage, his bride passed away giving birth to the couple's child. Xuma entered international waters yet again, this time pursuing the hand of Madie Beatrice Hall, a North Carolinian, and oldest daughter of H. H. Hall and Ginny Cowan Hall, two pillars of the Winston-Salem community. Hall's father served as the town's first Black physician, and like his son-in-law, a medical doctor, he followed the call to heal.[50] Marriage into this family was anything but easy for Xuma. A long courtship finally resulted in the African American finally saying yes to his hand in holy matrimony.

In 1940, following interruptions brought on by the Second World War, the blushing bride finally arrived in South Africa.[51] Madie Hall Xuma (MHX) pursued social justice, just like her father, but instead of Jim Crow's zenith, she conducted her work at apartheid's dawn. MHX "was a singular woman whose attitudes were informed by the ideas of the Talented Tenth, that a miniscule percentage of blacks with a college education who operated under the sentiment that they should become community leaders in order to help the entire African community as [the prominent activist and intellectual thinker] W. E. B. Du Bois argued."[52] This union represented more than an emotional and a spiritual bond; it also signified a political and social connection. Before Xuma passed away, and his wife moved back to North Carolina respectively in 1962 and 1963, the power couple blazed an important trail within the South African landscape.

From 1940 to 1949, Xuma held the reins of the nation's oldest Black political organization. This achievement followed his attainment of a Bachelor of Science degree at Tuskegee University in Tuskegee, Alabama (1920), a medical degree from Northwestern University in Evanston, Illinois (1926), and a Diploma of Health from London University's School of Hygiene and Tropical Medicine (1938). Even while holding down two Medical Officer positions in Sophiatown and Alexandra, Xuma cared for White and African patients. Xuma risked his credentials and even his reputation among his own people to support his principles. He opposed the artificial barriers that existed between European and African patients and African practitioners who, despite taking a Hippocratic oath, faced criminalization for not turning away the sick no matter their respective race.[53]

Several addresses further affirm Xuma's stance against segregation and his own ideological beliefs in support of multiracialism. 'The Policy and Platform of the ANC' and 'Africans' Claims in South Africa' are two key pieces that refute notions that this African, American, and South African all rolled into one relied exclusively on the gentleman's approach. His activism went beyond just the submission of memorandums or the configurations of deputations sent to appropriate government authorities. The ANC president released his political powder keg through his fiery ideas and consistent demands for his political body to take the lead in the country's destiny; for the government to grant Africans full citizenship; and lastly, for post-war South Africa to abolish discriminatory legislative measures that greatly impacted and inhibited the socio-economic growth of Africans.[54] This last suggestion explains why Xuma paid attention to the bussing situation in Alexandra, and elsewhere.

Systemic racism created the conditions under which Africans became a vulnerable, captive clientele for a capitalistic ABOA. Xuma uses his seven pages to discuss how transport affected the economy of hardworking Africans; to challenge the company's spending practices amid protestations of insolvency; and lastly, to push for changes within the transport industry. The ANC president littered his papers with potentially damaging albeit circumstantial evidence. He noted instances of excessive overcrowding, ferocious terminal scrambles, and what appeared to be ostentatious company acquisitions. Criticized by Nelson Mandela, Ahmed Kathrada, Walter Sisulu, and other younger ANC adherents, for being too diplomatic, Xuma left a conspicuous trail of being an opponent to the government's policy on segregation. His memorandum, which is just one of many examples, is interspersed with messages he conveyed on other platforms to illustrate his vision of nationalism holistically.

Xuma's memorandum uncovers several signs of alleged company affluence. He wrote:

> A statement has been made before this commission to the effect that it is nobody's concern what profits the bus owners are making as a result of providing the service at 4d for one single journey and 6d on weekends Saturday 1 pm to Monday 8 am and on holidays. We submit, that under the circumstances, that it is the concern of all interested parties in the dispute. The

> books are essential, and the information is material in order to justify the Transportation Board for raising the fare from 4d to 5d for one single journey during weekdays. We are under the impression that the bus owners want their fares raised because they're making no money.[55]

One of the first indications of suspected profiting was the monopoly's bold move from its modest workplace in Alexandra to a plush suite of offices in neighboring Wynberg. This new headquarters costs the struggling company $25 monthly which amounted to $300 yearly.[56] Eight additional employees rounded off this apparent spending spree. New acquisitions earned salaries ranging from £5.15.0d ($28.75) to £6.11.0d ($31.32) a week; in addition to drawing a yearly uniform allowance of £150 ($750). Reduced to relying on circumstantial evidence, Xuma concluded, "It [was] … [inconceivable] that a losing business would embark on such an expensive luxury in extra employees. … [he] find it difficult to believe … that they should incur this extra expense for the fun of it. They must be making some profit."[57] Xuma had every reason to believe this conclusion.

During the Second World War, a growing number of African women commuted to the industries and factories and bicyclists resorted to using the buses when tires became too scarce and expensive.[58] The ABOA became the sole beneficiary of the passenger influx with no competing transit. Former bus employee and Transvaal ANC President J. B. Marks put another nail in the cartel's coffin when he noted that only one route out of seventeen showed a loss in profits during his five years of employment as the cartel's bookkeeper.[59] Despite the solvent progress report, the Beardmore Commission concluded that the bus enterprise earned a relatively low return with a 4.5% profit margin from its capital investment. For an operation geared to maximize revenue, this appears unsubstantial, however, the figure supports Xuma's case. Seeing that the transit enterprise allegedly operated in the black, Xuma sought to empower the Africans he represented. He called for a national minimum wage, diversity in the transport industry, and for the AHC or a public entity to run the bus company.[60] Xuma sought these changes because he like the AWL, the Women's Brigade, and the Fourth International and the Africans they represented bore the economic brunt of segregation. Xuma noted the bus employees' salaries (Table 6.2) in his voluminous papers:[61]

Transport expenses made a huge dent in salaries that hovered below the poverty line. Washerwomen netted a mere 5d ($.10) or 2s 10d ($.70) per month for each bundle of wash. From this compensation, they deducted

Table 6.2 Bus Company Employees' Salaries

8 INSPECTORS	£2933.12s.0d	$14,658.00
4 INSPECTORS	£1310.8s.0d	$ 6566.00
2 OFFICE ASSISTANTS	£ 240.0s.0d	$ 1200.00
UNIFORMS	£ 150.0s.0d	$ 750.00
RENTAL	£ 120.0s 0d	$. 600.00
CONTROLLER'S SALARY	£ 600.0s.0d	$ 3000.00
7 DESPATCHERS	£1118.0s.0d	$ 5590.00
TOTAL EXPENDITURES	£6,472.0s.0d	$32,366.00

Table 6.3 Fare Structure

Location	*Fares-Weekday/Weekend*	*Distance*
Alexandra-Johannesburg	4d ($.08) 6d ($.12)	9 miles
Alexandra-Rosebank	4d ($.08) 6d ($.12)	2 miles
Alexandra-Union Grounds	5d ($.10)	2 miles
Alexandra-Wynberg	4d ($.08)	2 miles
Alexandra-Germiston	1s ($.25)	21 miles

the cost of supplies: 1s ($.25) for 2 bars of soap, 1s 3d ($.31) for a bag of coal, 3d ($.06) for a cord of wood, 4d ($.08) for starch in addition to monthly travel expenses. Charwomen earned even less. Performing laundry services at their employers' homes rather than away from their prying eyes, charwomen earned a 3d ($.06).[62] Out of that total, monthly transport expenses cost a staggering 1s 6d ($.37) with Alexandrans expending money for fares that ran from 4d ($.08) on weekdays and 6d ($.12) on weekends. Figures excluded possible double trips to attain highly contested seats. The AHC already noted that Orlando's residents had the option of buying coupon books to defray expenses and to lessen the daily economic burden of tendering fares. Xuma proposed a different resolution, but still along the lines of supporting the consumers when he suggested that the transit enterprise charge different prices for the distances traveled.

Commuters tendered the same 4d ($.08) tariff whether they journeyed two or ten miles from the township. Passengers being ferried to Germiston twenty-one miles south of Johannesburg, for example, would pay a higher fee than those disembarking the buses ten miles away at Noord Street in the city's downtown (Table 6.3). Surging tariffs represented a mushrooming economic concern. Foodstuffs were shooting up by an average of 46%

during the war years forcing many households to alter their eating habits, to impose rationings, to reduce meat consumption, or to eat animal entrails.[63] One mother "had to practically go without food [herself]..., to make sure the children ate enough. [She could] only buy one and half pounds of meat a week instead of the two pounds [she] got before."[64]

Another Alexandran resident criticized the bus company with this comment, "Operators say that their operating costs have increased. So have our living costs. Why should we have to pay another 1s a week for transport when we cannot even get mealie meal for our families?" Employers reduced pay even further when domestics broke dishes, arrived late, or fell sick. A pantry maid's story illustrates this liability. Maitland was in excellent health for many years, but as fate would have it, that picture perfect state changed, and she became sick. "Not once [did] [my employers] ... [send] a token of appreciation to care for my services, or even inferred after my health, [instead], the day's pay was deducted from the weekly pay. What a reward for faithful service!"[65] Xuma proposed that African employees earn at least 2.10s.0d ($11.92) a month since they already lived below the poverty line.[66] Absence of a minimum wage, a cost-of-living allowance, sick leave, or an eight-hour workday that existed in countries like the United States where changes began in 1938 further solidified the dehumanization of African people or conjured up experiences like Maitland's whose only 'crime' was a legitimate illness.

Fiscal economics and equitable opportunities reached Xuma's imagination on several occasions. One of the earliest times was on 21 July 1929 when he delivered a blistering speech before the British Association for the Advancement of Science. Officials sought to substitute professionally trained medical doctors and nurses with 'medical aids'. Xuma not only registered his strong objection to this proposal; he also called for the establishment of medical schools that would open its doors to Africans.[67] Possibly thinking about his own experience abroad, where he attended and graduated from an HBCU and a predominantly White institution, Xuma encouraged the state to provide funding for Africans to pursue medical training overseas. Xuma, who never stopped advocating for the political, social, and economic development of Africans, turned his attention from the disparities within the medical field to the problems associated with transport. His interest peaked immensely when he saw an African man on the brink of failing.

Other African bus owners came and went, but for fifteen years Baloyi (RG) gave the industry a run for its hard-earned money. Baloyi entered the commuter service industry in 1922, first as a taxi driver before he expanded his entrepreneurial skills and formed the United Bus Company five years later in 1927. He managed his enterprise from a garage behind his two-story brick-faced home. Baloyi's "Mighty Six" shuttled passengers from the bowels of Alexandra to the densely trafficked Johannesburg. Baloyi continued to take passengers from Ramokokastad to the Botswana (Bechuanaland) border until the government issued legislative measures that dramatically altered the ferrying arrangement.[68] Originally, the government created the 1930 Motor Carrier Act to prevent buses from operating in places already serviced by rail, but later however, it served another purpose when it started to regulate routes.[69] Standardization of both timetables, and fares meant that the 'pirate taxis' along with the fifty alternate conveyances which comprised the Emergency Transport Committee faced stiff competition with Alexandra's 'legitimate' bus monopoly, which later succeeded in muscling Baloyi out.

While this measure shook up already contested routes, and Alexandra's firm place within the transport industry, unsatisfied government officials went back to the drawing table. They issued amendments to the 1930 Motor Carrier Act respectively in 1939 and 1941. Inked with the death knell of their signatures, these new measures authorized Africans to pay a 100s ($25) application fee before considering their request. Stadler notes that throughout the 1940s, the Transportation Board repeatedly declined applications submitted by Africans.[70] Seeing things happening on the political forefront, Xuma joined Dr. James Moroka, his ANC successor, and partner, to save Baloyi's business from the auction block and the clutch of prospective White owners.[71]

When the Transportation Board (TB) rejected their application, the state called Baloyi's manhood, which was connected to his personal economy, into question. Baloyi owned one of the more modern homes in the township, a two-story affair covered in bricks, and framed by white posts. His home, buses, and other accoutrements allowed Baloyi to assume a role as a breadwinner, and to stake his claim to propriety. His social and political capital also afforded his wife Elizabeth Baloyi the luxury of participating and serving as an officer in the Tshabalala-led DOA. Baloyi's acquisitions, and the accompanying perks, allowed him to earn a passage into manhood. Dikobe who stars in this narrative yet again presents the powerful and emasculated Baloyi in his book of poems called *Dispossessed*. In a work that treats several subjects on Alexandra like the community's leaders, its wealth, and its squatters among other topics pays homage in an ode simply titled 'RG':[72]

None shall ever equal R. G.
Owning half of Alexandra Township
'Safe return Mighty Six'
Master of the road Roaring along Louis Botha Out-running
Green's Alexandra Limited Laub's Jackson's
From Second to Third Avenues
R. G. Proprietary Ltd.,
Rental pouring into leaking pockets
Signing cheques with the power of attorney
Charity at whim
"Stop the Rent Board."
In the confusion
All business stops
Adjourned sine die
A bull in the chinaman's shop.
Honour bestwed upon those
Who in service trusted
Not a sovereign unrecorded
Balance sheet as clean as a sheet
Great man was he—R. G.
In the N. R. C. chambers
Full two hours speech
Without banging.
Mourn Alexandra Township, Mourn the nation.
In poverty, he died Benevolent, charitable Signing cheques.
Poor he died. Proving his sincerity.

This elegy captures how Baloyi died as a pauper and as an exile. When Baloyi lost his home, he left northeastern Johannesburg to live in the city's southwestern quadrant in Diepkloof, one of the sprawling townships that occupy Soweto. Baloyi's move failed to improve his life, if anything, the relocation spurred on his impending deaths. He died twice, metaphorically in the year he lost evidence of his industry in 1942, and earthly when he passed away in 1962. Though occurring twenty years apart, each death had an impact on the nationalist goals of Africans, as they not only lost a tireless and fearless leader in Baloyi but also a positive and solvent dividend to the social account of racial respectability as Xuma's statement attests, "we [cannot] afford to see you, or any of our progressive people disappear from the limelight or fail to lead in certain directions, and [pulling] together, we can do a great deal, not only for ourselves but for our people in general."[73] Xuma's push to save Baloyi's floundering business exemplified his quest to improve the living standards of his people. The ANC leader saw the bigger picture that lay beyond transport, segregation, and race to issues of self-determination and liberation.

Xuma's approach stood in stark contrast to the ANC Youth League.[74] His version of mass mobilization failed to completely occupy the streets which the ANCYL championed. Instead, speeches before the United Nations, his hand in the creation of the African Charter (a spin on the Atlantic Charter), and his memorandum to the Beardmore Commission exemplified the wider audience he reached. His devotion to broadening the diversity within the transport industry mirrored Johannesburg resident J. K. Mahemane who in a letter entitled 'Response to the Nation' (Impendulo ku Zulu) expressed that:

> Ibuhlungu kakulu lendaba uma kuyiqiniso ukuti abapti bezinqola zabamnyama base Alexandra-bangaba nalo mcabango wokufaka abelungu bokuhlola amatikiti endawnei yaBantu.
>
> It is very disturbing to hear that the black bus owners of Alexandra would think of bringing in white inspectors into our area.[75]

Xuma went against the will of the African bus owners when he sought to change the terrain and to level the economic field in terms of transport costs, employment, and ownership for African patrons and proprietors. He wanted the numbers to increase within the transit enterprise so that his people could recycle money back into the Alexandran economy just like the AHC's and Xuma's proposal of turning the Alexandra Bus Owners Association over to the township's governing body. Thus, Xuma's push for nationalism differed from the Fourth International's advocacy for socialism, however, despite this ideological difference, his actions illustrate how this man was in the forefront of the struggle for economic liberation.

The Johannesburg Section of the Fourth International

A year before Alexandra's first modern bus boycott (1939), the Fourth International began as a small study group among Cape Town's intellectual circles before it developed into a larger organization that espoused

Trotskyism.[76] This form of Marxist Communism supported a continual revolution by members of the working class that bodies like the Fourth International under the leadership of Hosea Jaffe, future editor of the Communist Organ, the *Worker's Voice*, sought to liberate. Alexandrans and their struggle fit neatly into the body's philosophy, so it was no surprise that the Fourth International took the initiative to evaluate the transportation situation and to offer its critique, and its recommendations. The Fourth International differed from Xuma, the AHC, and the AWL on this ground: the body offered a more representative demographic mix when it went beyond the binary between Black and White to include Coloureds, Africans, and Asians as this statement confirms, "the mode of life in most urban and contiguous areas in South Africa, as these affect not merely the Bantu, but also the Indian and Coloured people."[77]

While race served as a defining factor in the government's policy of divide and rule, class also alienated people. No matter how paltry or substantial, incomes consigned people to the type of conveyances they took. Poorer laborers traveled in buses, trams, and trains, while the more affluent used private cars. Transportation magnified divisions "between European and non-European on the one hand; and ... between the Bantu on one side and the Indian and Coloured".[78] Bunche shares this observation during his visit to South Africa in the thirties, "The natives here are themselves terribly confused about the J. C. [Jim Crow] situations on trams and buses. They say there are no specific rules and no signs. ... It is left to the arbitrary decision of individual conductors ... to [decide] whether a native can ride upstairs or not."[79] Bunche is surprised by the lack of signage to enforce segregated public conveyances. He does note however that Africans, like their African American counterparts, always sat in the back, whereas in regard to Coloureds, "they were indefinite as to what happened to [them]".[80]

The Fourth International sheds some light on this issue. An examination of the bi-lateral color bar on the buses and the trams reveals that Coloureds or Indians rode on these respective vehicles under two conditions that they either sat upstairs or occupied the rear or front seats.[81] Placards defined racialized spaces on motor coaches in Montgomery, Alabama. Each time the designated White area filled up, the sign moved further backwards. This took away the ten rear seats from paying Black customers to accommodate White patrons who refused to stand over them or vice versa. Furthermore, African Americans tendered their fare at the front of the bus only to disembark and alight again at the back.[82] In one of the few times that Tshabalala addresses race, she offers this observation, "Negroes are excluded from Pullman cars south of the Dixieline."[83]

A similar system of differentiation existed within South Africa's railroad cars. Whites and so-called Coloureds occupied the First and Second Class respectively. Asians and Africans sat in the least expensive and very overcrowded Third Class. Numbers swelled up on these passages because people who lived far from their places of employment often congregated at a single spot. Africans ended up spending insurmountable time traveling. The situation was so dire that the Fourth International concluded that "money spent in travelling to and from work [took] a heavy slice out of the wage of the bread-winner, and thereby [worsened] the conditions to which the worker [returned] after his day's misery in the mining, transport, and commercial industry, and the sphere of domestic service" only to do it all over again as an exploited member of the economic world of capitalism.[84] Leading sociologist Dr. Kate Leipman's research *A Journey to Work*, which the Bus Commission Report cites, substantiates the Fourth International's, and the AWL's, assertion that constant travel, standing for long periods of time (from forty-five minutes up to an hour), sitting on overcrowded buses, and walking long distances reduced the laborers' productivity, and lessened their very important family time.[85] The Fourth International wanted the state to construct apartments near South Africa's industrial and commercial areas.[86] While this proposal kept laborers near the modes of production, its suggestion foreshadowed the deliberations and the decisions of the Mentz Commission.

Formed in 1952, Mentz Commission oversaw the enforcement of the Groups Areas Act and the Population Registration Act which respectively created racial enclaves and entrenched the definition of biological determinism to prevent social advancement through passing and skin lightening. Alexandra came under intense scrutiny and uncertainty with this regulatory group when the Mentz Commission ordered the state to turn this highly vibrant and ethnically diverse township "exclusively into a dormitory for northern peri-urban Johannesburg workers".[87] Alexandra was already encircled by a swath of affluent residential areas, and with industries also standing nearby, it presented the best case for a conversion from a family dwelling area to a place for single dwelling hostel residents. The state proceeded with its mission and began forcibly removing Alexandrans from their community beginning in the early fifties. By the time the hemorrhaged stopped in 1979, an estimated 44,700 people willingly or involuntarily left the township for one of Soweto's many locations—Pimville,

Meadowlands, and others where they, despite having gardens, went to homes without walls, flooring, or ceilings.[88]

Historical conditions and an apartheid policy bent on ensuring White minority dominance, and racial purity, warranted this stealth move. By the 1970s and with the establishment of ten homelands, the apartheid regime realized its grand policy of separate development. Bophuthatswana, Kwa/Zulu Natal, Ciskei, and the Transkei and six other areas represented a larger version of what the Fourth International and the Mentz Commission had proposed respectively in the forties and in the fifties. The South African government recognized these homelands (Bantustans) as nation-states created for its people to develop along their own cultural and political lines.[89] No other country responded in kind. Each homeland had a leader, but most of the inhabitants remained inextricably linked to South Africa's economy as workers in the country's factories, homes, and mines. The Homelands Policy was counter-intuitive to the apartment scheme that the Fourth International recommended principally because these areas skirted South Africa's peripheries, and therefore, moved them further away from employment and financial opportunities.[90] This option also enhanced the state's power over the community which stood in stark contrast to the Fourth International's philosophy which advocated for African people to control the means of production, distribution, and exchange. "Socialism [was] necessary [because] it would solve the transport problem and the expropriation of the workers by … private owners … and [eradicate] all race discrimination in transport, as in everything else."[91]

An Accounting of Segregation

The story of the Alexandra bus boycotts untangles many intersecting layers from the diverse narratives that defined and documented their occurrence. Commuters registered their dissent. Bus owners plead their case for raising fares. Socialists, nationalists, community dwellers, factory workers, housewives, and domestics offered resolutions to save the nation. Even Dikobe's short story offers a recommendation. Continuing from an interrupted meeting to a summation of activities, Dikobe transplants readers to a wintry day rather than end on a cliffhanger. The writer explains how the wheels of out-of-reach transport continued rolling on. Dikobe wrote: "A deputation is sent to City Council's transportation. It receives 'sympathetic' hearing. Capitulation [sic] is in process."[92] Despite supporting

Alexandrans, the Commission ultimately backed the bus owners following its lengthy investigation which ran from August 1943 to January 1944, with this important opinion:

> transport charges in relation to workers' wages, or even to the total family income, are beyond the capacity of the African workers to pay. Indeed, it may be said that they cannot afford to pay anything. They certainly cannot afford to pay anything more in any direction except by reducing still further their hunger diet.[93]

The body's turned-about-face occurred almost as if overnight. Political scientist Tom Lodge weighed in on this immense change of events, "…In 1943 the state appears to have played a conciliatory and defusing role, [while] in 1944 official attitudes were more combative. Despite the commission's evidence which suggested that no urban African community on the Rand could afford increased transport costs, the government gave its assent in November 1944 to the 5d ($.10) fare."[94] Lorentz stood by bus owners over the years and even warned passengers to accept the higher fares or face interruption or cessation of services. Lorentz and other officials made good on their threats. In 1942, the ABOA shortened the route. Alexandrans chose a symbolic protest. They only tendered the original 4d ($.08) fare but resorted to drastic measures when uniformed police officers rode the shuttles.[95] Commuters also got off at the next available stops, paid the full 5d ($.10) tariff, or walked the extra miles to board buses. Other instances of dissent occurred.

Protesters radicalized and attacked symbols of segregation like the buses and the police officers. In Dikobe's fictionalized account, his protagonist, Gaur Radebe, takes a definitive stand. "Expelled from the CPSA in 1942, he was associated with Paul Mosaka's efforts to launch the African Democratic Party in 1943. His name was again in the news when he helped lead the Alexandra bus boycotts of 1943 and 1944."[96] Dikobe captures Radebe vetoing the proposal that supported the government controlling the community's bus system. The short narrative also includes the owners' voices, "We have put Wynberg as an alternative terminus; how's that Mr[.] Gaur [Radebe]? who responds, I've already said no man's land [the strip of land from First Avenue Wynberg to Johannesburg-Pretoria main artery] is life risk."[97] Dikobe apparently had his ear to the ground. The AWL discussed this same concern. The imaginary conversation ends with Green, one of the original ABOA members, skirting around the topic and not explaining the rationale for an alternative pick-up location. This avoidance spilled over on to real life, leaving the AWL to conclude:

> the bus cartel [could not] be asked to be ... philanthropists. They [could] not be asked to waste [their time thinking and scheming how best they could] ... [to] satisfy the public. [Instead, they] spent all their time and energy thinking and serving how best to make [their] profit.[98]

Dikobe continued his reporting in another way. In newspaper articles, Dikobe utilizes his given name, Marks Rammitloa. Pieces appear in his native tongue, Sesotho, rather than the English he preferred to employ with his poems. His choice of language determined the vantage point from which he portrayed the bus boycotts. The time he submitted to the Communist-inspired *Inkululeko*, Rammitloa documents the residents' desire to renew the bus boycott in November 1944. They initiated the last transit strike of the forties (1944) by conducting weekly marches from the township's Number 2 Square to Johannesburg. Participants reconvened at the Noord Street terminus during the evenings for the procession back to Alexandra. Government officials took it upon themselves to launch reprisals. Authorities bombarded and interrupted the residents' meeting to read Proclamation No. 201 of 1939 which outlawed gatherings of more than twenty people at one time. Marchers foiled the police's attempt to disrupt their early dawn procession by retreating and continuing in groups of ten to fifteen people. Groups even remained off the sidewalks to avoid arbitrary arrests, but the police proved to be relentless in their harassment tactics despite the boycotters' precautions.[99]

During the succeeding days, they attacked the alternate transport pool, formed previously during the 1943 bus boycott. The Alexandra Emergency Transport Committee (AETC) replaced its motor vehicles with a fleet of horse-drawn trolleys which lessened costs to £1 ($5.00) per day.[100] Donations from passengers fueled this change in the carpooling system especially given the fact that government enacted a petrol embargo against the AETC's operations, but the body already had enough gas rationings to avoid delays in its operations.[101] The Women's Brigade, in turn, stepped up its efforts and formed a cordon across Ninth Avenue to prevent the bus cartel from capitalizing on the minority which still sought its transit services.[102] The state and the monopoly struck back when they pulled out the big guns and hired 'riders' to lure commuters back onto their motorcoaches.[103]

The patronage's opposition continued the assault when they made it a point to sully the movement's reputation and its motives. For example, the White-owned *Rand Daily Mail* alleged that "black goon squads" had chased away a shuttle that carried twenty-five odd passengers or that a black taxi cab driver held up a bus that contained one commuter by blocking the road and forcing the patron to walk.[104] Falsifications continued with parties fueling the growing gossip mill with rumors of a failed protest. Martial law also took place. Authorities sealed off streets. Heavily hit were Corlett Drive and Louis Botha Avenue. Motorists at those respective intersections faced a battery of threatening questions and intimidation tactics that consisted of the police jotting down the drivers' names, their addresses, and their license plate numbers. The police took another step in its reprisal campaign by arresting violators and sympathizers.[105] And in a move to really paralyze the protest, the Transportation Board suspended drivers' licenses even when offenders possessed the legal counsel of the Workers Transport Action Committee (WTAC), an umbrella group of four political organizations, and the Campaign for Right and Justice (CRJ), a pacifist organization founded by the Reverend Michael Scott sometime in the mid-forties.[106]

Like earlier bus boycotts, residents secured the restoration of the original 4d ($.08) tariff, but this time, the government answered the suggestions posed by the AWL, Xuma, Fisch, the AHC, and the Fourth International when they called for a transfer of ownership to the government, the AHC, or a non-private body. In 1945, officials made the decision to create a Public Utility Corporation (PUTCO). While this move appeared to show that Africans had the state's ear, and its endorsing signature, PUTCO, as future 1957 boycott leader Dan Mokonyane points out, in *Lessons of Azikhwelwa*, had a major shortcoming because "the venture discouraged the economies of large corporations. PUTCO and other entities like it, still supported controlling monopolies, which did not act for the public good."[107] This critique was a large reason for the opposition to the bus company by the AWL and the Fourth International. Xuma understood this moral obligation which he discerned:

> No transport scheme is a solution to the Non-European transport problem, unless it … recognizes … that Non-Europeans, Africans in particular, live at unreasonable distances from their employment [and] that [the state has a moral obligation to bear the whole transport charge] not as a charitable gesture or gift, but as a duty.[108]

In what may seem like a response to Xuma's criticism, and the Beardmore Commission's conclusion of Africans' inability to pay, the government under War Emergency Proclamation No. 1901 issued an Employer Travel Subsidy in 1944. This legislation required employers to defray transport expenses incurred by African laborers amounting to a daily expense of 10d ($.20).[109] In doing this, the state made it clear that these travel allowances did not constitute earnings to be deducted from wages, but rather they were subsidies granted to compensate for the appearance and continuation of segregation.[110] While officials finally assumed responsibility for segregation and the economic expense borne by Africans, some flaws in this legislation existed. The CPSA weighed in on the discussion with its pamphlet, 'They Marched to Victory', in which it declares that "[the Employer Travel Subsidy] only applied to certain classes of employment—[and] did not cover casual workers, washerwomen, women travelling to town for shopping, children, people attending hospital or visiting friends, the man looking for work".[111] Workers faced the onus of collecting subsidies from their employers. They either complied or ran the risk of enduring three months in prison and/or paid fines.[112] While intentional, the measure contained no rules for enforcement. Maitland's story now told in its entirety further reveals the problems that surfaced:

> when it is payday, you have to remind madam that shops are closing—she has completely lost her memory; and the sighs that take place before you are given your hard-worked-for earnings takes away all the blessings of an honest earned wage.[113]

Maitland's narrative illustrates that Africans faced humiliation daily and the Employer Travel Subsidy proposed to bear even more indignation. The DOA, the NCAW, and other emergent political bodies fought to erase and erode societal differences based on race and conditions of alleged inferiority. Like those who trumpeted their consumer purchasing power during Alexandra's historic bus boycotts, these bodies stood as moral compasses that pointed north in their words and actions just as those who followed its direction to travel along the Underground Railroad to escape American slavery. Tshabalala and Soga embodied the spirit and the vitality of America's Moses, Harried Tubman, through their efforts to attain freedom from the yokes of segregation while pursuing social justice at apartheid's dawn.

Notes

1. Tim Couzens, 'Nobody's Baby,' Belinda Bozzoli (ed.), *Labour, Townships and Protest: Studies in the Social History of the Witwatersrand* (Johannesburg: Ravan Press, 1979), 42-46.
2. Alan Gregor Cobley, *Class and Consciousness: The Black Petty Bourgeoisie in South Africa, 1924 to 1950* (New York: Greenwood Press, 1990), 222. Baloyi was a widely recognized politician, footballer, Native Representative Council (NRC) Officer, Transvaal African National Congress (TANC) treasurer, and a founding member of the Alexandra Bus Owners Association (ABOA). Bus owners included Mrs. T. Sacks, Robin Green, Northwestern, J. Combrink, Dick Mathole, Richard Baloyi, and D. Laub among other proprietors.
3. Dawne Y. Curry, "Community, Culture and Resistance in Alexandra, South Africa," PhD dissertation, Michigan State University, East Lansing, Michigan, 2006. The six-member Beardmore Commission of Enquiry consisted of its chairman, E. Beardmore; former Attorney General, J. D. Rheinallt Jones; a Senator in the Orange Free State; A. P. Brugman; a chartered accountant; S. J. Bezuidenhout; a businessman; S. C. Quinlan, a public prosecutor, and L. Meyer; Secretary, member of the Native Affairs Department. During a five-month investigation extending from August 1943 to January 1944, the Charles Beardmore Commission heard the testimony of over 192 witnesses, including deputations from both the bus monopoly and various Black protest organizations. While concluding that transport costs exceeded the patronage's ability to pay, the Commission ultimately decided in favor of the bus monopoly and supported its tariff increase.
4. Eddie Roux, *Time Longer than Rope: A History of the Black Man's Struggle for Freedom in South Africa* (Madison: University of Wisconsin Press, 1967), 318-321.
5. The Alexandra Bus Boycott, *Cape Standard*, August 5, 1943, 3. Noted activist Yusef Dadoo was involved in an array of political organizations, including the Non-European United Front, the Indian Congress, and a member of Alexandra's Emergency Transport Committee. He often spoke before mass meetings. After one such event, the government issued an order precluding his future participation in any public protest. The decree read: he shall not attend nor address any meetings convened by or held under the auspices of the Non-European United Front, Transvaal Indian Nationalist Youth Organisation, Transvaal Indian Nationalist Congress, the Communist Party of South Africa, or any other political meeting of a similar nature.

6. Memorandum of Evidence Presented by the Alexandra Health Committee to the Commission Appointed in Terms of Notice No. 1535, Xuma Papers, ABX 430927a (hereafter Alexandra Health Committee Memorandum).
7. Alfred Stadler, A Long Way to Walk: Bus Boycotts in Alexandra, 1940-1945 in Philip Bonner (ed.) *Working Papers in Southern African Studies* (Johannesburg: Ravan Press, 1981), 232.
8. Statement of the Johannesburg Section of the Fourth International, Xuma Papers, ABX 430922d (hereafter referred to as the Statement by Fourth International), 1.
9. Dawne Y. Curry, "Class, Community, and Culture and Resistance in Alexandra, South Africa, 1912-1985," PhD Dissertation, Michigan State University, East Lansing, Michigan, 2006, 23-24. See also Dawne Y. Curry, *Apartheid on a Black Isle: Removal and Resistance in Alexandra, South Africa* (New York: Palgrave Macmillan, 2012).
10. Mike Sarakinsky, From "Freehold Township" to "Model Township": A Political History of Alexandra, 1905-1983. Johannesburg: University of Witwatersrand Medical Library, 1984, 1 and Philip Bonner and *Noor Nieftagodien, Alexandra: A History* (Johannesburg: University of Witwatersrand Press, 2008), 3-5.
11. For more information on the 1913 Natives Land Act see Solomon T. Plaatje, *Native Life in South Africa* (Essex: Longman, 1987). On the 1923 Natives Urban Areas Act consult T. R. H. Davenport, *The Beginnings of Urban Segregation in South Africa: The Natives (Urban Areas) Act of 1923 and Its Background* (Grahamstown: Rhodes University, 1971).
12. Dawne Y. Curry, *Apartheid on a Black Isle: Removal and Resistance in Alexandra, South Africa* (New York: Palgrave Macmillan, 2012), 20.
13. Dawne Y. Curry, "Class, Community, and Culture and Resistance," 25-26.
14. David Duncan, "Liberals and Local Administration in South Africa: Alfred Hoernle" and the Alexandra Health Committee, 1933-1943, *International Journal of African Historical Studies*, 23, 3 (1990): 477.
15. Alexandra Health Committee Memorandum.
16. Dawne Y. Curry, "Class, Community, and Culture and Resistance," 30 and John Nauright. "Black Island in a White Sea: The Making of Alexandra Township, South Africa, 1912-1948," PhD Thesis, Ottawa: Queens University, 1992, 23.
17. Alexandra Health Committee Memorandum.
18. Ibid.
19. Baruch Hirson, *Yours for the Union*, 138.
20. Memorandum Representing the Residents of Alexandra Township in the Dispute over the Matter of Increased Fares between the City and

Alexandra Bus Owners Themselves, Xuma Papers, ABX 430711a (hereafter Memorandum Representing Alexandra Township Residents).

21. Walter B. Nhlapo, "The Women Are the Amazons," *Bantu World*, August 31, 1940, 12.
22. Miriam Basner, *Am I an African?*, 153.
23. Ibid.
24. Belinda Bozzoli (ed.), *Labour, Townships and Protest*, 42-43.
25. Judith Van Allen, "Sitting on a Man: The Lost Political Institutions of the Igbo," *Canadian Journal of African Studies / Revue Canadienne des Études Africaines*, 6 (1972): 173-175.
26. Ibid.
27. Ibid.
28. Henry Kam Kah, "Women's Resistance in Cameroon's Western Grassfields: The Power of Symbols, Organization, and Leadership, 1957-1961," *African Studies Quarterly*, 12, 3 (Summer 2011): 73-74.
29. Bus Service to Alexandra at Standstill: Natives Refuse to Pay Higher Fares, *Johannesburg Star*, August 3, 1943, 1.
30. Union of South Africa. Report of the Commission of Enquiry into the Operation of Bus Services for Non-Europeans on the Witwatersrand in the Districts of Pretoria and Vereeniging. UG 31 1944 (hereafter referred to as Bus Commission Report), 12.
31. "The Alexandra Bus Boycott," *Inkululeko*, August 5, 1943, 4.
32. Alexandra Women's League Memorandum, 1.
33. Ibid., 1-2.
34. Bus Commission Report, 20.
35. Alexandra Women's League Memorandum.
36. David Harries, "Daniel Koza: A Working Class Leader," *Perspectives*, 19 (1990): 13.
37. Alexandra Women's League Memorandum, 2.
38. Buses in Alexandra, *The Guardian*, August 5, 1943, 3.
39. Memorandum of Evidence Presented by the President-General of the African National Congress on Behalf of the Residents of Alexandra Township (hereafter referred to as ANC President-General Memorandum), 1-2.
40. Statement of Max, a bus conductor for ten years and a dispatcher for five, Xuma Papers ABX430711b.
41. Ibid.
42. Ibid.
43. Ibid.
44. Alexandra Women's League Memorandum, 2.
45. Ibid., 1.

46. Dr. A. B. Xuma, https://www.sahistory.org.za/people/dr-alfred-xuma, date accessed 15 February 2020.
47. Ibid.
48. Ibid.
49. Ibid.
50. Madie Hall Xuma, https://www.encyclopedia.com/education/news-wires-white-papers-and-books/xuma-madie-hall, date accessed 11 January 2020.
51. See Iris Berger, An African American "Mother of the Nation": Madie Hall Xuma in South Africa, 1940-1963, in Dawne Y. Curry et al., *Extending the Diaspora: New Histories of Black People* (Chicago: University of Illinois Press, 2009), 125-154.
52. Iris Berger,
53. Dr. A. B. Xuma online. See Steven Gish, *Dr. A. B. Xuma: African, American, South African* (New York: New York University Press, 2000).
54. Dr. A. B. Xuma online.
55. ANC President-General Memorandum.
56. Ibid.
57. Ibid.
58. Ibid.
59. Alfred Stadler, 'A Long Way to Walk,' 230-237.
60. ANC President-General Memorandum.
61. Ibid.
62. Bus Commission Report, 11-12.
63. "Food Prices Shot Up by 46%," *Guardian*, August 5, 1943, 5.
64. "Maitland, A Pantry Maid," *Cape Standard*, July 27, 1943, 8.
65. Ibid.
66. Ibid.
67. Dr. A. B. Xuma online.
68. R. G. Baloyi, Xuma Papers, ABX 430711c. See Alan Gregor Cobley, *Class and Consciousness*, 222.
69. Alfred Stadler, "A Long Way to Walk," 232.
70. Ibid.
71. Ibid.
72. Modikwe Dikobe, *Dispossessed* (Johannesburg: Ravan Press, 1983), 34-364
73. Alfred Stadler, "A Long Way to Walk," 234.
74. Formed in 1944, the African National Congress Youth League consisted of the following officers: Anton Lembede, President; Walter Sisulu, Treasurer; Oliver Tambo, Secretary; and the Executive Committee, David Bopape; A. P. Mda; Jordan Ngubane; Nelson Mandela; Lionel Majombozie and Congress Mbatha.

75. "Basebenzi Base Alexandra, (Workers of Alexandra)," *Bantu World*, August 13, 1938. Ngala ngakiti asifuni bhasi equtywa ngu mlungu. Indawo yabelungu iSophiatown ne Western Native Township, hai eAlexandra Township.
76. Baruch Hirson, "The Trotskyist Groups in South Africa: A Retrospective View," Encyclopedia of Trotskyism On-Line: Revolutionary History: 4, 4 (South Africa), 17-18
77. Statement of the Johannesburg Section of the Fourth International, Xuma Papers, ABX 430922d (hereafter referred to as the Statement by the Fourth International).
78. Ibid.
79. Robert R. Edgar, *An African American in South Africa*, 179.
80. Ibid.
81. Ibid.
82. Montgomery City Ordinance. See Jo Ann Gibson Robinson, *The Montgomery Bus Boycott and the Women Who Started It* (Knoxville: Tennessee, 1987).
83. Miss C. L. Tshabalala's Address.
84. Statement by the Fourth International.
85. Bus Commission Report, 20.
86. Statement by the Fourth International.
87. Philip Bonner and Noor Nieftagodien, *Alexandra: A History* (Johannesburg: Witwatersrand University Press (2008), 178.
88. Mike Sarakinsky, From "Freehold Township" to "Model Township": A Political History of Alexandra, 1905-1983. Johannesburg: University of Witwatersrand Medical Library, 1984, 55.
89. See Steffen Jensen and Olaf Zenker, *South African Homelands as Frontiers: Apartheid's Loose Ends in the Postcolonial Era* (Southern African Studies) (New York: Routledge, 2016), Anne Kelk Mager, *Gender and the Making of a South African Bantustan: A Social History of the Ciskei, 1945-1959* (Social History of Africa) (New York: Heinemann, 1999), Jeffrey Butler, Robert I. Rotberg et al., *The Black Homelands of South Africa: The Political and Economic Development of Bophuthatswana and Kwa-Zulu* (Volume 21) (Perspectives on Southern Africa) (Los Angeles: University of California Press, 1978).
90. Statement by the Fourth International.
91. Ibid.
92. Tim Couzens, "Nobody's Baby", 46.
93. Communist Party of South Africa, "They Marched to Victory" (1944), 9 and Bus Commission Report, 12.
94. Tom Lodge, *Black Politics in South Africa since 1945* (Johannesburg: Ravan Press, 1944), 14.

95. Memorandum Representing Alexandra Township Residents.
96. Gaur Radebe, https://www.sahistory.org.za/people/gaur-radebe, date accessed 18 September 2021.
97. Tim Couzens, "Nobody's Baby," 45-46.
98. Alexandra Women's League Memorandum, 4.
99. M. Rammitloa, Libese Tsa Alexandra, *Inkululeko* June 23, 1945, 4, and Alexandra Bus Boycott, *Rand Daily Mail*, November 15, 1944, 8.
100. John Nauright, "Black Island in a White Sea," 307. Alfred Stadler, "A Long Way to Walk", 234.
101. Ibid.
102. Alexandra Bus Boycott, *Rand Daily Mail*, November 15, 1944, 8.
103. Black Goon Squads, *Rand Daily Mail*, November 18, 1944, 1.
104. Ibid.
105. Ibid.
106. Baruch Hirson, *Yours for the Union*, 143-144.
107. Dan Mokonyane, *Lessons of Azikhwelwa* (London: Nakong ya Rena, 1994).
108. ANC President-General Memorandum.
109. Meshack Khosa, "Changing Patterns of 'Black' Bus Subsidies in the Apartheid City, 1944-1986," *GeoJournal*, 22, 3 (1990): 252.
110. Ibid.
111. Communist Party of South Africa, "They Marched to Victory," 14.
112. Meshack Khosa, "Changing Patterns of 'Black' Bus Subsidies," 252.
113. "Maitland, A Pantry Maid."

CHAPTER 7

Daughters of Africa and the Politics of Religious and Literary Sampling

Tshabalala's eighteen-year tenure on American soil led to several epiphanies that she revealed before South Africa's reading public. Many of her revelations articulate her understanding or miscomprehension about the African American Diaspora, the mounting need for solidarity, the lessons of travel, the beauty in forming a female sorority, and the significance of embarking upon cultural exchange. Tshabalala traveled to the United States with high hopes and conceptions about America. This descendant of the African continent revered African Americans like many South Africans who looked upon diasporic offspring as models—epitomes of social and political advancement—and as saviors chosen to free Africans as the title of Robert Trent Vinson's monograph, *The Americans Are Coming*, suggests.[1] To her surprise and dismay, Tshabalala found that America's Black community "were neither advanced nor succeeding," in spite of the fact, as she explained, that "the Negro woman in the States ha[d] … followed the … example of her older sister (Africa) with haste unequaled".[2] For some reason the DOA founder chose not to elaborate on why she had reached this conclusion which is unfortunate given her tenure on American soil for nearly two decades. Tshabalala forced scholars to rely solely on her editorials for a semblance of her honest interpretations unless of course, one day a scholar makes an incredible find and puts some of the missing pieces together.

D. Y. Curry, *Social Justice at Apartheid's Dawn*, African Histories and Modernities, https://doi.org/10.1007/978-3-030-85404-1_7

Something else gripped her immediate attention. In 1927, Tshabalala attended her first religious conference held annually in upstate New York's Chautauqua. She witnessed women from all over the world participate in a mutual fraternity for three consecutive weeks. This show of collaboration led her to realize that "there was strength in unity".[3] Tshabalala gleaned another lesson from the example of the Black women's club movement. The South African wrote, "CLUB life in America has really become a tremendous business because it has been proved it is a tremendous force."[4] Tshabalala started the DOA in Natal with all of these considerations in mind, fourteen years after Maxeke had established the Bantu Women's League in 1932. The DOA was: a conference of [African] women organizations [that met] … as a federal union with five principal goals: to promote sisterhood, to develop a community of mutual service, to organize African women into a National Movement that propagated the ideals of social, health, economic, educational, and cultural activities,…; to watch, protect and safeguard the inherent rights and privileges of African women; to seek an affiliation with any recognized political organisation on such terms and conditions as may harmonise with the ideals of the Association.[5]

This self-help group possibly boasted 5000 members at one time. Historian Healy-Clancy argues this number eclipsed the far more established ANC which came in at 4000 constituents.[6] A crucial letter written in Tshabalala's own hand, however, cites a more modest number between 100 and 500 members which may have represented the actual numbers in the Transvaal or the body as a whole.[7] Alexandra Township boasted the largest Daughters' branch on the Witwatersrand let alone the country. Leadership and members represented the wives of local luminaries like bus owner Richard G. Baloyi (Elizabeth Baloyi), Native Affairs employee Samuel Piliso (Ethel Maud Piliso or Topsie as she was called), political activist C. S. Ramahanoe (Violet Ramahanoe), and Reverend Paulos Mabiletsa (Clara Mabiletsa). African women aged eighteen and older joined the organization economically by paying dues, religiously by accepting God, communally by engaging in philanthropy, and symbolically by 'bambane ngesandla' (holding hands).[8] Affiliation costs two shillings, six pence ($.26).[9]

Tshabalala used Alexandra's overwhelming support and its headquarters at Number 5 Thirteenth Avenue (Fig. 7.1) to gain adherents on the Rand. She spoke in Pimville, Pretoria, Orlando, and Sophiatown among other sites that dotted her itinerary. Her overriding message "save the nation" guided everything she did; in fact Tshabalala's double economic

Fig. 7.1 Daughters of Africa Stamp. (Photo courtesy of Katie Mooney (Katie Mooney, Amadodakazi—Baradi Ba Africa, 1. See also (KJB, 402, N1192-N11212 and KJB 411) National Archives of South Africa in Pretoria.). Number 5, Thirteenth Avenue, stood downstairs along Alexandra's steep gradient. As the command center for the Daughters of Africa, its leaders and members met to arrange several activities to promote sisterhood. Among the body's many endeavors were its meetings where tea was promptly served, and an agenda carried out with military precision)

consciousness helped her inherent cross-over appeal as a 'bridge leader'. Sociologist Belinda Robnett originally coined the term 'bridge leader' to accord African American women a title for their unofficial participation in the American Civil Rights Movement (CRM) as liaisons between the male leadership and the African American community.[10] Tshabalala traversed both the secular and spiritual worlds as a modern-day missionary and as a club founder. Public addresses, compositions, and written editorials helped Tshabalala to spread the word of God by mixing religious proselytization with fervent activism. With a public life captured by editorials, and accentuated by pavement politics, Tshabalala left an indelible impression as one of a Daughter of Africa, as a bridge leader, and as a modern-day missionary.

The Philosophy Behind a Movement of African Daughters

"Miss Tshabalala [first became] a missionary" by attending the highly reputed Moody Bible Institute in Chicago, Illinois, and the New Britain Normal State School in Hartford, Connecticut.[11] After completing her studies at those institutions, Tshabalala went on to apply her education in the Gold Coast (present-day Ghana) as an employee of the African Methodist Episcopalian Zion (AMEZ) Church's Missionary Board. For three years (1919–1922) she worked as a principal at an all-girls school in Kwitta (Keta), a town seeped in international and trans-continental history.[12] Kwitta's geographical location on the Gulf of Guinea in West Africa and its situation within the Volta River region facilitated its once highly active participation in the selling of spices, ivory, gold, and even human chattel. From 1918 to 1919, an influenza epidemic ravaged the Ashanti, the Northern Territories Protectorate, and the British Togoland trust territory. American newspapers reported that another missionary Henrietta Peters accompanied Tshabalala to the Gold Coast (present-day Ghana) in West Africa. Print mediums allude to 'My Three Years in the Gold Coast', a speech that Tshabalala rendered before church bodies, but other than that there is no further detail nor a rendition of her experiences within the copy. Instead, we are left to rely on chronology to provide some context.

Tshabalala's missionary pursuits continued following her return to the United States in 1922. She conducted a string of presentations in Ohio, Pennsylvania, New York, Virginia, Indiana, and a host of other states. An *Ilanga laseNatal* article reported that she spoke passionately about her beloved continent: "Her Christian character and her presentation of … the needs of Africa in the twentieth century has won the love and sympathies of the American people."[13] Praise continued to pour from the New York Amsterdam as these statements attest:

> The Native people of South Africa ought to be proud of this brave young woman, who has broken up home ties in order that the kingdom of Christ may be extended to all the nations of the world. Pray that God might protect her from all dangers and give her a long life to be spent in His service for the redemption of the dark races of Africa.[14]

Tshabalala mirrored and refracted the zealous fervor carried out by the likes of David Livingstone. One of the most well-known explorers in the nineteenth century, Livingstone, an abolitionist, and an adherent of the London Missionary Society (LMS), joined his geographical sojourning contemporaries (Henry Morton Stanley, Richard Burton, etc.) in a campaign to civilize and to conquer the unknown, uninhabited lands of the insatiably 'wild' African continent. As part of the Scramble of Africa (SOA), an imperial race for geopolitical control over the Suez Canal, Africa's major rivers and the continent's plethora of minerals, missionaries, and explorers flooded the African continent to proselytize, to pursue mercantilist endeavors, and to gain scientific knowledge.[15] Tshabalala

'Africanized' the European 'civilizing mission' and the Scramble for Africa that she set off in spectacular fashion when she stoked a vigorous competition within the *Bantu World*'s pages to gain new adherents (colonies). Of course, she followed the letter of the DOA's governing principles.

An eleven-page constitution outlined the body's mission and its objectives. A Board of Directors oversaw the National Executive Committee (NEC) with the offices of a President, a Vice-President, a Secretary, a Treasurer, and a Vice-Treasurer. Each province and territory had their own respective presidents, two NEC delegates, and several committees that heard proposals and reports from different branches.[16] Sometimes conference participants recognized new members or heard regrets when, for instance, Tshabalala was unable to attend a meeting, or they announced the arrival of constituents who poured in from various 'homesteads'.[17] Places like the coal-mining area of Dundee situated within the Biggarsberg Mountains or the coastal city of Durban represented two of the thirty or so affiliates that dotted the isiZulu-speaking territory. Even the NCAW's secretary Eleanor Hlahle mentions the organization's ubiquitous presence there, "we tried to move into Pietermaritzburg (PMB), but that was a DOA stronghold."[18] Not satisfied with the DOA's overwhelming reach in Natal, Tshabalala on the behest of Alexandra's Elizabeth Baloyi (wife of legendary Alexandran bus owner, politician, and footballer Richard G. Baloyi) set up a branch in this fabled township that a swath of White, affluent residential areas encircled. 'Colonization' and 'proselytization' continued every time a new body emerged throughout the country. The DOA pounced on each and every 'annexation' to astronomically shoot up the organization's swelling numbers; in fact, the body modeled its territorial expansion on the African homesteads that its regional and national branches replicated.

Political scientist Judith Van Allen and former South African President Nelson Mandela explain how African villages stood as architectural feats on the landscape and served as an illustration of the community's political structure. Van Allen turns her gaze to Nigeria's southeastern ethnic group, the Igbo. She writes, "the Igbo ... lived traditionally in semi-autonomous villages, which consisted of ... scattered compounds of 75 or so patrikinsmen."[19] Mandela describes his birthplace, "Qunu [as being] situated in a narrow grassy valley of green hills with clear streams running through them, the homesteads consisted of no more than a few hundred people who lived in huts, which were beehive-shaped structures of mud walls, with a wooden pole in the center holding up a peaked, grass roof...."[20]

While no match for the idyllic and picturesque settings of Nigeria, and the Eastern Cape, the DOA's branches emerged within a terrain of mine heaps, slums, townships, and dense populations that littered the bursting seams of Johannesburg and Durban.[21] The DOA-styled homesteads, which differed from their expanse in the rural communities, covered an area of approximately sixty miles from Benoni in the East Rand to Orlando in southwestern Johannesburg. Streets, roads, townships, and political demarcations divided the branches geographically, and politically, but they acted in one accord nationally and socially at conferences where they converged.

Religion also seeped into her public consciousness. Tshabalala wanted Africans to undergo a metaphorical baptism by recommitting to God. Following comments made by Pietermaritzburg's Mayor during a 1930s conference, who argued that the "black nation has love of religion, [and] must follow in Jesus' footsteps", Tshabalala concurred as this statement corroborates:

> [Black people] were born in this country and they were happy to see the father of the house who was there to help and educate them how to work for the black nation. But [Africans] have forgotten about their originality in this nation so it is our duty to wake them up and to make [our] nation [dignified].[22]

Tshabalala punctuated this goal by using Bible passages to apply a moral to a contemporary problem. In doing this, she defies the notion that Christianity was a Western religion, instead as her employment shows, "…African-Christian modes of belief and identity, which have been powerfully evident in this country and across the continent in various forms, reflect neither the simple binary of colonial capitulation/negotiation nor heretical Christianity, but a powerful confluence of cultural and spiritual modes of being, ironically perhaps closer to originary Christianity than the beliefs and practices of the missionaries who often condemned such forms."[23] Tshabalala also incorporated the teachings and epiphanies that she gleaned while living in the United States.

Tshabalala was heavily influenced by the African American women's club movements, as historian Healy-Clancy contends, but she was also inspired by African American and South African male movements. She drew from both models through what I call *sampling*, which is to say employing a technique often utilized by artists to borrow the chords and melodies of other musicians.[24] Tshabalala similarly incorporated multiple speeches and songs to discuss, race, gender, leadership, world history, transnationalism, and business among other topics the activist intellectual interrogated. Her biggest sampling initiative came from a traditional African staple called the *manyanos* (prayer unions).

Sample 1: The *Manyanos*—The Structure of the Daughters' Version of a Prayer Union

Manyanos originated during the nineteenth century in the Eastern Cape where the AmaXhosa, one of four Nguni nations, predominated. The term *manyanos* comes from the verb *ukumanya* which means to join. Lore has it that when Methodist women migrated from the Eastern Cape to colonial Natal, they incorporated isiXhosa words into their Christian Zulu lexicon. For a long time, "...[*manyano*] remained the general term used by the Methodists for their Churchwomen's organizations, even amongst peoples speaking other Bantu languages. When more and more translations of the Bible and hymnbooks were made, other Bantu words came to be adopted."[25] *Manyanos* exercised their own individual styles:

> The general atmosphere of a Manyano is one of weeping and sighing. The air is heavily charged with intense emotion. Women stand up and speak out their troubles, sometimes wailing or screaming, sometimes in a frenzied whispering. Their bodies tremble. Their eyes are tightly closed or fixed heavenwards. Talk is of miracles, of the sick and the dead. The women in the audience, with many "AAHHHS!" and tongues in approval and understanding or exclaim in admiration of a particular rhetorical highlight.[26]

Manyanos and other female bodies provided Black women with alternative and parallel spaces that differed from mainstream White and African male-dominated organizations. As authentic African bodies, *manyanos* carried out practices of resistance, and theological projects, while at the same time, they were straddling multiple identities, and boundaries within and outside of them.[27] Each women's prayer union boasted colored uniforms, which consisted of a skirt, a blouse, and a girdle in a variety of hues that symbolized diversity, and unity concurrently.[28] Furthermore, "*manyanos* demonstrate the intertwining of... [God's power] as a spiritual reality with the material reality of survival through the wearing of a church uniform."[29] Tshabalala pursued the *manyano* style for the following reason:

Every club should be the center of a bureaucracy and as our Women's Federation is made up of individual clubs, here we should find a large circle of African Daughters radiating great principles of life-credoso of thought and speech, tolerance, sincerity and justice, service, and cooperation.[30]

Songs, scripture, and prayers sounded the invocation to 'social worship'. Some meetings opened with Tshabalala's original piece, the 'Daughters of Africa Litany' (cited later in text), while others commenced proceedings with the isiXhosa adaptation of *Nkosi Sikelel iAfrika* and ended with the Sesotho version *Morena Boloka* or they started off with different melodic tunes.[31] The Second Annual Daughters Federation held at Crown Mines began its festivities with this song:

O Sister Daughter hold to thy heart they Sister; Where pity dwells, the Love of God is there. To worship rightly is to love each other, Each smile a psalm, each kindly deed a prayer.[32]

Attendants initiated official business when they began issuing *Izimibuko* (reports) for their respective branches. An example of this round-robin roll call looked and sounded like this:[33]

DRIEFONTEIN: Sheshisa Miss Mkhize, usitshele usuku uMsunguli wama Dodakazi ayodlula ngalo eLadysmith eseqonde eJo'burgngoba uyokwehla endleleni amise ngokuphelele amaClub ayi (12). Izihlangano ezimbili ezinkulu ziyoba seWatersmeet nase Driefontein.

DRIEFONTEIN: Miss Mkhize, please inform us effectively on the day the founder will be passing our town of Ladysmith on her return to Johannesburg. We hear she will be stopping someplace to form 12 new clubs. Two big meetings will be held in Watersmeet and Driefontein.

UMTHWALUME: Bhalani nina nobabili dade iqondise kuMfundisi ukuze udaba lwethu lusilungele ngoba sesibona sengathi sesisele sodwa kuloludabaolusemlonyeni lobuDodakazi, ngoba nathi lapha sesizimisele, siyathanda ukujoyina.

UMTHWALUME: both you ladies please write to the Reverend so that our issues will be addressed. We are running out of time in this issue on being members of the Daughters. We are also eager to be part of it.

EDENDALE: Ngicela maDodakazi ase Africa angenzele isiguqo somthandazo ukuze nginikwe amandla, nokwazi, nokufaneleka kulendawo, nomsebenzi engiwuphathisiwe nina omncance kangaka.

EDENDALE: I would like the Daughters to hold a vigil for me so that I can have strength and knowledge to host this huge amount of work.

> DANNHAUSER: Indaba yobuDodakazi base Africa ngiyithandisa okobisi lona umuntu aluphuza angadinwa. Sitshele, Nkosazana, izinsuku oyodlula ngazo lapha nxa usukhuphuka uya eJohannesburg. Sukulindele.
>
> DANHAUSER: I love the matter of the Daughters like the love of milk. Please inform us Miss, of the days you will be passing by on your way back up to Johannesburg. We are waiting for you.

Tshabalala's image as respectable, popular, and forward-thinking etched everything that represented the DOA and what it became through evolution. These statements also detail the willingness of prospective participants to conduct organizational work, but with, of course, the body's blessing. For instance, the Edendale attendant requested a vigil before carrying out the organization's duties while other times, the DOA acted as a conduit to ministers, which was the case when an Umthwalume delegate made such a request. The roll call, which followed the chorus of reports, documented attendances and absences before formal agendas of varying items began.

One session taking place from 21 to 26 January 1948 at Dannhauser made it a point to place the National Fund of the Daughters of Africa Association on the agenda. Delegates from different provinces collected monies which they in turn presented before the Treasurer of the Union. Natal amassed a nice sum of money while the Transvaal failed to meet the Constitution of the Union's minimum funds that it stipulated for each province. Tshabalala recognized these financial shortcomings and at the same time praised the members for their efforts:

> In the name of this big Union of the D. O. Africa, we are very much thankful of all the attempts and initiatives from the big Provinces, a lot. We are pleading with our sisters in the Natal to please pay their dues to the Treasurer of the Union. Also, to the Transvaal to finish the huge work, it is intense, let us come together daughters and actively make our nation prosper. Thank you, Daughters.[34]

The DOA also grappled with position of African women. Customary and Civil Law regarded them as minors and men as their male guardians. African women never reached majority status regardless of their ages under this practice. Inheritances and accrued wealth went to male heirs or other male recipients rather than to widows or female laborers. In an editorial written originally in isiZulu and translated here, Natal's very own L. N. Msimang, a prominent DOA leader, had this to say about the women's economic disenfranchisement:

> Loku akusidumazile neze ngoba sisafuna umgwaqo kumnyango okuyiwona esingangqongqoza kuwo. Obuningi ubuntandane esifazanenei bubangwa yilobundlalifa. Umfolokazi oshiywa yindoda enefa makemukwe onke amalungelo okubusa ifa lendoda yakhe bengazishiyanga buze ngenxa yale NATIVE CODE.
>
> A whole lot of poverty among women is caused by this inheritance. A widow suffers and struggles to educate her children even though she was left her husband's inheritance because she is not allowed to have power over decisions because of this NATIVE CODE. If it is so easy to abuse women of our nation like this, then we are still far from getting back the Africa we seek. People are outraged over this despair that has befallen our women. Is this not destroying our nation?[35]

This issue weighed so heavily on Tshabalala's mind that she embarked on a concerted effort to place women on a political pedestal. Instead of championing African women's sexual virtue as White American men had done for their female counterparts during the Jim Crow era, Tshabalala exalted their innate worth. When women are "coordinating the home", she believed, "the black nation … [becomes] strengthened because the maker of everything helps those who are trying to establish themselves".[36]

Philanthropy, which appeared frequently as an agenda item, represented a DOA mainstay. Much of the body's charitable activities went to support the growing War Fund with the Second World War raging across the globe. Hertzog ultimately resigned during this time because he advocated for South Africa to remain neutral, but the country instead, threw its hat into the ring on the side of the British and the Allies—France and Poland. The nation's brave soldiers ended up fighting intense battles in Madagascar, Ethiopia, North Africa, and Italy. With the costs of war mounting, the DOA lent its support in the following ways. Nokukhanya Bhengu Luthuli single-handedly established a DOA branch in Groutville, a town with heavy connections to American missionaries that date back to 1840. She became so pivotal in canvassing the *amakholwa* (Christians) and the *Amagatsha* (non-Christians) in this African reserve that the DOA branch grew by leaps and bounds. Interest peaked so much that Luthuli held meetings and workshops in a home she shared with her husband Chief Albert John Luthuli, ANC President and the first African recipient of the Nobel Peace Prize, and their children. The Luthuli home turned into a makeshift cottage industry:

> during the war we come back from school and gather in our sitting room—the Daughters of Africa were there. My mother taught my brother and sisters to knit so that we could all support the war effort. We learnt to make balaclavas, jerseys, socks, and gloves.[37]

Support also came in monetary form. The *Bantu World* reported that on one occasion, cash-strapped Alexandra Township raised £60 ($300) and another £7.13.0d at another time while Crown Mines chipped £7 7s.7d in for the war cause.[38] The ever-popular Bantu Men's Social Club also factored into this monetary equation. Its owner Ray Philips showed the latest films on the silver screens. Proceeds went to the DOA's War Fund. DOA created a one-day fundraising initiative 'Red Letter Day' (Fig. 7.2) that Alexandra's Health Committee and the South African government endorsed with their respective signatures in 1942. This announcement, which promotes the collaboration between women's and church groups, comes with the encouraging invitation, "Rally to the Call!!"[39] The successful campaign raised much-needed funds for the world's second

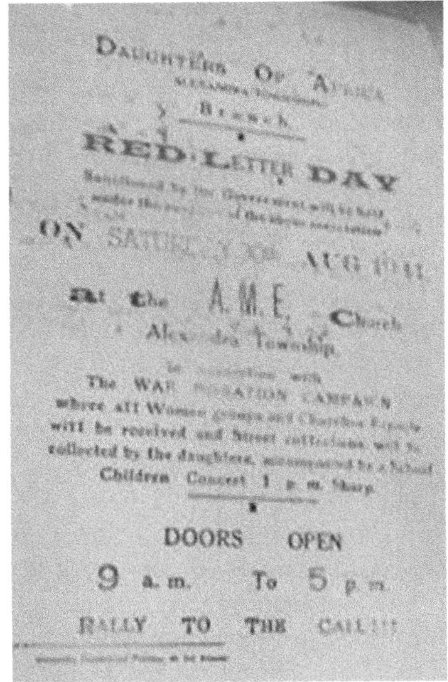

Fig. 7.2 Daughters of Africa Red Letter Day. This is a flyer that highlighted the DOA's attempt to attain funds for the war campaign at the African Methodist Episcopal Church in Alexandra. (Photo by Katie Mooney (Katie Mooney, Amadodakazi—Baradi Ba Africa, 2, 13))

heightening war. The DOA handed the proceeds over to the Native Commissioner who in turn thanked the body in a letter.[40]

The *Igugu le Sizwe* (Daughters Reserves) that the DOA's Board of Directors formed consisted of the nation's youth who collected monetary (Fig. 7.3) contributions from every street dotting Alexandra's gridiron pattern. Door-to-door fundraising culminated with a celebratory concert that began bright and early at 9 am and concluded just before sunset at 5 pm.[41] 'Daughters of Africa Day' and the Markets on the Number 2 Square provided additional opportunities for fundraising every August (former) or Saturday (latter).[42] Other efforts supported youth recreational centers and Young Women's Christian Association (YWCA)-like hostels. Social service fueled the DOA's identity, as its motto "All Service Ranks the Same with God" supported its dictum. This was not just lip service. Tshabalala reinforced this goal during her 'Message for the New Year' when she wrote, "let him that would be great among you be the servant of all. By your influence may you lead other women of your community to the joy of service, may we be drawn to realize as never the blessedness of living for others."[43]

Sample 2: Choral Music and the Bible

Choral music or *makwaya* has a long-sustained history in South Africa. It draws upon the nineteenth-century missionary style, the formal Western four-part harmony, and indigenous African traditional styles.[44] John Knox Bokwe (JKB) was one of choral music's most profound purveyors who helped to popularize the genre with his hymnal, 'Saviors and Sinners'. This celebrated Xhosa song composer, Presbyterian minister, and musician enjoyed prominence between 1875 and 1922.[45] South Africa's diamond industry boomed, and the deep-seated tensions between the British and the Xhosa over land reach a feverish pitch during the height of his career. Bokwe managed to look beyond this growing problem in his pursuit of unity between the Mfengu and the AmaXhosa by using his music, in much the same way as Reverend Tiyo Soga, to bridge the divide between ethnic groups and to retain indigenous African culture. Both men were swept up in a growing tidal wave of Black expressive culture that intersected with the confluences of African American spirituals and the choral performances of the Victorian Age. In the case of 'Umdengentonga' (the man with the big mind), as Bokwe was popularly called, he amalgamated genres. Bokwe devised and expounded upon missionary-styled music, African American minstrel shows, and the *isicathamiya* singing style of migrant men.[46]

In the 1870s and the 1880s, when Bokwe set out to create a style of music that incorporated Christianity, he also constructed a distinct indigenous African sound. Bokwe did take regular choral music, which was sung in acapella or accompanied by an organ or a piano, and merged four-part harmonies, and a diatonic scale of separate half steps with octaves sung in isiXhosa.[47] Compositions later featured the languages of Sesotho and isiZulu. Another exponent of this musical style, Enoch Sontaga, an educator at the Methodist Mission School, was born in the Eastern Cape's Uitenhage (Kariega, its current name) almost twenty miles away from coastal Port Elizabeth, lived from 1873 to 1905. He gained fame after penning the first verses of the popular national anthem, *Nkosi Sikelel iAfrika* (God Bless Africa) in 1897. "As a spiritual song, '*Nkosi sikeleli*' invokes the Holy Spirit, '*Yihla Moya*' while fusing Protestantism with African cleansing traditions."[48]

Originally, a B-flat major set the arrangement for the four-part harmony tune. Things changed when prominent Eastern Cape intellectual Samuel Mqhayi wrote seven additional verses in isiXhosa in 1927. The song went through another alteration when Moses Mphahlele published a Sesotho version in 1942. *Nkosi Sikelel iAfrika* gained increasing popularity when Reverend Dr. John L. Dube's Ohlange Zulu Choir belted out its lyrics throughout the mining capital of Johannesburg.[49] This church hymn later emerged as a popular anthemic tune at political meetings during apartheid at a time when it and others like Vuyusile Mini's *Nansi Endodyama Verwoerd* (Beware Verwoerd) served as rallying war cries.[50] Before *Nkosi Sikelel iAfrika* reached this heightened acclaim, Katie Makanya had a hand in its early development.

One day when Makanya was nearing her aunt's home, she heard vocals coming from the veranda. When Makanya walked inside, she had no idea whatsoever that two of South Africa's greatest composers, Sontaga and Bokwe, sat in the receiving room. The tall impressionable Bokwe broke the ice from the expansive armchair with this question:

> "were you one of the sisters that sung before the queen?" "Yes," Katie said shyly, "we sang your Vuka Deborah, and she liked it very much." During the course of the conversation, Makanya's aunt asked Bokwe to teach her a new song. Sontaga along with all the visitors began humming the unfinished and unpolished version of *Nkosi Sikelel iAfrika*. Without her thinking about it,

> Katie's voice rose up out of her throat, an octave higher than the others, until Sontaga nodded, satisfied, and hummed a few more bars, paused and shook his head. "It is not yet right," he said. Bokwe nodded, "Not yet, but it is a good song. When the notes come right in your head, you will know it is finished."[51]

This co-authored song, which enshrined the call-and-response pattern, acted as an invocation to politically worship. Its first and second stanzas call for alms and prayer.

Choral music entered the DOA's repertoire for several reasons. The founder had her roots in the African church. She also had missionary training in the Gold Coast and the United States where she served as a principal at all-girls school and as the Director of Religion for the Nazarene Congregational Church in Brooklyn, New York, respectively. Other evidence of her African musical roots surfaced when she gave talks. On one such occasion and in a celebration of the Missionary Society of Connecticut's Homeland Day, Tshabalala topped off her discussion before African American female youth with a song rendered with all of the clicks and intonations of her mother tongue.[52] In an essay called 'Life and Light for Women' published in 1898, Nokutela Ndima Dube proclaimed that "music [was] a great power among [her] people, and God [had] opened the way for [her] to learn better how to sing into [our] hearts".[53] The South African's interest in music is further shown with the original compositions she wrote. *Abakhayo Yabo Indlu* ('Those Who Build Their House'), 'The Daughters' Hymn' (*Ihlubo Lama Dodakazi*), and 'The Daughters of Africa Litany' are examples of her creativity. Like the poems of Mgqwetho and ACD, the songs that Tshabalala, Bokwe, Sontaga, and Reverend Tiyo Soga penned show how African women provided and articulated discourses on segregation that were similar to and different from their male colleagues.

As the first South African to become ordained, Reverend Soga pushed for the retention of isiXhosa. He made this a major objective as attested by his translation of the Bible, and John Bunyan's seminal work, 'Pilgrim's Progress', into his mother tongue.[54] Around the time that Reverend Soga wrote, and lived, the British busied themselves with expansionist endeavors, and that meant making their presence known in the Eastern Cape where the AmaXhosa predominated. From 1789 to 1889, nine frontier wars flared up between the two groups over land, water, and boundaries. Soga turned to music, faith, and Black people for sustenance amid these cost-consuming battles. Growing fear of Europeans increasingly encroaching upon AmaXhosa territory led Reverend Soga to implore Blacks to

"Fulfill/realize [their] promise" as the hymn *Lizalis' idinga lakho* translates. He argued, "All races, all nations, must be saved, All knees in this world, Must bow before you So that all tongues, Proclaim your glory."[55] Sontaga conveyed this same message. Passages from *Nkosi Sikelel iAfrika* read, "Lord, we ask You to protect our nation, Intervene and end all conflicts, Protect us, protect our nation, Protect South Africa, South Africa."[56]

The song's first verse, and in those that Mqhayi wrote, contains stanzas written in isiXhosa which signified several important things as a medium of communication. Tongues pass down traditions, reclaim and preserve languages; transmit lofty and attainable ideas; and espouse theoretical notions that proffer resolutions and words of advice. Tshabalala was also no stranger to the use of indigenous languages. She used her compositions similarly to Bokwe, Reverend Soga, and Mgqwetho as opportunities to teach and to champion racial upliftment. Both of them criticized European colonialism, while at the same time, they called out the continent's oppressors for the substantial debt owed to their people. Mgqwetho, however, went a step further, when she like Tshabalala chastised Africans for not paying back the indemnities that stood in arrears for themselves.

The DOA's main anthemic song, *Abakhayo Indlu Yabo* (Those Who Build Their House), made its debut in Mfume along Durban's South Coast at a meeting held within two years of apartheid's treacherous period in 1946. *Abakhayo Indlu Yabo* consists of six stanzas. This how-to-manual authorizes Black women to pray, to stand, to donate, to set a good example, and to work with God.[57] The opening verse proclaims, "Those who build their house, without you, waste their strength, God Almighty. Those who protect their house, if not protected by the Lord, keepers of all."[58] The song's other main purpose, 'to hold hands', represented a staple in Tshabalala's philosophy. She executed this activity whether she led the Women's Brigade or the Daughters of Africa to signal their unity and spirituality with clasped hands. 'Lizalis' idinga lakho' (Reverend Soga's song) and *Abakhayo Indlu Yabo* (Tshabalala's tune) are musical offerings that outline a pattern of requests that they issue to God. In the former song, its conveyor writes, "God, Forgive [their] sins," "do not send your wrath," "prohibit [them] God from disobeying," or "revive [them]" in turn Tshabalala makes the plea to her people (*Abantu bakhe*) explicitly to pray:[59]

Sizwe namuhla Thixo wethu	Hear us today Lord,
Nxa Sikhulekela isizwe	when we pray
Sikhulekela isizwe	praying for the nation
Sonke esinsundu	The whole Black nation
Amen	Amen

Abakhayo Indlu Yabo's penultimate stanza explains what they needed to do. Black people's salvation stood precariously on the line: "We must work with the creator, Women of Africa, let's hold hands, in this work."[60] Tshabalala insisted on this move. She sincerely believed that God guided everything. Homes faltered, disobedience developed, and nations struggled because:

> Isizwe esingakakwazi ukuziqoqa, nokufihla sigqibe amahlazo aso isizwe esingakabi bikho, esisakhasela eziko, sisendawnei yokubelethwa emhlane njalo.
>
> A nation that does not have responsibility over the caring of its people is a poor nation that is still dependent on charity.[61]

This statement calls upon the teachings of *Ubuntu* and *isivivane* that Tshabalala and Makanya both prescribed. It also relates to the principles that guide the monotheistic religion of Christianity. The religion's dictum, "Am I my brother's keeper", conveys the moral responsibility of mankind to one another. Tshabalala relied heavily on the Bible for its scriptures and for its psalms to build a moral foundation. In one example, she took a story from the Bible's first book, Genesis, to drive home an important point:

> in the early days, Adam and Eve survived by sleeping on any rock or beneath any roof at sunset like a school of wild birds that migrated miles away and had failed to plan or prepare … until the day found themselves jostled into a world of human beings like us, [and] … [they had] to find shelter over their heads. … ever since this Biblical couple's experience, a [roof] became a symbol of permanence and those who live beneath it have a certain feeling of security and their planning, their work, and their activities become more than a momentous thought and a day's affair.[62]

This passage, which is full of imagery, fits nicely into Tshabalala's lesson plan. The wild birds represent the African people who had turned to Western culture over the perpetuation of their own. A good example of this lies with the *amakholwa*, the Christian converts in Natal, who tried to emulate the West in dress, social mobility, and style. Tshabalala's critique marries nicely with the observations put forth by Mgqwetho, Maxeke, and others who intimated the same thing in their respective contributions to political thought. The phrase "a school of wild birds that migrated miles away" insinuates that they left the group, and thus their departure signifies the quest for the individualism that permeates Western societies. John chapter 15, verse 5 promotes unity and togetherness when it states, "Yes, I am the vine; you are the branches. Those who remain in me, and I in them, will produce much fruit. For apart from me you can do nothing."[63] Tshabalala provided her own version of this passage. She wrote, "Even though there's many routes that depart from home there's a place where they meet, like the many streams that meet a river."[64] The DOA represented the river, and its many branches, the streams. Each met at meetings held in the style of the *manyanos* they emulated and the African call and response pattern they followed.

Sample 3: The African Call and Response Pattern

Originating on the African continent above and below the massive expanse of the eye-alluring Sahara Desert, the call and response pattern has been adopted as an art form in other places around the world. Latin American musical styles of salsa, cha-cha-cha, rumba, and timba refer to this style as Coro-pregon while the genre forms part of the North American Western folk music that sailors, laborers, and members of the armed forces sung.[65] "Call and response patterns ... [involve a] technique [that is] ... related to audience (reader) participation [because the] text suggests or calls for an explicit response."[66] Tshabalala was a frequent practitioner of this improvised, oral tradition. In 1940, during a solemn and impressive initiation ceremony held in Alexandra Township, the DOA bellowed out a Tshabalala-authored litany that called on religion for communal protection and social justice:[67]

> LEADER: The wise woman buildeth her house but the foolish woman plucketh it down with her hands.
> PEOPLE: Oh, Jehova of old we beseech thee, make us willing to serve our homes, our communities, and our beloved country by working through thine guidance and thine love.
> LEADER: May the sisterhood household of the African race devote its energies in working for its youth morally and spiritually, socially, and otherwise.
> PEOPLE: Hear us, Good lord.
> LEADER: From thee alone may we learn to be teachers of peace and harmony in our abodes as we daily go about our duties.
> PEOPLE: Fill our hearts with thine Peace.
> LEADER: Help us to recognize the law of fairness, the right of all young and old, and desire not greedily others' share.

> PEOPLE: Lord help us to be broad and generous in thought and deed.
> LEADER: We pray for our sisters who have not as yet had the privilege of knowing the joys of service to others.
> PEOPLE: Lord keep us from pettiness, help us to be large in thought and encourage our efforts to aid our youth in its fight for high and noble living.

This invocation cites jealousy, pettiness, disharmony, immorality, unfairness, and selfishness as inhibitors of African development all the things that Tshabalala called on for guidance. She wanted to attain harmony and unity regardless of ethnic background, age, or social status. Her proposed goal, however, represented a paradox. The DOA leader spurned collaborations with Soga's NCAW even when sisterhood represented a significant quantification of the organization's success. Despite this apparent flaw between theory and practice, Tshabalala worked hard to uplift African people using myths, stories, tales, religion, and litanies to pursue social justice at apartheid's dawn. Traveling also informed her social service work. Experiences in America, the Gold Coast, and London exposed Tshabalala to the writings of contemporaries whose phraseology she sampled.

Sampling 4: Phraseology of African American Men

Even when Tshabalala formed the Daughters of Africa and acted as a social analyst or performed evangelical work as a modern-day missionary, she invoked the cultural ethos that had defined Ohlange and cemented its nickname as the 'Tuskegee of South Africa'. Tshabalala never strayed far from Booker T. Washington's core message that African Americans needed to pull themselves up by the bootstrap to advance. The 'Wizard of Tuskegee' dominated African American political thought for fifty years (1865–1915) in a period well recognized as the 'Age of Booker T. Washington'. Tshabalala was fortunate enough to reside in the United States during the last three years of Washington's life (1912–1915); however, her reticence to discuss her own personal experiences prevents scholars from knowing whether or not she ever met prominent African Americans like Washington. What is evident, however, is that his words reached Tshabalala's eyes and ended up as part of her written repertoire.

Long before Tshabalala sampled Washington's words, her fellow countryperson Pixley ka Seme, one of the ANC's early founders and leaders and Dr. John L. Dube's cousin, used Du Bois' verbiage in his own oratory. His

1912 speech echoes the diction of the first chapter of the African American's seminal study, *The Souls of Black Folk* where he incorporated the phrase "hewers of wood and drawers of water". Jaji further illustrates that Seme may have been familiar with 'Of Our Spiritual Strivings' of which Du Bois wrote:

> The double-aimed struggle of the black artisan—on the one hand to escape white contempt for a nation of mere hewers of wood and drawers of water, and on the other hand to plough and nail and dig for a poverty-stricken horde—could only result in making him a poor craftsman, for he had but half a heart in either cause.[68]

In 1899, Washington used similar phrasing, but his employment connotes a different meaning:

> it is said that we will be hewers of wood and drawers of water, but we will be more. We will turn the wood into machinery; into implements of agriculture. We will turn the water into steam; into dairy and agricultural products, and thus knit our life about that of the white man in a way to make us realize anew that "God made from one blood all people to dwell and prosper on the face of the earth."[69]

Washington believed in vocational work. He saw it as a stepping stone to racial progress, and political equality, which differed from Du Bois who pursued political equality and the ballot over industrial education and the bootstrap. During the period of American slavery, the bootstrap was employed as an instrument of control. Washington took this symbol of punishment and turned it into presumably a positive trope that epitomized his life. Tuskegee's founder, himself a former captive who went *Up from Slavery* as the title of his autobiography professes, to become a prominent educator, author, and orator, employed the bootstrap as a tool of imagery.[70] The goal was to get those at the top pulling those up from the bottom. This harks back to the same message that undergirded the NACW, an organization which operated on the motto, "Lifting as We Climb". The idea of helping others spilled over to Tshabalala whose employment of the rope symbolized her desire to band people together and make them responsible for each other, as *ubuntu*, the southern African salvation, prescribed. "Let's unite, by putting aside jealousy and greed, and make a long rope so that we can connect all Daughters of Africa."[71] In this statement appearing in *a Bantu World* editorial, Tshabalala made her objective as the

DOA's founder perfectly clear, "even ten people … [standing] together [holding a rope] [had] the strength of a hundred who [stood] singly, [because] a hundred in phalanx [could] overcome a thousand stragglers."[72] Tshabalala took this metaphor of unity a step further when she turned to Washington's words.

Dubbed the 'Atlanta Compromise' and given at the Cotton States and International Exposition in 1895, Washington addressed the American president, the Exposition's Board of Directors, and the country's citizens. This controversial speech garnered Washington the label as a sell-out and as an accommodationist after he called for African Americans to "cast down [their] bucket [where they were]—[to make] friends in every manly way of the people of all races by whom we are surrounded".[73] Southern Whites praised him for his stance on industrial education. Washington gained another admirer in Tshabalala, who sampled this line of his militant speech—which read, "In all things that are purely social we can be as separate as the fingers, yet one as the hand in all things essential to mutual progress"—garnered her attention.[74] Tshabalala made this reiteration of Washington's words which read: "imagine … both the illiterate and the literate comprising the dozens of club movements … in the union [coming] together, as separate as they are and yet alike, doing the same things at the same time as though some one powerful leader was directing the campaign."[75] While not using the hands to discuss the separation and togetherness between Black and White as Washington had done, Tshabalala chose instead to seek unity through religion and through the higher power of God.

James Weldon Johnson (1871–1938) and John Rosamond Johnson (1873–1954) also reached Tshabalala's attention. These two African American brothers reached national prominence as collaborators in a song that became the national anthem for their people. James Weldon Johnson was a civil rights activist, composer, politician, writer, and one of the initiators of the Harlem Renaissance which erupted in New York during the roaring twenties. As a student at Atlanta University, James Weldon Johnson took courses in English literature and ultimately edited the *Book of American Negro Poetry* (1922). Three years later in 1925, he and his brother JWJ published *The Book of Negro Spirituals*, an anthology which traces the earliest forms of sacred African American songs from their genesis to their more matured products.[76]

> His pioneering studies of Black poetry, music, and theater in the 1920s introduced many white Americans to the rich African American creative spirit, hitherto known mainly through the distortions of the minstrel show and dialect poetry. Meanwhile, as head of the National Association for the Advancement of Colored People (NAACP) during the 1920s, Johnson led determined civil rights campaigns in an effort to remove the legal, political, and social obstacles hindering Black achievement.[77]

His brother John Rosamond Johnson was equally credentialed. He acted, produced, sang, soldiered (he was 2nd Lieutenant in the 15th Regiment during the First World War), and wrote. Those around him witnessed his immense talent. At the age of four, the child prodigy began playing the piano. In later years, John Rosamond Johnson went on to enroll at the prestigious New England Conservatory, the oldest independent music outfit in the United States. He added another feather in his growing cap studying under the renowned musical maestro Samuel Taylor Coleridge-Taylor during his stint in grey-skyed London. Musical directorial skills also filled lines on his impressive resume. Time in New York accentuated his vibrant life. John Rosamond Johnson teamed up with Robert Cole to begin writing songs for vaudeville acts. This came after he had already written a piece for Williams and Walker's *Sons of Ham*.[78] One of his greatest achievements and long-lasting contributions came from a collaboration with his brother.

James Weldon Johnson wrote 'Lift Every Voice and Sing', a poem that he set to music. Composed in the popular A flat major, the NAACP declared 'Lift Every Voice and Sing' as the Negro National anthem, twelve years before the Star-Spangled Banner became the country's national tune in 1919. The Johnsons divided the song into three parts which consisted of praise, lamentation, and prayer.[79] Tshabalala samples the first stanza, however, she strays away from the composers' organization. She enumerates the past, the present, and the future in her articulation. Instead of singing "Facing the rising sun of our new day begun", as James Weldon Johnson had penned, Tshabalala interpreted his phrasing, melody, and chorus in the following way, "for you do see the gleam of the sunrise of our new day is already begun from the dark and gloomy past of our ignorance and complacency."[80]

Like her African American counterparts, Tshabalala engaged in the literary device of word painting. Word painting is when the music matches what is being sung.[81] For example, the phrase "Lift every voice and sing" is always sung on an ascending line, as is "Let all creation rise" in the first verse. This 'word painting' continues through the second section of the song. As the lyrics tell of the dark past and the blood of the slaughtered, the tune takes a mournful turn. Tshabalala does not dwell on a somber tone instead, her words are positive, and encouraging as this change in the original indicates, "Please do come to sing a song of joy with [them] all, a song full of hope that the present has brought [them]."[82] Tshabalala used this phraseology to encourage African women around the nation to attend the DOA's meetings. She wanted them to embrace the blessed sorority that awaited them. They also experienced the South African American nexus that their leader Tshabalala was a part of and continued to participate in through *sampling*.

Tshabalala's employment of this methodological device further cemented her role as a bridge leader who not only united African women, but also connected them to the African American diaspora of which they shared similarly related historical narratives. Had she been forthcoming regarding her sojourns in the Gold Coast and London, additional extrapolations could have teased out more connections between the African continent and its many diasporas. Tshabalala did, however, illustrate most emphatically through religious and literary *sampling* the significance of *ubuntu*. Tshabalala's desire to pursue a world that prevented exploitation could only be achieved, as she argued, if the social, spiritual, and economic well-being of everyone rose up.[83] For that to happen, the African nation needed to form a tight rope in order to overcome a thousand stragglers.[84] Tshabalala did her part. She formed the DOA, the Women's Brigade, and the Alexandra Women's League. She also had a hand in the formation of the African Democratic Party. During her thirty years of social service, Tshabalala catapulted the plight of African people by using the newspapers and her organizations as platforms for social justice.

Notes

1. Robert Trent Vinson, *The Americans Are Coming!: Dreams of African American Liberation in Segregationist South Africa* (New African Histories) (Athens: Ohio University Press, 2012).
2. "Miss C. L. Tshabalala's Address: Other Women," *Bantu World*, January 15, 1938, 11.
3. Ibid.
4. Ibid.

5. Dawne Y. Curry, "What is it that We Call the Nation": Cecilia Lillian Tshabalala's definition, diagnosis, and prognosis of the nation in a segregated South Africa, *Safundi: Journal of South African and American Studies*, 19, 1 (2018): 56.
6. Meghan Healy-Clancy, "The Daughters of Africa and Transatlantic Racial Kinship: Cecilia Lilian Tshabalala and the Women's Club Movement, 1912–1943," *Amerikastudien/American Studies*, 59, 4 (2014): 488.
7. Letter addressed to Senator J. D. Rheinallt Jones from Lillian Tshabalala. "South African Institute of Race Relations (SAIRR) AD843." Historical Papers, Cullen Library, University of the Witwatersrand, and Dawne Y. Curry, "What is it We Call the Nation?," 58.
8. Ibid.
9. Katie Mooney, Amadodakazi – Baradi Ba Africa, 6.
10. Belinda Robnett, *How Long? How Long?: African-American Women in the Struggle for Civil Rights* (Oxford: Oxford University Press, 1997), 19–23.
11. "Miss Tshabalala Becomes a Missionary," *Ilanga laseNatal*, October 26, 1917, 5.
12. "Native African to Teach Here," New York *Amsterdam News*, October 12, 1927, 1.
13. "Miss Tshabalala Becomes a Missionary."
14. "Native African to Teach Here," *New York Amsterdam News*, October 12, 1927, 1.
15. Erik Gilbert, and Jonathan T. Reynolds, *Africa in World History: From Prehistory to the Present* (Upper Saddle River: Pearson Prentice Hall, 2015), 4–6.
16. Katie Mooney, 'Amadodakazi-Baradi Ba Africa,' 6.
17. Daughters of Africa News, *Inkundla yaBantu*, July 14, 1945, 12. During a meeting held in Fortuna, the Daughters of Africa announced the body's newest members before seventy-five members.
18. Letter to Edith Rheinallt Jones from Eleanor Hlahle, National Council of African Women, Organisations, AD843/RJ/Pn 2.2, Historical Papers, Cullen Library, University of the Witwatersrand.
19. Judith Van Allen, "Sitting on a Man: The Lost Political Institutions of the Igbo," *Canadian Journal of African Studies / Revue Canadienne des Études Africaines*, 6 (1972): 173–175.
20. Nelson Mandela, *Long Walk to Freedom: The Autobiography of Nelson Mandela* (Boston: Little, Brown and Company, 1994), 7–8.
21. Branches included the following places: Newcastle, Vryheid, Pimville, Alexandra, Durban, Nkuthu, Kleinfontein, Sweden, Dundee, Edendale, Pietermaritzburg, Matiwane, Inanda, Imfume, Umgeni, Groutville, Eshowe, Entumeni, Impopala, Clermont, Umtwalamu, Colenso, Dannhauser, Boksburg, Benoni, Springs, Orange Free State, Swidee, Dundee, Western Native Township, and Slangspruit.

22. Vukani Sekusile Madodakaz Ase Africa, *Bantu World*, January 28, 1939, 3.
23. Duncan Brown, 'My Pen is the Tongue of a Skilful Poet,' 25.
24. Dawne Y. Curry, "What is What We Call the Nation," 56.
25. Mia Brandel-Syrier, *Black Women in Search of God* (London: Lutterworth Press, 1962), 34 and Beverly Haddad, "The Manyano Movement in South Africa: Site of Struggle, Survival, and Resistance," *Agenda*, 61 (2004): 4.
26. Mia Brandel-Syrier, *Black Women in Search of God* (London: Lutterworth Press, 1962), 34.
27. Beverly Haddad, "The Manyano Movement in South Africa," 9, Megan Healy-Clancy, "The New African Family: Women and the Making of an African Nationalist Body Politic, African Women Constructing and Healing Communities in 20th Century South Africa." Conference paper, North Eastern Workshop on Southern Africa, Burlington, Vermont, 2009, Peter limb, *The ANC's Early Years: Nation, Class and Place in South Africa before 1940* (Pretoria: University of South Africa Press, 2010), 119–20.
28. Mia Brandel-Syrier, *Black Women in Search of God*, 34.
29. Beverly Haddad, "The Manyano Movement in South Africa," 9.
30. Miss C. L. Tshabalala's Address-Other Women, *Bantu World*, January 15, 1938, 11.
31. Bertha Mkhize, "Amabala Engwe NgobuDodakazi base Afrika," *Ilanga laseNatal*, April 6, 1946, 9.
32. Katie Mooney, "Amadodakazi-Baradi Ba Africa," 9.
33. Amabala Engwe NgobuDodakazi baseAfrika (Leopard spots about the Daughters of Afrika), *Ilanga laseNatal*, April 6, 1946, 22.
34. Ingosi YaBesifazane Amadodakazi AseAfrika, *Ilanga laseNatal*, November 8, 1943, 9.
35. "Amadodakazi Eziveza Ngamazwi," *Ilanga laseNatal*, December 28, 1946, 24.
36. Miss C. L. Tshabalala's Address-Other Women.
37. Peter Rule, *Nokukhanya: Mother of Light* (Braamfontein: The Grail, 1993), 96.
38. War funds.
39. Katie Mooney, Amadodakazi – Baradi Ba Africa, 13.
40. Ibid.
41. Ibid.
42. *Alexandra News Bulletin*, Alexandra Township, South Africa, 1963.
43. "The Message for the New Year, C. L. Tshabalala," *Bantu World*, February 13, 1937, 8.
44. David K. Rycroft, Black South African Urban Music since the 1890s: Some Reminiscences of Alfred Assegai Kumalo (1879–1966), *African Music*, 7, 1 (1991): 6.

45. Grant Olwage, John Knox Bokwe, Colonial Composer: Tales about Race and Music, *Journal of the Royal Musical Association*, 131, 1 (2006): 1–37.
46. John Knox Bokwe, *The Journalist*, August 2015, https://www.thejournalist.org.za/pioneers/john-knox-bokwe/ date accessed 26 October 2020.
47. Grant Olwage, John Knox Bokwe, 19.
48. Enoch Sontaga, https://www.sahistory.org.za/people/enoch-mankayi-sontonga, 6 June 2021.
49. Ibid. and National Anthem, https://www.gov.za/about-sa/national-symbols/national-anthem#:~:text=Nkosi%20Sikelel%27%20iAfrika%20The%20words%20of%20the%20first,were%20later%20added%20by%20the%20poet%2C%20Samuel%20Mqhayi, date accessed 11 June 2021.
50. Lee Hirsch, Amandla!.
51. Margaret McCord, *The Calling of Katie Makanya*, 104.
52. "Homeland Day," *Hartford Courant*, May 1, 1926, 4.
53. Tsitsi Ella Jaji, *Africa in Stereo*, 32.
54. Tiyo Soga Translated Pilgrim's Progress into Xhosa, https://www.christianity.com/church/church-history/timeline/1801-1900/tiyo-soga-translated-pilgrims-progress-into-xhosa-11630543.html, date accessed 4 April 2021.
55. The hymn "Lizalis' idinga lakho" written by rev Tiyo Soga (with English translation) https://kairossouthernafrica.wordpress.com/2016/04/05/the-hymn-lizalis-idinga-lakho-written-by-rev-tiyo-soga-with-english-translation/, date accessed 22 November 2017.
56. South Africa's national anthem, with English translation, https://kairossouthernafrica.wordpress.com/2011/08/10/south-africas-national-anthem-with-english-translation/ date accessed 12 December 2019.
57. Dawne Y. Curry, "What is it We Call the Nation?," 71.
58. "Amadodakazi eMfume M. S.," *Ilanga laseNatal*, February 5, 1944, 7–8.
59. Ibid.
60. Ibid.
61. "Amadodakazi Eziveza Ngamazwi," *Ilanga laseNatal*, December 28, 1946, 24.
62. "Nomabunu's Article Discussed," *Bantu World*, May 21, 1938, 12.
63. John 15: 5, https://www.biblegateway.com/passage/?search=John%2015:5-8&version=NLT, date accessed 6 June 2016.
64. "Amadodakazi Eziveza Ngamazwi."
65. Maggie Sale, Call and Response as Critical Method: African American Oral Traditions and Beloved, *African American Review*, 26, 1 (Spring 1992): 41 and African Traditional Religion, https://www.sahistory.org.za/article/african-traditional-religion, date accessed 11 December 2020.
66. Ibid.
67. "The Daughters of Africa Litany," *Bantu World*, May 25, 1940, 9.

68. Tsitsi Ella Jaji, *Africa in Stereo*, 29.
69. Ibid., 30.
70. See Booker T. Washington, *Up From Slavery: The Autobiography* of Booker T. Washington (South Carolina: CreateSpace Independent Publishing Platform, 2012).
71. "Facing Facts: Leadership by C. L. Tshabalala," *Bantu World*, April 15, 1938, 12.
72. "What is the Club Woman? C. L. Tshabalala-Organising Secretary," *Bantu World*, April 4, 1936, 12.
73. Booker T. Washington Delivers 1895 Atlanta Compromise Speech, http://historymatters.gmu.edu/d/39/ date accessed 11 June 2021.
74. Ibid.
75. "Nomabunu's Article Discussed."
76. About James Weldon Johnson, http://jamesweldonjohnson.emmory.edu/home/about/index.html, date accessed 9 November 2020.
77. Ibid.
78. J. Rosamund Johnson, https://www.loc.gov/item/ihas.200038845/ date accessed 9 November 2020.
79. "What Makes Lift Every Voice and Sing So Iconic," https://www.cnn.com/interactive/2020/09/us/lift-every-voice-and-sing-trnd/ date accessed 19 November 2020., Hawn, Michael. "History of Hymns: 'Lift Every Voice and Sing'." Disciple Ministries: The United Methodist Church, https://www.umcdiscipleship.org/resources/history-of-hymns-lift-every-voiceand-sing (accessed April 1, 2017).
80. Ibid. and "Facing Facts."
81. "Word Painting in Songwriting," https://www.thesongwritingdesk.com/word-painting.html, date accessed 2 May 2019.
82. "Miss C. L. Tshabalala's Address, 11.
83. Ibid.
84. "What is the Club Woman?" C. L. Tshabalala.

CHAPTER 8

National Council of African Women and the Minutes of a Moral Agenda

In 1938, the second conference of the officially one-year-old National Council of African Women (NCAW) spectacularly took off. Port Elizabeth's Lily May Nikiwe, the meeting's "very nattily and well dressed-sporty hat, short fur coat [wearing] pretty chairperson", warmed up the crowd before Maxeke, the main attraction, ascended upon the stage.[1] Nikiwe handled her ceremonial duties flawlessly. The Healdtown-trained teacher discussed the NCAW's significance; in fact, she likened the body to a "canoe sailing to a distant unknown land, with a need of a far-seeing captain".[2] Nikiwe spoke highly of Maxeke—she was after all the reigning 'Mother of Politics'. Well-known South African educator and activist Ellen Kuzwayo explains why Maxeke was poised to serve as the NCAW's 'far-seeing captain' in her autobiography, *Call Me Woman*:

> When I first encountered her, her hearing, her upright head and clear eyes, proclaimed her as a woman of character and principles. She appeared fun and composed, a woman of values and standards. She gave me the impression of being conscientious and very business-like in her dealings but, above all, a woman very clear about the purpose and direction of her church and her community involvement. I did not find her easy to approach—unlike Minah (sic) Soga. I longed to get near her and talk to her; but except for hearing her address the conference, I never had an opportunity to speak of her. Now that I look back, perhaps the disparity in our ages was a barrier to my reaching her.[3]

D. Y. Curry, *Social Justice at Apartheid's Dawn*, African Histories and Modernities, https://doi.org/10.1007/978-3-030-85404-1_8

When Maxeke finally took the podium and stood before the forty or fifty female delegates in attendance, she delivered these words in her capacity as an elder and as a mentor:

> This work is not for yourselves—kill that spirit of 'self' and do not live above your people but live with them. ... Do away with that fearful animal of jealousy—kill that spirit and love one another as brothers and sisters. The other animal that will tear us to pieces is tribalism; I saw the shadow of it and it should cease to be. Stand by your motto, [do unto others as they do unto you] 'The golden rule'.[4]

Maxeke's excerpted speech conjures up the NACW's slogan, "Lifting as We Climb", Tshabalala's 'rope' metaphor, and *ubuntu*'s and *isivivane*'s principles as this statement by Soga attests, "If you can rise, bring someone with you". Black people had a social contract and a moral responsibility to eschew colorism and tribalism (Maxeke's term) for the collective's advancement.[5] This speech came on the heels of intense and transformative discussion raised by attendants at the All-Africa Convention (AAC). South Africa's foremost Black leaders descended upon the Free State to discuss the infamous Hertzog Bills (see Chap. 2) that levied additional restrictions on the already economically and politically deprived Black population. Land ownership changed, and so did the ability to move around and to procure labor. The AAC allowed Black women to do more than observe. They spoke, mobilized, and strategized, but there was one central and inherent problem.

African men failed to address the lingering 'Woman Question' when it came to their participation in male-led bodies. Maxeke had faced this dilemma.[6] At the ANC's inaugural meeting in 1912, Maxeke pushed to become an ANC member only for forty less-credentialed men to spurn her earnest request.[7] The AAC also annoyed the assembled female participants because they had little autonomy; as a matter of fact, anytime they wanted to challenge the South African government, they could only do so with the AAC's approval and under its aegis.[8] A similar experience occurred with the ANC. "In 1943, thirty-one years after the ANC's formation, women were allowed to become full members of the movement, with rights to vote and participate in all levels of its deliberations, ... the league remained under the political direction of the Congress."[9]

The AAC disrespected African women yet again when it failed to recognize or historically muted the contributions they made. All these apparent roadblocks led Maxeke and other women to take matters into their own hands. They became even more determined and "anxious to care for Non-European welfare and to train African women to interest themselves in social welfare. … [10] These pioneering women envisaged a Nationally organized society with local Branches" from the very beginning. Maxeke held the reins from 1937 to 1939. For some time, following Maxeke's death, the NCAW failed to have a definitive leader until Soga stepped forward from her position as the organization's secretary to assume the body's highest mantle. From 1939 to 1954, Soga served as the NCAW President. Those fifteen years saw the NCAW open clinics and district nursing services and support the Lads Hostel Juvenile Delinquent Facility and other organizations and causes like the DOA, the AAC, the ANC, and the Bantu Welfare Trust.[11] Furthermore, Soga's tenure exemplified her capitalization of Maxeke's mentorship; her carrying over of missionary work as a form of social justice; and her illuminating the body's story through copious minutes. As a matter of fact, her presidential addresses detailed and outlined a moral agenda and a philosophy of social service.

Philosophy of Social Service

Soga was ripe for the NCAW's discriminate picking. She had already distinguished herself in an ambassadorial role. The South African represented her country in India as the only female African delegate to the Madras Conference sponsored by the International Missionary Conference. Attendance at that successful world event led to Soga's participation in post-meeting deliberations in the United States, Canada, the Netherlands, and other European countries. Seabury chronicles this adventure by providing a good overview of this extensive traveling; however, a more detailed afterword is needed to understand the mission that Soga embarked upon following such eye-opening foreign experiences.[12] Soga's trip appeared in abbreviated form on the agenda during a meeting held in Queenstown where she was born. The highly credentialed Soga worked for many years as an educator. Although she traded professions, the passion to teach never died out; if anything, it evolved in her capacity as the NCAW President. Minutes outline, two principal themes that undergird the body's structure and its ideology: philosophy of social service and interracial collaboration. Soga emphasized this mandate in many of her presidential addresses. They reinforced the notion of *ubuntu* as this statement and the following attest: "the movement depends upon the sacrifice, service, and co-operation of all its members. Most African movements died because members lacked perseverance."[13] Of all the things that Soga raises with this brief aforementioned quote, the reminder she gives her people about their agency is perhaps its most impactful statement for several reasons. Soga and her contemporaries participated in a campaign to uplift the morale of the flocks they led. In 'gearing them up for war', an immense burden lay on their very broad shoulders because these women had to erase years of psychologically debilitating treatment. They had to lead by example to attain that lofty goal. That meant turning every opportunity into a teaching moment.

Soga, who was cognizant of this problem and immense necessity, made it a point to tell African people that they had to "[c]irculate [their] work and distribute as much info as possible, simply because this is not [their] Council, but the Council of African women from here right up to Egypt".[14] The female leader invokes the concept of communalism in this statement when she let her audience know that the NCAW belonged to all women-inhabiting areas that stretched from the Cape to Cairo. Her vision differed from diamond entrepreneur Cecil John Rhodes who had a colonialist dream to connect the two sites by rail. Soga, on the other hand, spoke about Black internationalism through the formation of relationships on the ground. She saw the unity of continental Africans as a holistic Pan-African experience in much the same way as scholar Kwame Nantambu or former Ghanaian President Kwame Nkrumah. They refuted the Eurocentric view, and instead privileged the African experience by making the continent the central focus rather than the Diasporas.[15] Soga employed their articulations in the following way. She pushed for sisterhood along transnational lines across the African continent even if it meant following the proposed route of a former colonizer that went south and across the Sahara to north. In the end, Soga's approach underscored her quest to pursue this philosophy as both an aspiration and an advocation. This goal reverberated throughout the NCAW's branches.

Situated seventy miles from the inviting white sand beaches of Port Elizabeth (PE) and eighty miles southwest of the Buffalo and Nahoon Rivers, Grahamstown (present-day Makhanda) maintained an NCAW branch. By the end of the Second World War in 1945, it boasted eighty members. Grahamstown began as a frontier garrison that Colonel John Graham founded (1812); however, today the city is known for its much-reputed Rhodes University and its annual Arts Festival. The town earned even more lore from the violent cultural clashes and mortal combat between the marauding British and the dominant ethnic group, the AmaXhosa. Amid this historical iconicity and this highly attractive landscape, the Grahamstown branch practiced what the president and its constituents preached. Philanthropic activities represented elements and components of the social service that yearly membership fees of £1/10/5 ($7.25) and fundraising supported. Money-generating activities included choral singing; for instance, a £15 ($71.53) admission fee enabled audiences to hear male choirs render song.[16]

Grahamstown's African communities fell prey to the same racially designated enclaves that demarcated the country's major cities. For example, a railway line which stretched from Johannesburg to Port Elizabeth and that cut through Grahamstown provided an artery for migrant laborers to descend upon the city of gold where they lived for months on end. Those that remained in Grahamstown benefited from the NCAW's philanthropic efforts.[17] Rhodes University students, for example, assisted in dispensing rations of meat and vegetables to the townspeople. In Queenstown where the body held its headquarters, the NCAW maintained a soup kitchen. When this social service appeared on the brink of dissolution, the organization stepped in and offered laborers a remittance from the £18 ($85.84) the body had raised. Suffers of tuberculosis (TB) and other illnesses received some medical relief from the NCAW's donations made on their sickly behalf.[18]

Northwest Province's Vryburg, on the other hand, compartmentalized social service. Sub-committees addressed the needs of the unemployed, prospective constituents and volunteers. Health rose as a significant concern and for good reasons.[19] Several townships failed to receive good bills. Probably at the top of an amassing list stood Alexandra in northeastern Johannesburg. As one of the epicenters for subsistence struggle protests, Alexandra gained further acclaim during a city-wide squatters' movement that had initially erupted in Orlando and rapidly spread to other parts of Johannesburg and the Rand. The latter protest, however, conjured up the bubbling fears of White suburbia over poor sanitation. High incidences of smallpox, enteric, and other communicable diseases festered nearby.[20] Queenstown fared no differently than Alexandra even with the NCAW pushing hard for health reform. TB rampantly ran throughout the area going as far back as the mid-nineteenth century.[21]

By focusing on these issues, Soga's NCAW attacked a myriad of segregation's injustices: the environment, which left unattended or improperly equipped led to disease; the inability to consult physicians due to exorbitant costs or lack of facilities or medical personnel; and if those items were not enough to cause alarm, the existence of inefficient social services. The DOA also made health one of its mandates. Albertina Mnguni, who was at one time the DOA's secretary and an SAIRR member, carried out what she called piecework. That activity entailed her finding extremely impoverished individuals, particularly those suckling, to distribute milk to fortify their emaciated bodies.[22]

In 1942, during its conference held in Queenstown, the NCAW highlighted the Nuffield Fund's philanthropic work because it provided monetary assistance for those in need of medical treatment, but it did not stop there. An action item immediately followed this announcement. The NCAW drafted an important, militant, and foresighted memorandum which the organization forwarded to the Health Commission based in Pretoria, one of South Africa's capitals and the seat of the Presidency. The NCAW sought to address this issue's entirety by turning to education, access to books, and labor as examples of other social disabilities. Even with the presence of the nation-wide ICU that Maxeke helped to form, Black workers in Queenstown spearheaded a union so that residents could meet their immediate needs as the NCAW strongly encouraged.[23] Segregation wreaked havoc, but in fashions like African Americans, Soga used her presidency to attain political equality as the soup kitchens, the resolutions, and the pivoting to well-known White leaders suggest.

Interracial collaborations were on the rise despite the impending threat of police surveillance or the danger of being arrested, banned, or ostracized for 'consorting'. Courting of Whites also occurred at a time when the body had already formed an alternate and parallel organization that differed from mainstream political groups. Distance from other female bodies also fostered these relations. Some promoted Pan-Africanist collaborations instead of interracial engagements. Soga ended up doing an accounting of the NCAW's achievements during its first ten years at the presidential address she gave in East London, a year before apartheid's soon-to-be repressive and brutal rise occurred in 1947. She noted the NCAW's success in becoming a voice for African people, bringing forward cases for old age pensions and maintenance grants for men, women, and children and introducing clinics, crèches (day-care centers), and soup kitchens for school-going and non-school-going children.[24] Soga and her followers accomplished all of these things despite the nation's unparalleled moral and physical deterioration that ignorance, poverty, overcrowded conditions, and unemployment fostered.[25] In a statement that reinforces the NCAW's role as the nation's custodians, she stated:

> We have to consider seriously the education of our children. Are they being really educated or are they being stuffed up to pass examinations? Can we not help in the shaping of the syllabus? Are we satisfied with all those who help in the training and shaping of their characters? Do we fully realise that the teachers of our children should be the very best men in the world? If not, let us go back home and do something about these things. We are the trustees.[26]

This abbreviated text illustrates the body's resolve in carrying out its role as the custodians of the African nation. Soga alludes to a social responsibility that lay upon Black women's shoulders. They had to live up to the NCAW's creed, "Do onto others as ye do onto you" or form a tight rope as Tshabalala advocated. Corporeality, which played a large part in their lives, modeled a different form of social justice that the women waged. Female organizations represented an extension of the language that their bodies displayed and internalized. The NCAW pursued the guidance, the direction, and the financial support of White benefactors, observers, and consultants in a move that seems an eerie reminder of the path taken by African male-led organizations.

The Social Piano of the Black and White Keys of Interracial Collaboration

The black and white keys of an upright piano and the singing of Reverend Soga's '*Lizalis Idinga*' flooded the conference hall where the first historicized entries of the NCAW's existence began. As a selection chosen by Reverend Richard Zacchaeus Mahabane, who was one of Maxeke's mentees, the hymn incorporated the traditional platform of choral music (see Chap. 5). The selection met with a resounding response. An array of voices captured the tenor, alto, baritone, and soprano ranges of the members and leaders present. The song's message also added to its importance, for it, like the NCAW, employed God in the quest to save the nation. Mahabane was no stranger to the limelight. He had led the ANC prior to, during, and after this meeting (1924–1927, 1937–1940); furthermore, he had his own congregation in several places, with his first one being in Bensonvale near Herschel in the Eastern Cape, quite far from his birthplace in the Free State's Thaba 'Nchu.[27]

Mahabane crossed the racial line when he brokered a relationship with Dr. Abdullah Abdurrahman, African Political Organisation (APO) leader, who fought for the rights of Coloureds. The two men combined their political aspirations when they initiated the Non-European Unity conferences. They brought together Africans, Indians, and Coloureds to discuss the government's policy of segregation that they all literally and figuratively financed.[28] As a member of the AAC's Executive Committee, Mahabane used his position to oppose the infamous Hertzog Bills (see Chap. 2).[29] Before Mahabane fulfilled his duties for the NCAW's event, he issued remarks about Elizabeth Rheinallt-Jones (ERJ), the guest speaker whom he called the "kaffir ousi".[30] Maxeke had the distinct honor of introducing the University of Leeds graduate following prayer and song. The two women had met twenty years before this occasion. As the wife of statesman David Rheinallt-Jones, ERJ carved out her own space within the political and educational arena. She taught in the Cape, Basutoland (present-day Lesotho) and the University of Witwatersrand (she taught Shona).[31] As an advisor for the South African National Council of Women (SANCW), she consulted on 'Native Affairs'. ERJ also lent her expertise to the NCAW. Of her many contributions to social activism, ERJ gave the NCAW great advice with these encouraging words uttered on 16 December 1937, "you are writing a page in the history of South Africa. The importance of your determination shall be rewarded manifold in the future. [It is important that you form a committee to archive your body's story]."[32]

Several issues lay on the table; however, ERJ focused exclusively on the body's structure. The ensemble agreed on a couple of things: the organization's name and to strike the word 'Bantu' from the title. ERJ felt that the word 'Bantu' excluded other African-descended women from the Rhodesias (Zimbabwe and Zambia) and the Protectorates (Lesotho and Swaziland) with a term that the South African government explicitly used to denigrate its Black inhabitants.[33] She suggested three other things: for the body to choose its organizational colors, to approve the International Council of Women's (ICW) motto, and to create a constitution. The NCAW ended up choosing green and mauve for the body's colors, and adopted the ICW's slogan, 'do unto others'. Constitutionally, they outlined organizational guidelines to establish rules of order.[34]

On another occasion, NAD officer Douglas Laing (DL) Smit came from a different angle. Within months before the Nationalist Party (NP) assumed power under the election slogan of apartheid, which unleashed a more brutal form of racial oppression that Black South Africans had ever known, experienced, or seen, Smit greeted the NCAW's leadership and its constituents for the third honorific occasion on 17 December 1947. Rather than stand at the podium and explain the roles that African women could play in helping the government, he focused on the activities that the NAD was carrying out. Updates came with this confession, "We usually make the mistake of addressing only the men on these subjects, but I think it is time we took the women into our confidence. The men have not always co-operated, and in any case, it is wise to seek the help of the women too."[35] His foreboding talk alludes to the difficult times that Black South Africans faced; however, he made it a point to focus on opportunities rather than grievances.

Smit argues that Africans and Whites issued complaints that depicted their stage of development. Black South Africans lamented about the loss of land, insufficient allotted plots, poor educational facilities, color bar in the mining industry, extremely low wages, and inadequate housing. White South Africans, by contrast, bought into stereotypes of their darker-hued counterparts. Of the many that littered their minds, unreliability ranked high because it forced South Africa's White minority to import labor from neighboring countries rather than supply Africans with employment opportunities.[36] Smit makes his case literally in black and white and perhaps this is too simplistic and unnuanced. South Africa consisted of multiple racial groups beyond those buffeted by the minority and majority populations. Seen in its entirety in Chap. 5, the Fourth International's treatise elaborates upon the complexity of segregation for this primary reason.

Smit only touches upon one of the symptoms rather than the larger problem borne by differentiated transport and geographical sequestration. More than anything, Smit fails to assign culpability to either party nor did he acknowledge the structural issues that created the social ones. His only admission of fault comes with this sentence:

> [U]nfortunately, the teachings of a certain type of person have been to set the two races against each other rather than to bring them together. The great thing to remember is that the White man needs the African and the African needs the white man.[37]

This theory of political and social symbiosis spelled of cooperation, but it wreaked of condensation as it discounted all of the generations in which

Africans worked the land, communed with it, and established different nations on it as Tantsi, Plaatje, Maxeke, Mgqwetho, and others had contended.

While Smit's remarks raise some consternation, they indicate several things in his thinking. Smit incorporates the dependency theory when he lays out how the core (Whites) fed the periphery (Africans). His call for a symbiotic relationship challenges Soga's view on African custodial responsibilities because he situates that outcome within the prism of race relations. Smit's own argument for interdependence and its continuation outlined a step in the push for social justice; however, his argument is intertwined with labor and its supply, and its demand. Up until that time, and beyond, Africans received far lower salaries than their White and even Coloured counterparts. Both the NCAW and the ANC called for equity in this regard. Signs of paternalism surfaced yet again through the commentary issued by Union Secretary of Health Dr. Gale who stated the following:

> I am glad to be here, because I have tremendous faith, in what women can do in health matters. I see in front of me the chosen leaders of your people and I see behind you, millions of followers. There are some people who expect the Government to put things in their hands. But remember, we are given fingers to work, to pick up or do anything. As a servant of the Government, I wish to advise you, not to expect everything from the Government, but learn to do things yourselves. The Government at present has a plan for your people but cannot put it into practice without your assistance. You must explain the plan to your people intelligently. The 1942 Health Commission's Report boldly exposed the true situation. It revealed that many people are ignorant about health matters.[38]

One might question, why Soga allowed Whites to appear before meetings given the incidences and tinges of paternalism that framed most of their 'uplifting' and 'sterile' words. All of this was important to consider for one primary reason. Soga encouraged her people to remember their agentic powers in preserving the nation. A question emerges worth pondering. Did the collaborations infringe upon or assist in the BYL's, the NCAW's, and the DOA's push to secure the youth's future that these bodies so ably championed? Bunche questions this very notion when he criticizes the reliance upon interracial comradeships with this summation:

> the ANC and the NCAW tended to lean heavily on the advice of Europeans. (To what extent is this a deliberate effort to draw women away from the

established African organizations, thus weakening them?) Ma and Pa Jones working hand in glove on moderation and splitting tactics. Mrs. B., Mrs. Jones, and Mrs. Marquard were invited as advisors (intimation that Mrs. B. and Mrs. Marquard on the one hand and Mrs. Jones on the other, don't quite see eye to eye on aspects of the Council).[39]

When Tshabalala spurned several offers and opportunities for the NCAW and the DOA to work together, Soga possibly turned to powerful White leaders for advice and financial support. There was no doubt that the NCAW intended to live up to the charge bellowed by ERJ who when in Kimberley stated, "[the body was] to organize and organize until [it] had about 300 branches in the Union".[40] The NCAW did amass quite a number of branches.[41] They littered the Eastern Cape where the body had its stronghold. Smaller tallies resided in Natal and the Rand where the Tshabalala-led DOA already had a commanding lead. Soga dissected this situation and concluded that the body needed to ramp up its publicity. To attain that goal, she established the 'Morning Watch', a leaflet that highlighted organizational activities across all the branches. Soga encouraged contributors to support the leaflet by punctually and regularly supplying news to fuel the copy on its pages and to alert others of the paper's existence.[42] While public awareness represented a main feature in all of the women's nation-building activities, the NCAW's minutes offer an intimacy that the printed mediums fail to broker. A plethora of organizational documents touched at the heart of the intellectualism that Soga, and the interracial collaborations she sought, and fostered. Given the racial climate of South Africa's segregation era, what prompted such a bold, militant move? Lessons Soga learned while at Madras and other places abroad perhaps can shed some light on her style of bridge leadership.

The Method of Soga's Political Madness: The Moral of it All

As the link to several worlds: the racial and gendered; the secular and the spiritual; the political and the social; and the young, and the old, Soga used her innate gift to capture the magic and the message of her foreign travel. Soga understood the importance of Christian fellowship as a unifying tool. During a closing session in Amsterdam, Soga surprised Seabury when she taught the conference forum the Xosa [sic] hymn. First, she sang it alone and then led them together in repeating it[43]:

Let the gospel go on Let all the nations hear it Till all have learned of it In every part of the world. Amen	Mali hambe, e li li zwi Ma zi live zonk'I zi zwe Li de li fundi se bonke A ba senda we ni zonke.

Soga turned to spirituality at a crucial moment in her religious and social education. Her recognition of the universe's importance echoes Tshabalala, Tantsi, Plaatje, Maxeke, Mgqwetho, and Smit because they each talk about interdependence. Despite the great awakening that she experienced on American, Indian, European, and Canadian soil, Soga's relationship with religion seems to be amiss in the NCAW's minutes save the openings by male African ministers, the inclusion of hymnal singing, and the invocation of prayers. The proverbial separation of the church and state appears here in this regard, but did her affiliation with God require explicitness as was the case with Tshabalala and the DOA that she led and the compositions she wrote and sang? Further light, however, is shed through Soga's engagement with missiology. "Missiology is the area of practical theology that investigates the mandate, message, and mission of the Christian church, especially the nature of missionary work." [44] Soga embodied this theory. She entered the life of another by wearing the appropriate garment as the NCAW's President.[45]

For fifteen years, Soga's primary objective was to learn the language of respective communities and to study their contexts. She did this through the NCAW's charitable acts and social justice pursuits. All of this resulted in the passing of resolutions, the formation of hostels for wayward youths, the promotion of adequate healthcare, and political work based on ethical reconstruction; in fact, it could be said that the moral of it all is captured in two different scenarios. The first one involves the well-known South African author Alan Paton, who wrote works like *Cry, the Beloved Country* and *Too Late the Phalarope*, and the second one teases out a quote given by Soga herself.

In 1944, when the NCAW's main consultant, ERJ, passed away, Paton attended the funeral. He expressed his astonishment by what he had witnessed, "I myself have undergone one unforgettable experience of racial unity, when I saw a great congregation of white people, black people, coloured people and Indian people-not all of them Christians, assembled in St. George's to give thanks for her life and work".[46] Attendants epitomized the core of Soga's philosophy of multiracialism. The funeral service merged together different historical and social narratives. Tshabalala witnessed what Soga describes when she attended the Chautauqua religious conferences where "women from all [climes, denominations, and ethnicities] came together in an educational and spiritual federation".[47] Makanya also believed in this type of fraternity as this statement attests, "Africans [were] one of the rainbow people, owing allegiance to one country where all people's languages and religions would be entrenched in the constitution".[48] Newspaper accounts like this one cited here, read:

> Of course, South Africa is the "rainbow nation", a term first used by Desmond Tutu and later by Nelson Mandela in a post-apartheid South Africa that yearned for prosperity and peace.[49]

This copy fails to trace this concept's etymology to people like Makanya who had theorized about this type of democracy long before the transition of power in 1994. Instead, the nation's first democratically elected President Nelson Mandela elaborates on what appears to be Tutu's originality with this statement, "Each of us is as intimately attached to the soil of this beautiful country as are the famous jacaranda trees of Pretoria and the mimosa trees of the bushveld—a rainbow nation at peace with itself and the world".[50] Despite history's glossing over of Makanya's contributions, her discourse marries well with the ANC's adoption of multiracialism. The body persistently advocated for equitable representation and social acceptance something that Makanya put forth when she acknowledged the moral responsibility to all who lived within South Africa.

Notes

1. Robert R. Edgar, *An African American in South Africa*, 277.
2. "Personal Sketches: Mrs. Lily Nikiwe," *Bantu World*, August 22, 1939, 9. Nikiwe was also a leader of the Wayfarer Movement and the founder of an industrial school where young women and girls learned to dress make, crochet, and kneading and National Council of African Women, Minutes of Annual Conference 1937–1954, Organisations, Pn2.2, AD843/RJ.
3. Ellen Kuzwayo, *Call Me Woman* (London: The Women's Press, 1985), 103.
4. National Council of African Women, Minutes of Annual Conference 1937–1954, Organisations, Pn2.2, AD843/RJ.
5. Ibid.
6. Ibid.
7. Zubeida Jaffer, *Beauty of the Heart*, 80.

8. National Council of African Women, Minutes of Annual Conference.
9. Shireen Hassim, *The ANC Women's League* (Auckland Park: Jacana Media, 2016), 28.
10. National Council of African Women, Minutes of Annual Conference.
11. National Council of African Women, ncaw.org, date accessed 18 May 2021.
12. See Ruth Isabel Seabury, *Daughter of Africa*.
13. National Council of African Women, Minutes of the 6th Annual Conference of the National Council of African Women held at the Mallet Hall, Queenstown, December 16th–19th, 1942, Organisations, Box 263, Pn2, AD843/RJ (hereafter NCAW, Queenstown, Mallet Hall).
14. National Council of African Women Minutes of the Conference Held in the Abantu-Batho Hall, No. 2 Location, Kimberley on the 14th–17th December 1937, Organisations, Box 263, Pn2, AD843/RJ.
15. Kwame Nantambu, "Pan-Africanism versus Pan-African Nationalism: An Afrocentric Analysis," *Journal of Black Studies*, 28, 5 (May 1998): 561–574.
16. National Council of African Women, Grahamstown Branch, Report of the Year Ending in 1945, Organisations, Box 263, Pn2, AD843/RJ.
17. Ibid.
18. Ibid.
19. National Council of African Women Minutes of the Conference Held in Vryheid, Organisations, Box 263, Pn2, AD843/RJ.
20. See Dawne Y. Curry, 'Their World is a Ghetto,' 277–293.
21. NCAW, Queenstown, Mallet Hall.
22. Albertina Mnguni Mzimela, Campbell Collections Oral History, KCAV329.
23. NCAW Queenstown, Mallet Hall.
24. The National Council of African Women at East London on Wednesday the 17th December 1947, Organisations, (hereafter NCAW, East London) Box 263, Pn2, AD843/RJ.
25. National Council of African Women Minutes of the Conference Held in the Abantu-Batho Hall, No. 2 Location, Kimberley on the 14th–17th December 1937, Organisations, Box 263, Pn2, AD843/RJ.
26. Ibid.
27. National Council of African Women, Minutes of the Conference Held in the Bantu Social Institute, Batho Location, Bloemfontein on Tuesday the 20th December 1938 (hereafter NCAW, Batho Location), Organisations, Box 263, Pn2, AD843/RJ.
28. Reverend Richard Zacchaeus Mahabane, https://www.sahistory.org.za/people/reverend-zaccheus-richard-mahabane, date assessed 6 June 2021.
29. Ibid.

30. National Council of African Women, Minutes of the Conference Held in the Bantu Social Institute.
31. Papers of Elizabeth Rheinallt Jones, Historical Papers Research Archive, 1923–1959, ZA HPRA AD1428.
32. NCAW Bloemfontein.
33. Ibid.
34. Ibid.
35. NCAW, Address by Dr. D. L. Smit at the Annual Conference of the National Council of African Women at East London on Wednesday the 17th December 1947, Organisations (hereafter NCAW, East London) Box 263, Pn2, AD843/RJ.
36. Ibid.
37. Ibid.
38. Ibid.
39. Robert R. Edgar, *An African American in South Africa*, 278.
40. NCAW, East London.
41. Port Alfred, Queenstown, Evaton, Lady Selbourne (Pretoria), Umtata, Kimberley, Mafeking, Randfontein, and other sites across the country.
42. NCAW, East London.
43. Ruth Isabel Seabury, *Daughter of Africa*, 127.
44. Nico A. Botha, Towards the En-Gendering of Missiology, 105–116 and Definitions of Missiology, https://www.definitions.net/definition/missiology, date accessed 15 December 2020.
45. Nico A. Botha, Towards the En-Gendering of Missiology, 111.
46. Ibid.
47. Miss C. L. Tshabalala's Address-Other Women.
48. Umehani Khan, A Critical Study of the Life of Sibusiswe Makanya, 74.
49. "South Africa: The Rainbow Nation," https://www.insidethetravellab.com/south-africa-called-rainbow-nation/, date accessed 23 August 2021.
50. Why South Africa is Called the Rainbow Nation, https://www.insidethetravellab.com/south-africa-called-rainbow-nation/ date accessed 26 May 2021.

CHAPTER 9

Conclusion: Blueprints for the Nation They Left Behind

When the votes with their weary, social justice feet were tallied, and preserved and illuminated in the annals of history, the book's featured subjects bequeathed blueprints for the nation they left behind. Everyone concurred that the progeny of the nation rested with African men and women working with each other. While it was true that many of them promoted African women's self-development, they also understood the inextricable link that African men had in the development and the promotion of the community's salvation. Tshabalala viewed this collaboration through the proscriptions of ***ubuntu***, ***isivivane***, Washington's 'bootstrap', the DOA's rope, and even the NACW's motto, "Lifting as We Climb". Tshabalala also turned to spirituality as another way of **fostering male/female comradeships** because she believed that "[e]verything that breathes human, an animal or plants or roots that grows on its own, proves that they are alive and breathing and bearing fruit (or young)".[1] Well-known ANC leader and Father of African Nationalism Anton Lembede also championed connections to a higher force. He stressed geography over religion as this quote attests, "the African natives ... live and move and have their being in the spirit of Africa, in short, [because] they are one with Africa".[2]

As much as Lembede wanted Africans to tap into their innate connection with the continent, he saw and understood the importance of indigeneity and its relationship to cosmology. Tshabalala also welcomed this synergy. She wanted Africans to be in tune with God. Her notion on

D. Y. Curry, *Social Justice at Apartheid's Dawn*, African Histories and Modernities, https://doi.org/10.1007/978-3-030-85404-1_9

'one-ness' also called for African women to commune with the ancestral spirits through hand-holding to promote intimacy and the union of energies into one, all-being force. She wrote:

> Through the value of our efforts and our labours may we with the passing year think of the past tenderly and thank God for the bitter experiences that have been ours by pressing forward to join hands with the SONS OF AFRICA known as the All-African Convention, fraternally walking hand in hand with the DOA standing together in friendship and mutual confidence.[3]

Angeline Khumalo Dube offered her own example of an inclusive approach during a meeting where she both chastised and encouraged her listeners, "husbands [were] the ones on the forefront, arranging meetings, strategizing for the betterment of our country. African women could not afford to be silent and not make [their] voices heard. They needed to help their men."[4] African women first had to overcome ethnic divisions. During a meeting before the DOA, Dr. John L. Dube urged his audience to forget that they were "Zulu, or that [they were] Mosutho (sic), or that [they were] Xhosa, and … be … African".[5] Dube pushed for this goal and outcome so that the African nation could "co-operate wholeheartedly to improve living conditions, … to fight for better educational facilities, old age pensions, [higher wages] and to teach the people to strive for freedom by joining with [Africans residing] in other provinces".[6] Baloyi, who echoed Dube, encouraged "the Mothers of Africa to continue taking steps towards unity because if they did, the nation could look forward to better things".[7] Baloyi hit upon a touchy subject with tensions brewing between the DOA and the NCAW.

A copious paper trail captures the 'family feud' in this organizational version of the game show. Trouble potentially started when the NCAW pushed to gain adherents. The body eyed the DOA stronghold, Pietermaritzburg (PMB). NCAW leader Eleanor Hlahle proclaims in her secretarial hand that people in PMB were DOA-minded and highly unlikely to turn the tide in the body's favor. The NCAW tested the Alexandran waters, but DOA leaders Elizabeth Baloyi and others vetoed the suggestion. Soga and her leadership reached the same dead end in the East Rand where Benoni, its targeted area, began originally as a mining camp in 1887.[8] Affiliation with the DOA also failed to materialize even after Tshabalala addressed the NCAW and refused to answer any questions about the body's dense constitution.[9] Soga tried to tell her on several occasions that NCAW represented a bigger organizational entity than the provincial body she led, but her efforts fell flat.[10] Also, the DOA and the

NCAW both sought the same limited resources. A letter written by Soga to one of the body's benefactors, Elizabeth Rheinallt Jones (ERJ), provides evidence to this effect. Professor John Tengo Jabavu received funds and decided to split the bounty of £70 roughly $33.81 between the DOA and the Home Improvement Societies.[11] This sort of acrimony was not confined to females; Congress of Racial Equality (CORE) co-founder James Farmer expresses his own disappointment in his autobiography, *Lay Bare the Heart*. This early proponent of African American liberation, prominent sit-in activist, advocate, and participant of the Freedom Rides, felt politically invisible when Reverend Dr. Martin Luther King, Jr., rose to prominence as the leader of the Montgomery bus boycott:

> The great day has come at last. The nonviolent movement in America is airborne. Why am I not more exuberant? Is it because it is not I who leads it? Is there a green-eyed monster peering through my eyes? I had labored a decade and a half in the vineyards of nonviolence. Now, out of nowhere, someone comes and harvests the grapes and drinks the wine.[12]

When Soga inherited the NCAW's rein, she began drinking the wine that Farmer describes and that Tshabalala longed to taste. From 1930 on, Tshabalala had been tilling the fields, but her illumination dimly shown which perhaps explains her angst, her bellicosity, and her competitiveness toward Soga or any other woman or female organization which appeared to steal her historic thunder. The DOA founder possibly spurned these overtures for a reason enclosed in a letter addressed to ANC President-General Dr. Alfred B. Xuma.

Written eight years after the NCAW's founding in 1945, Tshabalala asks Xuma to speak at THE FIRST FEDERATION OF AFRICAN WOMEN meeting. Tshabalala used enlarged font to convey the event's magnitude and to entice her proposed guest of honor.[13] Tshabalala's dream of an umbrella national female body finally materialized when struggle stalwarts Helen Joseph, Lillian Ngoyi, Frances Baard, Winnie Mandela, and others created the Federation of South African Women (FSAW) in 1955. It is not known if Tshabalala allowed herself to participate in this momentous feat but given her inability to broker relations between the DOA and the NCAW, and her own desire to go down in history as the originator of this type of collaboration, the possibility is highly unlikely. Thus, after competing for the same limelight, for limited funding and for geographical turf, Tshabalala's DOA and Soga's NCAW met different fates. The former became moribund despite pleas by leaders to resuscitate the organization following Tshabalala's death (1961 or 1962) whereas the latter still exists today in the twenty-first century.

Female-to-Female Comradeships

In 1921, the ICU began as a trade union for Coloured and African workers before it expanded under Clement Kadalie's direction to a popular mass-based movement influenced by UNIA founder Marcus Garvey and the Industrial Workers of the World (IWW). The body's focus and emphasis on everyday problems drew Mkhize in like a magnet.[14] Kadalie and his constituents had several things going for them: their advocacy of Black self-determination, their promotion of blackness, and their accrued results like the clothing shop, Vuka Africa. Natal activist and political leader Allison Wells George (A. W. G.) Champion managed this store that catered to the delectable buying tastes of an emerging Black middle class in Durban until it closed in 1929.[15] It was at this shop, where the ICU attempted to attain the commercial, personal, and financial autonomy which Garvey championed, that Nhlumba Bertha Mkhize met Alexander (later Simons).

Alexander immigrated from Latvia when she was only fifteen. Her family wanted to avoid the rampant persecution of Jews and Communists that were beginning to sweep Europe in the late 1920s. They ultimately landed in Cape Town where Alexander immediately threw herself into the political arena.[16] Within a few days of her arrival, Alexander met Zainunnisa 'Cissie' Gool and John Gomas, both of whom were high-profile political figures. Gool was no stranger to the limelight. Her father was none other than Dr. Abdullah Abdurrahman, a descendant of Muslim Malay slaves and a prominent Capetonian medical doctor who founded the African Political Organisation (APO) in 1902. The APO dominated Coloured protest politics until the National Liberation League (NLL) eclipsed it beginning in the 1930s. Abdurrahman's death put the final nail in the body's coffin in 1940.[17] By that time, Gool had married her husband, Abdul Hamid Gool, and had established the NLL with her collaborators Johnny Gomas, a tailor by profession, and James La Guma, a career labor activist, on 1 December 1935, the same date of the annual celebration of the emancipation of slavery.[18] Alexander had already learned about socialism and Communism from her father and his best friend so her turn toward the CPSA came as no surprise, if anything it represented a natural extension of the internal politics spewing around in her home.[19]

Alexander's study went on to oppose retrenchment of African mine workers and to fight against extremely low wages, and excessive and restraining curfews. She also took a definitive stance against the imposition of passes onto women in 1931 and 1936. During the first anti-pass protest, Mkhize engaged in another female comradeship when she summoned a legion of 500 militarized African women to participate in a procession to the Magistrate's office in Durban (*eThekwini*). Trouble brewed over the government's decision to require African women to attain permission to move around by forcing them to go all the way to Ndwedwe, thirty-seven miles north of Durban, the original, prescribed site. Ndwedwe's distance and its 'long-bare table land ensconced within the Valley of the Thousand Hills' made it nearly impossible for persons dependent upon public transport to make the trek without missing valuable work hours or expending additional money on travel.[20]

When the standoff or 'sitting on a man' happened like the actions taken by the Alexandra Women's Brigade and Nigeria's Igbo women, White people came out of their shops to observe the protest happening right before their very eyes. The group's elected spokesperson Mkhize used the opportunity conjure up a scenario for the Native Commissioner to consider. Mkhize (Fig. 9.1) stated:

> supposing a man's child is dead in Durban here, and she was to go to Ndwedwe first and get perhaps a week or a month, and then what happens? The surprised Native Commissioner responded, 'It's the first time I've been here for about ten years ... that I've seen people come to tell me their troubles, therefore I understand what they are talking about, and now, from today, onwards no Native woman shall carry a pass?' The women ululated with Awu! were so happy, and jubilant that they all shouted, 'what is our national anthem? *Nkosi Sikelel iAfrika*', before they disappeared.[21]

No African woman carried a pass until the '*dompas*' (dumb pass) which the 1952 Native Act introduced the Reference Book under apartheid. Coloured, Asian, African, and White women stormed the grounds at the Union Buildings in Pretoria on 9 August 1956 to protest this imposition and to tell Minister Strijdom that "he had struck a rock, [and had] struck the women". That statement which became a frenetic chant exemplifies how on that very wintry day participants cultivated the soil by engaging in inclusive immersion as a form of resistance.

Fig. 9.1 Following the abolition of apartheid, government officials began to honor the names of African heroes and heroines of the struggle. Bertha Mkhize replaced Victoria Street. That artery contains the famed market which is a major tourist attraction. Charlotte Maxeke Street picture below replaced the name John Brandt who had once served as one of South Africa's Presidents (https://www.ulwaziprogramme.org/no-longer-at-this-address-from-victoria-street-to-nhlumba-bertha-mkhize-street/, date accessed 28 November 2021)

Cultivating the Soil/Inclusive Immersion

Tshabalala commonly utilized the phrase 'cultivating the soil' to explain the need to conduct social service in the urban and rural areas. The DOA made this such an important goal that the organization sent envoys to different parts of Natal and the Transvaal. On one occasion, DOA leaders Mkhize and Mnguni traveled around Natal where they had hoped to spread their political and ideological wings. The ensemble's first stop was Eshowe, one of Natal's oldest European settlements nestled in the Dhlinza Forest having been established sometime in 1860. The group continued from Eshowe by bus further south to Entumeni by traveling up and down unpaved roads snaking around hills and valleys that welcomed and swallowed them up in the country's vastness and its jaw-dropping scenery. This picture-perfect postcard transported Mnguni back to her idyllic roots.

Mnguni was born in Entumeni; however, despite this affiliation, she worried about the kind of reception that the indigenous population would bestow upon her entourage. She was after all a transformed 'city girl', who had left home to pursue a cosmopolitan life while her cohort already had 'real-life' experience living in Inanda, a stone's throw away from metropolitan Durban.[22] Despite her apprehensions, the community warmly embraced the two DOA leaders and allowed them to 'cultivate the soil' for Entumeni was ripe for political planting. Mnguni went a step further in carrying out the DOA's philosophy when she told this forest-tucked community that "[t]heir land [was] fertile for vegetation. [They] [could] grow what [they] [needed] and then sell the surplus and make profits for [their] clubs."[23] This informal exchange illustrated how the DOA sought to build the nation from the bottom up as Tshabalala states in that aforementioned Pimville, Soweto, speech.[24]

Makanya contributed similarly to the development of her people. Believing strongly in equipping rural inhabitants for the transition to urban life, she conducted 'rounds' throughout Natal. The country's first rural sociologist also tested the heavily guarded racial line when she removed some of the mystery between White and Black by having the former conduct inclusive immersions. The premise behind this idea was simple. She wanted non-indigenous people to witness how the policy of segregation impacted those occupying Natal's most bucolic, land-endowed sites, and for them to understand the isiZulu language and culture. One of these studies was White American missionary Dr. Lavinia Scott who set sail for South Africa, the same year of the DOA's establishment in 1932. Her forty-two year missionary career found the American studying at the prestigious Adams College situated twenty-three miles south of Durban where she learned isiZulu. Scott successfully passed a comprehensive exam which consisted of a twenty-minute conversation.[25] The American supplemented and complemented her language training with additional immersion at Makanya's Imbumbulu home where she spent two weeks.[26] Visitors and missionaries learned language, but also the community's (*umphakati*) history so that they could better understand the protests that erupted over cattle dipping regulations, liquor disputes, and the pass laws. Makanya explained why this move was important:

> [M]ore European young people would then grow up determined to see that the living conditions of the Natives were made more wholesome. There would appear also as something of a sympathetic spirit towards the Natives that is so sadly lacking at the present time.[27]

Soga also believed in this type of inclusive engagement. In "The Need for the Missionary Today: His Place and Foundation", Soga argues that "missionaries should learn languages, and study backgrounds to appreciate the good in that [respective] tradition and look at things from the other man's point of view and only then lay [down] the Christian foundation".[28]

Soga got her intellectual and spiritual feet wet when she traveled to India to participate in an all-important religious conference, which she compounded with an ambassadorial role to both North America and Europe. The South African stayed a short time in England before she ventured to the Netherlands where Amsterdam, the 'Venice of the North', awaited the brand of Christian gospel that she and other adherents professed at the international religious conference that the city hosted.[29] Every national fountain quenched Soga's intellectual thirst. Soga drank so much that she went home and taught the youth everything she had learned. This action appears noble and forward thinking but it also appears disingenuous to Soga's ideological beliefs. Her quest to bring Africa and its people into the world of tomorrow rested on a western model rather than on African-established practices. Nokutela Ndima Dube presented another option. She pulled no punches in reminding her American audience "[that Africans did] not want to teach their people all of [their] civilization [they only wanted] to better their conditions [so as] not to make them unnatural or unhappy". [30] Africans needed to attain their own identity and engage in processes that prohibited the disintegration of traditions, mores, and cultures which is a belief they all held even when calling for syncretism between the Global North and the Global South.

Afrofuturistic Models for Democratic Pan-Humanity

Of all the things, African women left behind their call for a global, symbiotic relationship based on an Afrofuturistic model for democratic panhumanity that still resonates today. These women sought to "balance neocolonial developments in the modern world through visions of utopic (ideally perfect) and dystopic (wretchedly dehumanized) tomorrows".[31]

Chautauqua's religious conferences embodied the utopia that Tshabalala pursued through the DOA. Women from India, China, Japan, South Africa, and other nations around the world filed in singly, doubly, and in threes for twelve intensive weeks of religious immersion. With its idyllic setting in upstate New York and its stellar conference, Chautauqua impressed Tshabalala so much that after witnessing women from different social, political, and religious backgrounds come together in a sorority of mutual cooperation, she knew then that 'there was strength in unity':

> It was during the year 1927 that I was seized by the desire to visit the Chautauqua conference held annually at Chautauqua, New York. For the first time in my life the everyday phrase UNITY is strength had a lasting meaning in my mind. Here gathered women of all climes, the Christian women termed missionaries from home and abroad and come together into an educational as well as spiritual federation mind you. These women represented almost all denominations acknowledged as such. From different foreign countries these workers brought to the home—women varied knowledge and experience gathered, which I am certain were in turn recorded for the future studies at home and abroad. ... Some of these women brought reports on various topics and also to listen with the masses anxiously to what the speakers had to say.[32]

This inspiring event gave Tshabalala another model besides the National Association of Colored Women to emulate.[33] Her contemporary Soga found her spiritual awakening in India when she realized this epiphany that Seabury narrates, "Brought up in a land of the colour bar, the fact that all races could live together in such a beautiful fellowship was a never ceasing source of wonder. That is why she called it heaven."[34] The Solomon Mahlangu Freedom College (SOMAFACO) epitomized what these women sought.

Established in 1978, this revolutionary educational institution bore the namesake of freedom fighter and Mamelodi-native Solomon Mahlangu. Mahlangu joined the ANC's militant wing, *Umkhonto weSizwe* (Spear of the Nation), which the body founded following the clampdown after the Sharpeville Massacre in 1961, the same year that the riveting Soweto Uprising erupted on 16 June 1976.[35] Students left Morris Isaacson High School to oppose Afrikaans as a medium of instruction for math, science, geography, history, and other classes. Protesters viewed Afrikaans as the language of the oppressor (the White minority government) while English was seen as the tongue of liberation.[36] Mahlangu, whom the state accused of murder, violently lost his life when a noose draped around his bulging neck extinguished his last breaths.[37] The ANC honored the assassinated militant posthumously by building SOMAFACO. The center rested on land in Morogoro, Tanzania, where the body held its educational headquarters. SOMAFACO ended up serving as a home to many displaced South African youth following the Soweto Uprising when they fled the country for fear of retribution by the government.[38]

SOMAFACO also provided exiles with primary and secondary education that was far different from the Bantu Education that they had been receiving—"the white-washing of African history and the repeated drumming of their ordained positions as laborers.[39] 'Bantu education' was not introduced as a means of raising the cultural level of the Africans, nor of developing the abilities of the African child to the full, but as one of the devices which aims at solving the cheap labour problems of the country."[40] SOMAFACO changed the rules of the game. It also provided a prototype for the future and perhaps the past through a concept that mirrors the ideas that this book's subjects championed. Barbara Bell speaks about SOMAFACO in Lauretta Ngcobo's anthology, *Prodigal Daughters*. Bell was a former pre-school teacher, who lived in exile in Zambia, Botswana, and New Zealand before ending up in Tanzania. Bell further explains the significance of this institutional enterprise:

> At the Mazimbu complex that housed the Solomon Mahlangu Freedom College (SOMAFACO) we had what I now think of as post-1994 South Africa in microcosm, a de-racialised hierarchy where the leadership enjoyed a relatively privileged lifestyle down to being provided with four times more toilet paper than the rank-n-file where black women, again, were at the bottom of the pile. … It was a rude awakening, but we thought, naively, that the Mazimbu community could still become the sort of democratic model of the South Africa of our dreams and hopes; anti-racist, anti-sexist, and egalitarian.[41]

Tshabalala expressed the same sentiments. "[She saw] beyond a world that [prevented] exploitation, [fostered] just distribution and guaranteed the rights of freedom", all things that SOMAFACO promoted and inculcated.[42] Soga, on the other hand, infuses her narrative by discussing the encounter between Black and White and the implications for each group. She also explained Africa's role in the making of an egalitarian and a democratic society.

> The white man did his very best to make us as near like himself as possible. We adopted his clothes, his manner of speech. We learned his history, his geography, his language, his poetry, and his literature. Only now are scientists and anthropologists beginning to discover and dig up the treasures of Africa's past. Pray God it is not too late. Pray God we can still find them, for the world will be poorer without Africa's part. Africa's part! It was that we felt in our contact with Miss Soga and that we should like to bring to people everywhere—a part in building and giving to the world the resources of the earth, of transmitting beauty, and discovering truth along with all the rest of us. In tribal days life was unselfish and the concern of all was for the good of the tribe, of society. Perhaps we are rediscovering the need for that in these totalitarian days. To free Africa from superstition and dirt and fear that were parts of tribal life was one thing, but to take from her the tribal structure, the fellowship, and the togetherness that the Anglo-Saxon has lost and perhaps never had is tragedy, and we shall do well to help Africa rediscover herself. Perhaps she will teach us all to be part of a tribe, within a people, within a nation, within a world, where all are needed, and no one will exploit another.[43]

Makanya further threads this idea in "Glimpses of Native Life in South Africa". Like Soga, she explicates the importance behind some of the traditions that her people carried out:

> It is my hope that the western culture with all the means of understanding at its command will understand and appreciate what my people can give to the world. Our background is different from yours, but it has been the background that has made us. We have no beggars. We never turn a hungry person from our door. We are taught from early childhood to help our fellowmen. We too, follow the Christian precept: "I am my brother's keeper".[44]

Nairobi, Kenya, gives Sisonke Msimang a rude awakening in this more contemporary example of pan-humanism. Msimang weaves together the chronicles of two continents and two countries—Canada and Kenya—in *Always Another Country* and the heartbreak of child who understood the concept of pan-humanity. Msimang's beloved two-wheeler, which she saved her money for several weeks in Canada, gets stolen. When a good Samaritan returns the bike to Msimang to restore the streets' code of ethics, racially intra-divided Nairobi partially stitches its seams between the wealthy and the impoverished. All hope is further lost when the good citizen arranges for the victim to meet the perpetrator.[45] Msimang subconsciously wants a relationship with her bike's temporary possessor, but her dream is interrupted by her reflection's unapologetic irreverence, and his cultural blackness, and by her expectative demand, and her assumed whiteness. The bicycle is the symbol and the metaphor for class tensions, which prevent two African-descended people from forming a lasting bond based on their shared heritage.

Msimang wishes to rectify the impact of colonialism, neo-colonialism, and Black-ruled governments with one fell swoop. This is not partially her fault, after all, she had at one time resided in Zambia, a free Black country where its President Kenneth Kaunda preached and practiced Pan-Africanism. Kenya's Daniel Arap Moi, who stood in stark contrast to Kaunda, failed to include Pan-Africanism in his nationalist or Afrofuturist agenda; instead, he widened the divide between the wealthy and the poor. Msimang also envisions the encounter as a micro-version of the political union that Ghana's Kwame Nkrumah and Ethiopia's leader Haile Selassie championed, envisioned, and materialized with the Organisation of African Unity (OAU) and the African Union (AU) formed, respectively, in 1963 and 2002.[46] Bell and Msimang offer two different versions of institutionalization that considers varied organizational structures. SOMAFACO, the OAU, and the AU represent formalized institutional bodies whereas the intra-relationships that Msimang seeks foster an unwritten code between and among Africans.

ANC activist Baleka Mbete, who offers another example of a democratic institution, spent fifteen years in exile beginning around 1976. She lived in Swaziland, Mozambique, Tanzania, Kenya, Botswana, and Zimbabwe. In 1990, Mbete returned home as part of the first group of ANC women that stalwart Gertrude Shope led back to South Africa. Mbete rose up the ANC's ranks to perform a major role in the women's regional and national structures. She was also a presenter on the ANC's clandestine station, Radio Freedom, which the body created in 1967.[47] Headquartered in Lusaka, Zambia, Radio Freedom broadcast in Tanzania, Ethiopia, Angola, Madagascar, and South Africa (the apartheid regime considered it subversive and arrested anyone found listening to its contents). In another interview appearing in *Prodigal Daughters*, Mbete discusses how exiles embodied the concepts of *ubuntu* and *isivivane* in more contemporary times. Mbete's words articulate how journeying to another place changed the mindsets of Africans not only about the world but also their own cultures:

> The 'exile kids' have a different perspective on life or sense to a different reality and set of values early on in their lives—non-racial human and social interactions in other countries and seeing of living in different parts of the world.[48]

Living as citizens of the world temporarily or permanently promoted cultural diplomacy and the pan-humanism that Tshabalala and others passionately pursued at apartheid's dawn. Yet, while they blazed a conspicuous trail that promoted societal betterment, these daughters of Africa missed some obvious nation-building moves. Two things sounded the alarm: the myopic depiction of Black women's internationalism and, lastly, the need to redefine cultural diplomacy.

Omissions from the Blueprint

Of all the things African women addressed, they failed to leave a prototype for an international body that sought social justice on the global stage. Pursuits of equity in gender, ameliorations within a system of segregation, and continuance and expansion of their roles as mothers and wives led Tshabalala, Dube, and others alluding to greater societal issues rather than creating the institutions to address them. When the Women's World Congress for Peace and Liberty (WWCPL) called for Black women to represent South Africa on its behalf, the NCAW replied with regrets. Held in October 1939, this Cuban conference represented a prime opportunity for the NCAW to establish international ties that the South African government prohibited with the National Council of Women (NCW) of White females. A letter dated 2 June 1939 sent from an NCAW representative explains how the exorbitant costs of obtaining passports and passages for Africans was to dear for the body to handle financially. In lieu of their actual attendance, the correspondent proposed two resolutions one of which included them extending good wishes to the Cuban conference's deliberations regarding "the tragedy of war, its toll of broken homes, of orphaned children, of refugees uprooted from their native lands, its destruction of civilisation's valued heritage".[49] The NCAW pledged on the South African home front to meet to suggest recommendations on topics listed in the conference's program.

Discussions possibly occurred, but what results did they produce given that the country already had examples of globalizing local problems? For example, the African Association that Alice Victoria Kinloch (Chap. 3) founded along with Trinidadian Henry Sylvester Williams and Sierra Leonean Thomas John Thompson, for example, sought "to benefit people in Africa by helping them to bring some of the dark side of things [like South Africa's abuse of mine workers] in Africa and elsewhere to light … by [working] to educate and mobilise (sic) people in the fight against colonialism and imperialism".[50] The Women's Enfranchisement Association of the Union (WEAU) tried to attain women's suffrage by taking its call to the Parliament floor (1908–1909, 1912, 1920, 1921, and 1929), and through affiliations with the British Dominion's Suffrage Union (BDSU) and the International Women's Suffrage Alliance (IWSA). In 1923, a small group from elite, Cairo families formed the Egyptian Feminist Union (EFU). In rhythm with both the African Association and the WEAU, the EFU sought nationalist goals in Egypt all the while brokering transnational ties to the International Women's Suffrage Association (IWSA).[51]

The EFU took its platform a step further when the organization established two journals. Appearing in French and Arabic, *L'Egyptienne* (1925–1940) and *Al-Misriyya* (1937–1940) outlined its demands for legal reform.[52] Their existence raises a question, were these bodies' dress rehearsals for something bigger on the horizon or did they represent evidence of a major theoretical oversight on behalf of the activist intellectuals featured in *Social Justice at Apartheid's Dawn*? For example, Tshabalala wrote about the Italian occupation of Ethiopia (1935–1936) when she expressed her concern about the Red Sea country being wiped off the map. Unlike the DOA, the EFU made this topic a major agenda item. Dissent against Italy's aggression subsequently aligned the organization with other nations and bodies that sought to extricate the European country from Eritrea's geographical neighbor.

Across the pond in the United States, African America's Madame C. J. Walker, the hair and beauty product entrepreneur and billionaire, launched an international organization during early twentieth century by which two global wars, colonial rule in Africa, and American expansion overseas set the stage for its dire need. Walker established the International League of Darker Peoples (ILDP), a short-lived but significant Black internationalist organization in the United States. Founded in 1919, the ILDP highlighted Walker's contributions to the international world as a donor and as a supporter of Garvey's United Negro Improvement Association (UNIA), and as a donor of mission schools in South Africa and other educational initiatives.[53] In her seminal essay, Internationalism

Noir (Black Internationalism) Martinican intellectual Jeanne "Jane" Nardal posits that African-descended people needed to study the Black race.[54] Historian Keshia N. Blain, who saw Nardal as a pioneer in this field, pushed the envelope further by analyzing global struggles for freedom whereas I propose to unearth the micro-psychosomatic feelings of everyday Black internationalism by exploring the 'self'. If we consider the politics of energy, then a transnational network is in fact a part of their legacy, or is it? Take Tshabalala and Soga, for example, when they held hands or worshiped God, they like the AWL whose memorandum acted as the housewives, domestics, and the factory workers' hands linked their DNA to a cosmological, cartographical map.

While the AWL participated in this interconnective feat, these commuters, and others like them, only understood segregation as it applied to South Africa rather than the continent where European powers like the British or the French created racially segregated enclaves in their respective African colonies or beyond Africa. Xuma, by contrast, saw the bigger, looming picture. When the United Nation's passed the Atlantic Charter that American President Franklin Delano Roosevelt (FDR) and British Prime Minister Winston Churchill spearheaded in 1941, Xuma and Amy Jacques Garvey (AJG), Marcus Garvey's second wife, ignited a robust rebuttal to the document's aims. They both took issue with the fact that neither drafter envisioned the freedoms of African-descended people rather as Churchill put it, "the African invasion was just beginning … if all [went] well … [they] might control the whole North African shore … thus saving some of the masses of shipping now rounding the Cape. This is our first great prize."[55] Xuma saw the writing on the political wall. He used the African Charter which he authored to oppose aggrandizement and territorial changes. Support for self-government, an open door trade policy, economic collaboration, abolition of Nazi tyranny, freedom of the seas, and no use of force in international disputes clearly spelled out the inherent problems of the Atlantic Charter.[56]

Amy Jacques Garvey galvanized every activist she could. Adam Clayton Powell, Jr., one of the editors of the Harlem's People's *Voice*, and Nigeria's own Nnamdi Azikiwe, director of the *West African Pilot*, a Black nationalist newspaper running out of Lagos, topped the growing list who represented her arsenal. Her goal was to do the following.[57] She wanted to draw up a memorandum to present before the UN that showcased the talents from different parts of the world and from diverse constituencies. For instance, AJG commissioned Azikiwe to draft the West African Press

Delegation Memorandum while she worked on the Memorandum Correlative of Africa, the West Indies, and the Americas, in which she "[called] on the United Nations to extend democratic principles to African peoples around the globe".[58]

Even with these contemporary examples, African women who helmed some of the most prominent female organizations of their time appeared not to have left behind a pronouncement of their own. Perhaps, the reason for this absence has to do with apoliticism. Black Studies Africanist Maria Martin argues that gender relations in Nigeria centered on Yoruba cosmology, which based its principles on complementarianism and duality—the good/bad, unseen/seen, or heaven/earth. Nigerian women like Martin's subject, Funmilayo Ransome-Kuti (FRK), who had formed the Abeokuta Women's Union and other bodies, turned to apoliticism as a strategy because "[they] saw their personal fight for equality as separate from the political elite narratives that were formed during the nationalist movement. … They were not interested in holding the power to rule the state but the power to affect change, instead of constricting them to proscribed doctrines that called for their unwavering support."[59]

I initially thought that Martin's explication only applied to African men whom their female counterparts failed to curry, which as another critique of their legacy which possibly forestalled the nationalist movement during its early stages. Additional reading of the women's bequeathed corpus changed my scholarly assessment. They made assertions similar to Xuma, AJG, the ILDP, and other people and bodies. The following 'document' is an imagined construct extracted from different statements made by Mpama, Tshabalala, and Soga. They illustrate how their thoughts mirrored others around the globe. It 'reads':

> We, women, should come to the field as strugglers. … We can no longer remain in the background or concern only with domestic and sports affairs. The time has arrived to enter the political field and stand shoulder to shoulder with [our] men in the struggle.[60]
>
> We want communication that are extensive of the home, where we shall be friends with each other with people of all races and creeds, where good schools, high standard of living and public health, recreation beauty and the moral atmosphere shall tempt the finest type.
>
> We cannot get these things unless, we work together. We must put them into daily intercourse and into politics. There is no community so small that cannot realize these ambitions and when you, have put them into your

> home town you have helped to make your race one hundred percent African.[61]
>
> [We] must pray for us for those who rule and are ruled. [We] must pray that there will be brothers to help us, that we may have the strength to find the things we need that we shall receive our trust in men and ourselves because we trust God. [We] must pray that we shall walk always upward toward the light and that there may be Christian love and hope for us all and for all.[62]
>
> Women of Africa, I appeal to you to loose [sic] no time, but come forward and take your place in the struggle against the oppressive laws inflicted on you [and other marginalized groups].[63]

Several things emerge from this montage of collated statements. Of most important is the message that African people deserved human rights. The call to address oppressive legislation and other strangleholds ties in nicely with AJG in her pitch to "free [Africans] from their present disabilities—economically, socially, educationally, politically, spiritually, and morally".[64] Secondly, the 'document' leans toward pacifism when it calls upon brotherly and sisterly love as an antidote to militarism and violence—symbolic, gendered, and physical alike. Thirdly, the 'call' for pan-humanism stands out in this declaration. The women 'push' for equitable relations among all races and creeds while also advocating for self-determination something that the Atlantic Charter outlines, but that Xuma and AJG dispute in both of their responses.

Even with these foci, economic autonomy is missing from this exercise. Tshabalala and the DOA often taught rural inhabitants to grow their own produce for subsistence and for sale, but like the NCAW and its soup kitchens, their attempts to attain economic empowerment never rose to the scale that Garvey envisioned or carried out. The Jamaican established an alternate and parallel community by creating the UNIA's newspaper, the *Negro World*, an independent shipping line in the guise of the Black Star Line and other commercial ventures that promoted self-determination.[65] This 'intellectual fabrication' of an envisioned collaborative statement provides a prototype for a global audience that they were remised in reaching despite exposure to overseas travel and Black women's club movements. They also had organizational precursors like the African Association that Kinloch had established with a Trinidadian and a Sierra Leonean—two men that indicated her interest in comradeships across the lines of gender. A surging movement of Black internationalism stood in their wake. Perhaps their reluctance or short-sightedness prevented their 'welcome' on the global stage where clearly their ideas registered with others around the world.

The Welcomes and the Send-offs of Legacy Makers

Transformation often took place during the welcomes and the goodbyes of Africans who entered foreign soils. South Africa welcomed its own citizens back home through the melancholic and ballistic sounds of war, through the celebrations of joy, through the presence of opportunities, through the roars of thunderous applause, and through the exhibition of *hlonipha* (respect). Geographic landscapes, sculptures, topography, sound, smells, and varying colored skies greeted South Africans wherever they went throughout the world and on the African continent. Several returnees enjoyed parties in their esteemed honor while a raging war delayed a family reunion. Maxeke's return occurred amid the second South African War which stopped everything from travel to and from the north where her family resided in Ramokgopa and the delivery of mail.[66] But while she waited to see her fiancé Marshall Maxeke and other loved ones, the AME Church in the Cape Province provided Maxeke comfort and support. During her time waiting out the war in Cape Town, Maxeke formed the Women's Mite Missionary Society (WMMS). She had experience with this type of body. As a student member of the North Ohio Conference of the Women's Mite Missionary Society, she learned how to engage in social service within and outside the Black community. Maxeke upon the urging of her American hosts often gave them her opinion on the struggles of her people back home at those meetings.[67]

After witnessing America's splendor of towering New York City skyscrapers, an underground subway system, and a montage of people from different nations, ethnicities, and backgrounds, Matta went home to South Africa where "On Sunday 4th November in the New Brighton hall, scores of people … gathered to welcome her. P. D. Swaartz and Prince Nikiwe accompanied Matta for this celebratory occasion."[68] Speeches, music, and dance demonstrations filled the night. In 1930, Tshabalala and Makanya came back together on the same vessel headed to South Africa after changing boats in Southampton, England. Not long after they arrived in Durban, receivers held a grand reception in their honor at the Methodist Church. Tshabalala seized the opportunity to render an inspiring speech.[69] An offer to serve as the first African female grantee formed another part of Tshabalala's welcome, but she turned down the position "to serve her own people—the Africans. She left Durban for her place: 'Kwa Zamonwake' (Kleinfontein) just three miles from Driefontein".[70]

Soga's return mirrored the extensive overseas tour that she carried out while abroad. Her South African adventure began in Johannesburg. She spoke before a racially mixed crowd downtown at the Bantu Men's Social Centre on Eloff Street. At another event 600 people honored Soga with showers "during a triumphal tour of South Africa where … she bought a blessing to white and black alike".[71] Perhaps:

> the most compelling meeting took place at the Wilberforce Institute, an educational center that the Maxekes, Marshall, and Charlotte along with assistance from the African Methodist Episcopal Church, established for their brothers and sisters on the continent. "[The Wilberforce Institute] experience was one of the most delightful opportunities of her African tour. It was the place where her year in America, her time in Madras, and her return home all seemed to have special significance."[72]

During a school event where its skeptical principal thought to himself, "A woman speaker today. That's very unusual. We never have women speakers. Who can this woman be? African, they say—that's even more unusual for there are so few African women able to speak. And a princess, they say—but we don't have princesses any more! (sic) What will she speak about—religion?"[73] The guest soon taught the principal and the students a valuable lesson:

> In response to [the] introduction and the tumultuous applause that followed, Miss Soga rose and stepped smiling to the front of the stage. Just at that moment the door beside the platform suddenly opened and six or eight seniors looked in, saw that there was no room, and hastily withdrew. At once Miss Soga said to the principal, "Please call those young men in. I have something I want to say to them." A little astonished, the principal directed one of the teachers to call the boys back. They came, looking a little sheepish and feeling a bit conspicuous. Very dramatically, beckoning them expressively with her whole arm, and yet smiling all the time, Miss Soga said, "Please come in and stand right there. I have something important to say." Then she looked very serious. "When did you get too proud to sit on the floor?" she asked. "Since when have Africans required chairs to sit? Is there one of you in whose home there are enough chairs for everybody? I don't believe it. Are you too soft? Or is it beneath your dignity to sit on the floor in the presence of your elders or even your peers? I saw a teacher the other day too proud to carry his books, with a little boy running along obsequiously at his side carrying them. I was shocked. What is our country coming

> to? What is happening to education if that is so? Dignity is a strange thing—there is a right kind of dignity and a wrong kind. The dignity of labor and the pride of self-respect must be retaught to young Africa." [74]

By the time the speech concluded, Soga's stern critic had changed his original tune as this glowing comment conveys, "if this is Africa, my motherland, I am proud to be a son of Africa".[75] The principal turned a new leaf simply because Soga's passion, message, and style kept him captivated. She also reminded the youth and the principal of a heritage filled with integrity and pride. Despite leading one of the most prominent female organizations of her time, the years reduced Soga to a small figure "who was forced to eke out a living in dire circumstances, despite having been engaged in many causes that pushed for an increase for Black pensioners".[76] Soga's contribution to South African politics appeared to end unspectacularly with poverty encapsulating her 'send-off' from this world to the eternal one.

Send-offs

Send-offs (treatment after death) consist of commemoration and eulogies. Some examples illustrate both occurrences. For example, Seabury published one of few sources that capture Soga's travels abroad. *Daughter of Africa* is a collaboration between Seabury, the author, and Soga, the willing subject.

> Realizing Miss Soga's greatness afresh one day when we were together, I [Seabury]had asked her, 'Are there many great personalities among the women of South Africa?' 'Oh, yes', she said, 'a number, and in many walks of life'. 'And they, I suppose', said I, 'represent much of Africa's future hope'.[77]

The minute that Seabury published this book in 1945, Soga became a scholarly and theoretical subject. This went beyond Seabury's offering to include the Mina Soga Missionary Societies (MSMS) that sprung up all over the United States. For example, Indiana's Pleasant Union Lutheran Church's MSMS brought women together to discuss 'Growing as World Friends'.[78] Soga's overseas trips and her philosophy as NCAW President encapsulated the spirit in which Pleasant Union Lutheran's Church embodied and professed.

Honorifics also came in the form of scholarly research. Healy-Clancy brought Tshabalala from the margin to the center with her analysis of her transatlantic kinship ties. Curry drew on literary corpus to explore how she defined, diagnosed, and prognosed the nation. Still even with their scholarship, this historical figure deserves a full-length biography that situates her even further within the global struggle for freedom that goes beyond the transatlantic paradigm to examine her missionary work in the Gold Coast and in London, England. The NCAW preserved its minutes whereas the DOA's remain hidden within files like those at the National Archives of South Africa in Pretoria, or they are lost to history. They could provide a more intimate road map to the DOA's governance, trajectory, evolution, and legacy. Makanya supplied this type of information and left her voice in several places. For instance, when Makanya participated at NEC hearings, she advocated for cultural retention, while also accommodating changes in modernity. She spoke yet again through the BYL's organizational documents, and through journals like *The South African Outlook* and newspaper outlets such as *Umteteli waBantu* and the *Bantu World*, print mediums where the Natal leader etched out the theories and the principles that guided her application of *isivivane*. Myrtle Trowbridge's biographical account supplements and complements the theses and dissertations written by Umehani Khan and Brandy Thomas. The next step is for a full-length book either in the form of Ohio University's Short History Series or another form so that Makanya gets her due for greater analysis.

Maxeke has also garnered the attention of several chroniclers. Thozama April wrote an award-winning thesis that documents not only Maxeke's life but also her intellectual one. Zubeida Jaffer's *Beauty of the Heart* traces Maxeke's life from her childhood to her last days on earth. Like Thozama's work, Jaffer's offering is methodologically sound as she provides a framework that juxtaposes her contributions alongside men and the changing political climate under segregation. Accolades continue to follow Maxeke even in death. In 1939, when Maxeke passed away at the age of sixty-five, journalist Walter M. B. Nhlapo wrote a eulogy in poetic form that appeared in the *Bantu World*. It read[79]:

O lady great! Art thou gone
To where golden light of the day is fair
No night to dull the perfumed air
Where with kins thou'll not be lone?
In the land of fadeless day
With lasting sights and perfumed breeze
Hills in tapestry and calm blue seas
O thou art gone there to stay.
Sleep! Thou art happy and free

With radiant wings, thou shalt ee'r be
They people wait for those in blue sky
And what is our grief to thee
To fadeless daylight thou'rt gone
Where there's life and glory, dance, and song
Of Africans and heavenly throng
Go home! Thou art not alone!
When though art in land of sunshine
And we seem to hear they voice once more
From those scented realms of glowing shore
Be spirit to this land which's thine.
Sleep lady! We shall meet again
Thine grave we bedeck with richest flowers
Which the sunny day rears in our flowers,
Thou wilt not be lur'd again.

Nhlapo describes the place where Maxeke entered upon transitioning. He captures nature and its abundance of sunshine, an array of beautiful flowers, and a fadeless daylight. Nhlapo punctuates this home-going with dance and song. Maxeke triumphantly goes on to her glory with the nature's warmth and its charm wrapping themselves around her. She becomes one again with the earth, which differed for those that Plaatje and Adelaide Charles Dube feature in their respective works which critiqued the 1913 Natives Land Act.

Pretoria's Groen Kloof Nature Reserve, by contrast, immortalizes the leader with a life-sized bronzed statue portraying Maxeke in her best attire with one hand over the other. This monument is poetry in visual form. For it shows Maxeke among the people she had valiantly championed.[80] The Charlotte Mannya-Maxeke Institute (CMMI) "[which] preserves, promotes, elevates, and leverages the legacy left behind by Mme Charlotte" is another reenactment of Maxeke's legacy. The CMMI and the University of South Africa (UNISA) gives the Charlotte Mannya-Maxeke Award which Thozama won for her groundbreaking work on her as an intellectual figure in 2019.[81] Streets also honored some of these African women like Maxeke and Mkhize whose own quest to save the nation replaced the names of figures of apartheid lore (Figs. 9.1 and 9.2).[82]

Accolades also poured in for Mpama. The ANC awarded Mpama the highly prestigious Order of Luthuli Award for her life-long activism. Scholarship also immortalized her legacy. Edgar's pocket-sized book packs a powerful intellectual punch. His interrogation and homage address the

Fig. 9.2 http://www.auswhn.org.au/blog/charlotte-maxeke/ date accessed 28 November 2021

multi-dimensional ways that Mpama fought for social justice as a mother, as a grandmother, as a community organizer, as a churchwoman, and as a healer. Edgar meticulously reads all of her intricacies. Like her colleagues, "Josie was indeed an 'untidy hero'[83] who troubled the waters and challenged racial, ethnic, gender, and class conventions and boundaries—set by segregation and apartheid or by communities themselves".[84] We learned through these activist intellectuals how Africa stabbed itself; how the loss of land led to social death; how the nation, a spiritual living being, represented the wealthy, the impoverished, and the in-between; and how cultural art forms of poetry, songs, and editorials provided blueprints for the future. Throughout all of their angst, pain, and hope, their intellectual soundtrack kept playing the same tune: the African nation must be saved. They 'sung' this refrain repeatedly to the state and to their people's soul like the thundering chant of *Senzeni na* (What have we done?) would reverberate at apartheid's dawn.

Notes

1. Nomabunu's article discussed.
2. Robert R. Edgar, *Freedom in Our Lifetime: The Collected Writings of Anton Muziwakhe Lembede* (Athens: Ohio University Press, 1996), 21.
3. Cecilia Lillian Tshabalala, 'Other Women,' contd., *Bantu World*, January 22, 1938, 11.
4. Inkulumoka KaNkosikazi A. J. L. Dube.
5. "Daughters of Africa in Maritzburg Amalgamation, the War Discussed," *Ilanga laseNatal*, February 1, 1941, 9.
6. Ibid.
7. Ibid.
8. Letter to Edith Rheinallt Jones from Eleanor Hlahle, National Council of African Women, Organisations, AD843/RJ/Pn 2.2, Historical Papers, Cullen Library, University of the Witwatersrand.
9. National Council of African Women, Organisations, Cullen Library, University of the Witwatersrand, AD843/RJ/Pn2.1.
10. Letter to Mrs. Rheinallt Jones from Mina Soga, 27 July 1942, National Council of African Women, Organisations, AD843/RJ/Pn 2.2, Historical Papers, Cullen Library, University of the Witwatersrand.
11. Ibid.
12. James Farmer, *Lay Bare the Heart: An Autobiography of the Civil Rights Movement* (San Antonio: Texas Christian University, 1998), 55–60.
13. Letter to Dr. Alfred B. Xuma from Cecilia Lillian Tshabalala, "South African Institute of Race Relations (SAIRR) AD843." Historical Papers, Cullen Library, University of the Witwatersrand.
14. Bertha Mkhize Interview, A. Manson and D. Collins, interviewers, Oral History Programme, Killie Campbell library, KCAV151, August 14, 22, 1979.
15. Peter Limb, *The ANC's Early Years*, 263.
16. Ray Alexander (Simons), https://jwa.org/encyclopedia/article/alexander-simons-ray, date accessed 6 March 2021.
17. Dr. Abdullah Abdurrahman, https://www.sahistory.org.za/people/dr-abdullah-abdurahman, date accessed 1 November 2021.
18. Zainunnisa 'Cissie' Gool: The Jewel of District Six, https://capetownmuseum.org.za/they-built-this-city/zainunnisa-cissie-gool/ date accessed 2 April 2021.
19. Ray Alexander (Simons).
20. A. Manson and D. Collins, Bertha Mkhize Interview and P. E. Raper, *Dictionary of Southern African Place Name* (London: Jonathan Ball Publishers, 1989) 330 opp. cited, https://en.wikipedia.org/wiki/Ndwedwe, 8 June 2021.
21. A. Manson and D. Collins, Bertha Mkhize interview.

22. Amadodakazi kwaZulu (Daughters in KwaZulu), *Ilanga lase Natal* (August 31, 1946), 4. Translations conducted by Mpumelelo MaBiyela Bhengu Ngizoke ngithi qaphu ngo hambo lwethu, ngezomhlangano wamaDodakazi ase Afrika. Ngomhla ka July 19, 1946 sehla Eshowe sathatha iBus eliqonde Entumeni. Ngahamba neNkosazana yodumo uMiss Bertha Mkhize. Lentokazi ngiyifunde ngokunye nje Ngangihamba ngesaba, phela ngise Umuntu wase silangweni Kwa Zulu. Cabo bo idumbe lesiZulu lahlungile kuye, lapho kuhanjwa ibanga phansi kuye kulungile. Izikhalizakhe zisolimini, cha induku nemali. Ngisho njalo ngoba lezindawo esa sikuzo nganginvola lokuthi ngexe sa ukeleke kahle. Ngisho njalo ngoba lezindawo esa sikuzo nganginvola lokuthi ngexe sa ukeleke kahle.
23. Ibid.
24. Umbumbi wePimville.
25. Lavinia Scott, General Letter, Adams, June 7, 1933, written by Lavinia Scott, 1907–1959, in American Board of Commissioners for Foreign Missions Papers, Harvard University, Houghton Library, ABC 77.1, Box 47, individual biography (hereafter Lavinia Scott letter) and The Chapel Then and Now, https://inanda.org/events/inanda-stories/94-the-chapel-its-place-in-the-life-of-the-school.html#:~:text=American-born%20Dr%20Lavinia%20Scott%20set%20sail%20for%20South,thereafter%20becoming%20head%20of%20the%20school%20in%, date accessed 7 June 2021.
26. Ibid.
27. Sibusisiwe Makanya, Social Needs of Modern Native Life, *South African Outlook* (September 1, 1931): 167–168.
28. Mina Tembeka Soga, "The Need for the Missionary Today: His Place and Function," *IRM* 28, (1939): 217–220.
29. Ruth Isabel Seabury, *Daughter of Africa*, 113.
30. "Ideas of a Zula Woman."
31. Alondra Nelson—'Afrofuturism: Past-Future Visions' (22nd of Oct), https://blog.bham.ac.uk/englitpostgrad/2019/10/15/alondra-nelson-afrofuturism-past-future-visions-22nd-of-oct/ date accessed 15 April 2020.
32. "Miss C. L. Tshabalala's Address: Other Women," *Bantu World* (January 15, 1938), 11.
33. Meghan Healy-Clancy, "The Daughters of Africa and Transatlantic Racial Kinship," 486.
34. Ruth Isabel Seabury, *Daughter of Africa*, 73.
35. See Janet Cherry, *Spear of the Nation: Umkhonto WeSizwe, South Africa's Liberation Army, 1960s–1990s* (Athens: Ohio University, 2011).
36. See Alan Brooks, *Whirlwind before the storm: The origins and development of the uprising in Soweto and the rest of South Africa from June to December 1976* (International Defence and Aid Fund for Southern Africa, 1980),

Lynda Schuster, *A Burning Hunger: One Family's Struggle against Apartheid* (Athens: Ohio University Press, 2004), Pat Hopkins and Helen Grange, *The Rocky Rioter Teargas Show: The Inside Story of the 1976 Soweto Uprising* (Cape Town: Zebra, 2001), Noor Nieftagodien, *The Soweto Uprising* (Athens: Ohio University Press, 2014), Sifiso Ndlovu, *The Soweto Uprisings: Counter Memories of June 1976* (New York: Pan Macmillan South Africa, 2017), and Julian Brown, *The Road to Soweto: Resistance and the Uprising of 16 June 1976* (Suffolk: James Currey Publishers, 2016).

37. "Solomon Mahlangu," https://somafcotrust.org.za/about-the-trust-2/solomon-mahlangu/ date accessed 26 May 2021.
38. Lauretta Ngcobo, *Prodigal Daughters: Stories of South African Women in Exile* (Scottsville: University of KwaZulu/Natal Press, 2012), 24, 25, 26, 83.
39. Ibid., 24–26.
40. Duma Nokwe, The Meaning of Bantu Education, https://sahistory.org.za/sites/default/files/DC/Lin954.1729.455X.000.009.1954.7/Lin954.1729.455X.000.009.1954.7.pdf, date accessed 26 May 2021.
41. Lauretta Ngcobo, *Prodigal Daughters*, 24.
42. "Facing Facts."
43. Ruth Isabel Seabury, *Daughter of Africa*, 139.
44. Glimpses of Native Life in South Africa, Radio Talk by Sibusisiwe Makanya, 2.
45. Sisonke Msimang, *Always Another Country* (New York: World Editions, 2017), 126–137.
46. See Kwame Nkrumah's Vision of Africa, https://www.bbc.co.uk/worldservice/people/highlights/000914_nkrumah.shtml#:~:text=Nkrumah%20was%20born%20Kwame%20Francis%20Nwia%20Kofie%20in,was%20demanding%20freedom%20and%20independence%20for%20the%20colonies, date accessed 4 March 2021, Lansine Kaba, *Kwame Nkrumah and the Dream of African Unity|* (New York: Diasporic Africa Press, 2017), MulukenTeshager Abegaz, OAU 1966: Organization of African Unity (South Carolina: CreateSpace Independent Publishing Platform, 2017), and Jeffrey S. Ahlman, *Kwame Nkrumah: Voices of Liberation* (Athens: Ohio University Press, 2021).
47. Lauretta Ngcobo, *Prodigal Daughters*, 73–92.
48. Ibid., 91.
49. Women's World Congress for Peace and Liberty, Organisations, Cullen Library, Historical Papers, AD 843/RJ/Pw2.
50. David Killingray, Significant Black South Africans in Britain before 1912, 404.
51. Vijay Prashad, *The Darker Nations: A People's History of the Third World* (New York: The New Press, 2007), 54–55.

52. Ibid.
53. Keshia N. Blain, Madam C.J. Walker wasn't just a positive force for African Americans. She also pioneered global black activism, https://timeline.com/madame-cj-walker-history-50d6d7090076, date accessed 16 September 2021.
54. Keshia N. Blain and Tiffany M. Gill, *To Turn the World Over*, 2.
55. Ula Yvette Taylor, *The Veiled Garvey: The Life & Times of Amy Jacques Garvey* (Chapel Hill: University of North Carolina Press, 2002), 151.
56. Alfred B. Xuma, 'The African Charter,' Xuma Papers, ABX
57. Ula Yvette Taylor, *The Veiled Garvey*, 154.
58. Ibid.
59. Maria Martin, "More Power to Your Great Self": Nigerian Women's Activism and the Pan-African Transnationalist Construction of Black Feminism, *Phylon*, 53, 2 (Winter 2016): 54–78.
60. Robert R. Edgar, *Josie Mpama/Palmer*, 177.
61. C. L. Tshabalala, "What is the Club Woman?" *Bantu World*, April 4, 1936, 12.
62. Ruth Isabel Seabury, *Daughter of Africa*, 142.
63. Robert R. Edgar, *Josie Mpama/Palmer*, 177.
64. Ula Yvette Taylor, *The Veiled Garvey*, 154.
65. See Colin Grant, *Negro with a Hat: The Rise and Fall of Marcus Garvey* (Oxford: Oxford University Press, 2010).
66. Brandy S. Thomas, 'Give Them Their Due,' 32.
67. Ibid.
68. Translation by Nomvula Sikakane, Reporter from the Eastern Cape Ngu "Qalazive" wese Bhai, Ulwamukelo luka Rilda Matta (sic) e Bhai (The welcoming of Rilda (Matta sic) in the Eastern Cape), *Umteteli waBantu*, November 17, 1934, 11.
69. Viyella, Miss L. C. (sic) Tshabalala's Career, *Bantu World*, March 14, 1936, 10.
70. Ibid.
71. Ruth Isabel Seabury, *Daughter of Africa*, 1–4.
72. Ibid.
73. Ibid., 1, 2.
74. Ibid., 3, 4.
75. Ibid., 4.
76. Janet Hodgson, *Black Womanism in South Africa: Princess Emma Sandile* (Cape Town: Best Red, 2021), xviii.
77. Ruth Isabel Seabury, *Daughter of Africa*, 134.
78. "Pleasant Union Church to Make Aprons," *Indiana Gazette*, May 26, 1959, 8.

79. Walter M. B. Nhlapo, Mrs. Charlotte M. Maxeke, B. Sc., *Bantu World*, December 2, 1939, 9.
80. Zubeida Jaffer, *Beauty of the Heart*, 13.
81. The Charlotte Mannya-Maxeke Institute, About CMMI, https://cmmi.org.za/, date accessed 30 May 2021 and Dr. Thozama April awarded The Charlotte Mannya-Maxeke Award, https://www.chrflagship.uwc.ac.za/dr-thozama-april-awarded-the-charlotte-mannya-maxeke-award/#:~:text=Dr%20Thozama%20April%20awarded%20The%20Charlotte%20Mannya%20Maxeke,in%20documenting%20the%20life%20history date accessed 30 May 2021.
82. Charlotte Maxeke: Tireless campaigner for women's rights, http://www.auswhn.org.au/blog/charlotte-maxeke/, date accessed 28 November 2021.
83. *The Star*, November 19, 2012, opp. cited Robert R. Edgar, *Josie Mpama/Palmer*, 20.
84. Robert R. Edgar, *Josie Mpama/Palmer*, 11, 168.

Bibliography

Primary Sources

Newspapers
African Drum
Bantu Forum
Bantu World
Cape Standard
Drum Magazine
Guardian
Ilanga Lase Natal (Natal Sun)
Inkululeko (Freedom)
Inkundla ya Bantu
Rand Daily Mail
Star (Johannesburg)
UmAfrika
Umsebenzi (The Worker)
Umteteli wa Bantu (The African Mouthpiece)
World
Workers Voice

Papers

Historical Papers, Cullen Library, University of the Witwatersrand, Johannesburg, South Africa

D. Y. Curry, *Social Justice at Apartheid's Dawn*, African Histories and Modernities, https://doi.org/10.1007/978-3-030-85404-1

Dr. Alfred B. Xuma Papers
John David Rheinallt Papers
Helen Joseph Papers
National Council of African Women
Bantu Youth League
Institute for Commonwealth Studies, London, England
Hyman Basner Papers
Josie Palmer Papers
Campbell Collections, Durban, South Africa
Sibusisiwe Makanya Papers
H. M. S. Makanya Papers
Albertina Mnguni Papers
Bertha Mkhize Interviews

Commission Reports

Transvaal Province. T. P. 6-'37 Report of the Johannesburg and Germiston Boundaries Commission Part Three. (Feetham Commission), Pretoria: Government Printer, 1937.

Union Government (UG). Report of the Native Affairs Commission Appointed to Enquire into the Workings of the Provisions of the Native (Urban Areas) Act Relating to the Use and Supply of Kaffir beer. Pretoria: Government Printer, 1925.

UG. 39'25 Report of the Native Affairs Commission. Pretoria: Government Printer, 1925.

———. Report of the Inter-Departmental Committee on the Social, Health and Economic Conditions of Urban Natives (Smit Committee). Pretoria: Government Printer, 1942.

———. 42-'41 Report of the Native Affairs Commission 1939–40. Pretoria: Government Printer, 1932.

———. 31-'44 Report of the Commission Appointed to Inquire into the Operation of Bus Services For Services for Non-Europeans on the Witwatersrand and in the Districts of Pretoria and Vereeniging, 1944. Pretoria: Government Printer, 1944.

University of Witwatersrand, Historical and Literary Papers and Government Publications Libraries.

Secondary Sources

Achebe, Nwando. *Female Monarchs and Merchant Queens in Africa* (Athens: Ohio University Press, 2020).

Adi, Hakim. *Pan-Africanism: A History* (London: Bloomsbury Academic, 2018).

Alexandra, Peter. *War and the Origins of Apartheid: Labour and Politics in South Africa, 1939–48* (Athens: Ohio University Press, 2000).

Atkins, Keletso E. Atkins, Origins of the AmaWasha: the Zulu Washermen's Guild in Natal, 1850–1910, *Journal of African History*, 27, 1 (March 1986): 41–57.

Baines, G. "The Origins of Urban Segregation: Local Government and the Residence of Port Elizabeth c. 1835–1865", *South African Historical Journal*,22, 6 (1990): 61–81.

Baldwin, Alan. "Mass Removals and Separate Development," J*ournal of Southern African Studies,* 1, (1974): 32–46.

Ballentine, Christopher. "Music and Emancipation: The Social Role of Black Jazz and Vaudeville in South Africa between the 1910s and the Early 1940s," *Journal of Southern African Studies*, 17, 1 (March 1991): 25–36.

Ballinger, Mary. *From Union to Apartheid: A Trek to Isolation* (Johannesburg: Witwatersrand University Press, 1969).

Basner, Miriam. *Am I an African? The Political Memoirs of H. M. Basner* (Johannesburg: University of Witwatersrand Press, 1993).

Beinart, William. *Twentieth-Century South Africa* 2nd ed. (Oxford: Oxford University Press, Benson, Mary. *South Africa: The Struggle for a Birthright* (New York: Funk & Wagnalls, 1969).

Berger, Iris. *Women in Twentieth-Century Africa* (Cambridge: Cambridge University Press, 2016).

——— *Threads of Solidarity: Women in South African Industry 1900–1980* (Indianapolis: Indiana University Press, 1992).

———. "Sources of Class Consciousness: South African Women in Recent Labour Struggles," *International Journal of African Historical Studies*,16, 1 (1993): 49–66.

Bernstein, Hilda. *For Their Triumphs and for Their Tears: Women in Apartheid South Africa* (London: International Defence Fund, 1975).

Berry Ramey, Daina. *The Price for Their Pound of Flesh: The Value of the Enslaved, from Womb to Grave, in the Building of a Nation* (New York: Beacon Press, 2017).

Blackwell, Basil. *Unfairly Structured Cities* (Oxford: Oxford University Press, 1994).

Blain, Keshia N. *To Set the World on Fire: Black Nationalist Women and the Global Struggle For Freedom* (Philadelphia: University of Pennsylvania Press, 2018).

Bloch, R. and P. Wilkinson. "Urban Control and Popular Struggle: A Survey of State Urban Policy, 1920–1970," *Africa Perspective*, 20 (1982): 23–37.

Blomley, Nicholas. "Law, Property, and the Geography of Violence: The Frontier, the Survey, and the Grid," *Annals of the Association of American Geographers*, 93, 1 (March, 2003): 121–141.

Bloom, H. "The South African Police: Laws and Powers," *Africa South*, 2, 2 (1958): 63–74.

Blyden, Nemata. *African Americans and Africa: A New History* (New Haven: Yale, 2019).

Boahen, Adu. *African Perspectives on Colonialism* (Baltimore: Johns Hopkins University, 1989).

Bonin, Debby. "Claiming Spaces, Changing Places: Political Violence and Women's Protests in Kwa-Zulu-Natal," *Journal of Southern African Studies*, 26, 2 (June 2000): 301–317.

Bonner, Philip and Noor Nieftagodien. *Alexandra, A History* (Johannesburg: University of Witwatersrand Press, 2008).

Bonner, Philip et al., (eds.). *Holding Their Ground: Class, Locality and Culture in 19th and 20th Century South Africa* (Johannesburg: Ravan and University of the Witwatersrand Press, 1989).

Bonner, Philip. "The Politics of Black Squatter Movements on the Rand, 1944–1952," *Radical History Review* (Winter 1990): 46–60.

———. "Family, Crime and Political Consciousness on the East Rand, 1939–1955," *Journal of Southern African Studies*, 14, 3 (April 1988): 393–420.

Botha, Nico. 'Towards an Engendering of Missiology:' The Life-narrative of Mina Tembeka Soga, *Missionalia*, 31, 1 (2003): 11–21.

Bozzoli, Belinda. *Theatres of Struggle and the End of Apartheid* (Athens: Ohio University).

———. *Women of Phokeng* (Johannesburg: Ravan Press, 1991).

——— (ed.). *Class, Community and Conflict: South African Perspectives* (Johannesburg: Ravan Press, 1987).

——— (ed.). *Town and Countryside in the Transvaal: Capitalist Penetration and Popular Response* (Johannesburg: Ravan Press, 1983).

——— (ed.). *Labour, Townships and Protest: Studies in the Social History of the Witwatersrand* (Johannesburg: Ravan Press, 1979. Press, 2004).

Bradford, Helen. *A Taste of Freedom: The ICU in Rural South Africa, 1924–1930* (Johannesburg: Ravan Press, 1988).

Brandel-Syrier, Mia. *Black Women in Search of God* (London: Lutterworth Press, 1962).

Brooks, Pamela E. *Boycotts, Buses, and Passes: Black Women's Resistance in the U. S. South and South Africa* (Amherst: University of Massachusetts, 2008).

Brown, Duncan Brown. My pen is the Tongue of a Skilful (sic) Poet: African-Christian Identity and the Poetry of Nontsizi Mgqwetho, *English in Africa*, 31, 1 (May 2004): 23–58.

Butler, Kim D. *Freedoms Given, Freedoms Won: Afro-Brazilians in Post Abolition Sao Paulo and Salvador* (New Brunswick: Rutgers 1998).

Callinicos, Luli. *Gold and Workers 1886–1940: Factories, Townships and Popular Culture on the Rand. Volume II. A People's History of South Africa* (Johannesburg: Ravan Press, 1987a).

———. *A Place in the City: The Rand on the Eve of Apartheid: A People's History of South Africa* (Johannesburg: Ravan Press, 1987b).

Campbell, James T. *Songs of Zion: The American Methodist Episcopal Church in the United States* (Chapel Hill: University of North Carolina, 1998).

Cell, John W. *The Highest Stage of White Supremacy: The Origins of Segregation in South Africa and the American South*, Cambridge: Cambridge University Press, 1982.

Christopher, A. J. "Race and Residence in Colonial Port Elizabeth," *South African Geographical Society*, 69, 1 (1987): 3–20.

———. "Segregation Levels in South African Cities, 1911–1985," *International Journal of African Historical Studies*, 25, 3 (1992): 561–582.

———. "The Roots of Urban Segregation: South Africa at Union, 1910." *The Journal of Historical Geography*, 14, 2 (1988): 151–169.

Cobley, Alan Gregor. *Class and Consciousness: The Black Petty Bourgeoisie in South Africa, 1924 to 1950* (New York: Greenwood Press, 1990).

Cobbing, Julian. The Mfecane As Alibi: Thoughts On Dithakong and Mbolompo, *Journal of African History*, 29 (1988): 487–519.

Conference, International Missionary. *The World Mission of the Church: Findings and Recommendations of the Meeting of the International Missionary Council, 4th Meeting, Madras, 1938* (London: International Missionary Council, 1938).

Cooper, Brittney. *Beyond Respectability: The Intellectual Thought of Race Women* (Women, Gender, and Sexuality in American History (Chicago: University of Illinois, 2017).

Coplan, David. *In Township Tonight!* (London: Longman, 1985).

Curry, Dawne Y. "When Apartheid Interfered With Funerals: We Still Found Ways to Grieve in Alexandra, South Africa." *International Journal of Interdisciplinary Social Sciences*, 2, 22 (2007): 245–252.

———. *Apartheid on A Black Isle: Removal and Resistance in Alexandra, South Africa* (New York: Palgrave Macmillan, 2012).

———. "Their World Was A Ghetto:" Space, Power, and Identity in Alexandra's Squatters' Movement in Wendy Z. Goldman and Joe Trotter (ed.). *The Ghetto in Global History: 1500 to the Present* (New York: Routledge, 2018), 277–293.

Davenport, T. R. H. "African Townsmen? South African Natives (Urban Areas) Legislation through the Years," *African Affairs*, 68, 271 (1969): 450–462.

———. "The Triumph of Colonel Stallard: The Transformation of the Natives (Urban Areas) Act between 1923 and 1937," *South African Historical Journal*, 2, (1970): 320–335.

———. "The Beginnings of Urban Segregation in South Africa: The Natives (Urban Areas) Act of 1923 and Its Background." Occasional Paper 15, Institute for Social and Economic Research, Rhodes University (1971).

Dikobe, Modikwe. *Dispossessed* (Johannesburg: Ravan Press, 1983).

Draymond, M. J. et al. *Women Writing Africa: The Southern Region* (New York: Feminist Press, 2003).

Dubow, Saul. *The African National Congress* (Johannesburg: Jonathan Ball Publishers, 2000).

———. "Holding 'a Just Balance Between White and Black': The Native Affairs Department in South Africa, c. 1920–33," *Journal of Southern African Studies*, 12, 2 (April 1986): 217–239.

———. *Racial Segregation and the Origins of Apartheid in South Africa, 1919–1936* (Oxford: Oxford University Press, 1989).

———. "Afrikaner Nationalism, Apartheid and the Conceptualization of 'Race'", *The Journal of African History*, 33, 2 (1992): 209–237.

———. *Scientific Racism in Modern South Africa* (Cambridge: Cambridge University Press, 1995).

———. "Ethnic Euphemisms and Racial Echoes," *Journal of Southern African Studies*, 20, 3 (September 1994): 50–63.

Dudziak, Mary. *Cold War Civil Rights* (Princeton: Princeton University Press, 2002).

Duncan, David. "Liberals and Local Administration in South Africa: Alfred Hoernle and The Alexandra Health Committee, 1933–1943," *International Journal of African Historical Studies.*

Edgar, Robert R. *Josie Mpama/Palmer: Get Up and Get Moving!* (Athens: Ohio University Press, 2021).

——— (ed.). *An African American in South Africa: The Travel Notes of Ralph Bunche* (Athens: Ohio University Press, 1992).

———. *Freedom in Our Lifetime: The Collected Writings of Anton Muziwakhe Lembede* (Athens: Ohio University Press, 1996).

——— and Hilary Sapire. *African Apocalypse: The Story of Nontetha Nkwenkwe, a Twentieth-Century South African Prophet* (Athens: Ohio University, 2000).

Eldredge, Elizabeth. Sources of Conflict in Southern Africa, C. 1800–30: The 'Mfecane' Reconsidered, *The Journal of African History*, 33, 1 (1992): 1–35.

Erlmann, Veit. "Black Political Song in South Africa: Some Research Perspectives," in International Association for the Study of Popular Music, *Popular Music Perspectives* 2. Goteborg: IASPM, 1985.

Everett, David. "Alliance Politics of a Special Type: The Roots of the ANC/SACP Alliance, 1950–1954," *Journal of Southern African Studies*, 18, 1 (March 1991): 19–39.

Fanon, Frantz. *A Dying Colonialism* (New York: Grove Press, 1994.

Farmer, James. *Lay Bare the Heart: An Autobiography of the Civil Rights Movement* (Fort Worth: Texas Christian University Press, 1998).

Fatton, Robert. *Black Consciousness in South Africa: The Dialectics of Ideological Resistance to White Supremacy* (Albany: State University of New York Press, 1986).

Feinberg, Harvey M. "The 1913 Natives Land Act in South Africa: Politics, Race and Segregation in the Early 20th Century," *International Journal of African Historical Studies*, 26, 1 (1993): 65–109.

Feit, Edward. *African Opposition in South Africa: The Failure of Passive Resistance* (Stanford: The Hoover Institution on War, Revolution and Peace, 1967).

———. *Urban Revolt in South Africa, 1960–1964* (Evanston: Northwestern University Press, 1971).

Fortescue, Domenic. "The Communist Party of South Africa and the African Working Class in the 1940's," *International Journal of African Historical Studies*, 24, 3 (1991): 481–512.

Frankel, Philip. "The Politics of Passes: Control and Change in South Africa," *Journal of Modern African Studies*, 17, 2 (June 1979): 199–217.

Fredrickson, George. *White Supremacy: A Comparative Study on American and South African History* (New York: Oxford University Press, 1981).

———. *Black Liberation* (New York: Oxford University Press, 1995).

Gaitskell, Deborah, and Elaine Unterhalter, Mothers of the Nation: A Comparative Analysis of Nation, Race and Motherhood in Afrikaner Nationalism and the African National Congress, in: Yuval-Davis N., Anthias F., Campling J. (eds) *Woman-Nation-State* (New York: Palgrave Macmillan, 1989).

Gaitskell, Deborah. "Hot Meeting and Hard Kraals: African Biblewomen in Transvaal Methodism, 1924–60," *Journal of Religion in Africa*, XXX, 30, 3 (2000): 277–309.

Gasa, Nombonisa (ed.). *Women in South Africa History* (Pretoria: Human Sciences Research Council, 2007.

Gerhart, Gail M. *Black Power in South Africa: The Evolution of an Ideology* (Berkeley: University of California Press, 1978).

Gordon-Chipembere, Natasha (ed.). *Representation and Black Womanhood: The Legacy of Sarah Baartman* (New York: Palgrave Macmillan, 2014).

Gordon, Suzanne. *A Talent for Tomorrow: Life Stories of South African Servants* (Johannesburg: Ravan Press, 1985).

Gqola, Pumla Dineo. "'Like Three Tongues in One Mouth': Tracing the Elusive Lives of Slave Women in (slavocratic) South Africa," in Nombonisa Gasa (ed.), *Women in South Africa History*, 21–31.

Grundlingh, Albert. *Fighting Their Own War: South African Blacks and the First World War* (Johannesburg: Ravan Press, 1987).

Harries, D. (pseudonym). "Daniel Koza: A Working-Class Leader," *Africa Perspective*, 19 (1981): 2–38.

Hart, D. M. "Political Manipulation of Urban Space: The Razing of District Six, Cape Town", *Urban Geography*, 9, (1990): 603–628.

Hassim, Shireen, Hassim. *ANC Women's League* (Athens: Ohio University Press, 20.

———. *Women's Organizations and Democracy in South Africa: Contesting Authority* (Women in Africa and the Diaspora), (Madison: University of Wisconsin Press, 2006).

Healy-Clancy, Meghan. "The Daughters of Africa and Transatlantic Racial Kinship: Cecilia Lilian Tshabalala and the Women's Club Movement, 1912–1943," *Amerikastudien/American Studies*, 59, no. 4 (2014): 481–500.

———. Women and the Problem of Family in Early African Nationalist History and Historiography, *South African Historical Journal*, 64, 3 (2012): 450–471.

________. Meghan Healy-Clancy, "The Self, the Nation, and the World: The Scale of Clubwomen's Work," 24th Biennial conference of the Southern African Historical Society, University of Botswana, Gaborone 27–9 (June 2013).

Hellmann, Elle. *Rooiyard: A Sociological Survey of an Urban Native Slumyard* (Oxford: University Press, 1948).

Hetherington, Penelope. Women in South Africa: The Historiography in English, *The International Journal of African Historical Studies*, 26, 2 (1993): 241–269.

Hine, Darlene Clark. "Rape and the Inner Lives of Black Women in the Middle West: Preliminary Thoughts on the Culture of Dissemblance," *Signs: Journal of Women and Culture in Society*, 14, (Summer 1989): 912–20.

——— Wilma King, and Linda Reed (eds.). *'We Specialise in the Wholly Impossible': A Black Women's Reader* (New York: New York University Press, 1995).

——— and Jacqueline McCleod. Darlene Clark Hine and Jacqueline McCleod, *Crossing Boundaries: Comparative History of Black People in Diaspora* (Bloomington: Indiana University Press, 2001).

Hirson, Baruch. *Yours for the Union: Class and Community Struggles in South Africa, 1930–1947* (Johannesburg: University of the Witwatersrand, 1989).

———. *Year of Fire, Year of Ash* (London: Zed, 1979).

Hoare, Quinten and Geoffrey Novell (eds.). *Selections from the Prison Notebooks of Antonio Gramsci* (New York: International Publishers, 1971).

Holmes, Rachel. *The Hottentot Venus: The Life and Death of Sarah Baartman* (London: Bloomsbury, 2007).

Horrell, Muriel. *The Pass Laws* (Johannesburg: South African Institute of Race Relations, 1960).

Huddleston, Trevor. *Naught for Your Comfort* (Johannesburg: Hardingham and Donaldson, 1956).

Hughes, Heather. *First President: A Life of John L. Dube, Founding President of the African National Congress* (Bloomington: Indiana University, 2012).

Hyslop, Johnathan. "Teacher Resistance in African Education from the 1940s to the 1980s." in Mokubung Nkomo, ed., *Pedagogy of Domination: Toward a Democratic Education in South Africa* (Trenton: Africa World Press, 1990).

———. "State Education Policy and the Social Representation of the Urban Working Class: The Case of the Southern Transvaal 1955–1976," *Journal of Southern African Studies* 14, 3 (April 1988): 446–476.

Jaffer, Zubeida, *Beauty of the Heart: The Life and Times of Charlotte Mannya Maxeke* (Cape Town: ZJBooks, 2016).

Jaji, Tsitsi Ella. *Africa in Stereo: Modernism, Music, and Pan-African Solidarity* (Oxford: Oxford University Press, 2014).

Joseph-Gabriel, Annette K. Feminist Networks and Diasporic Practices: Eslanda Robeson's Travels in Africa in Keshia N. Blain and Tiffany M. Gill (eds.) *To Turn the Whole World Over: Black Women and Internationalism* (Chicago: University of Illinois Press, 2018).

Karis, Thomas and Gwendolyn Carter. *From Protest to challenge: Documents in South African Politics, 1882–1964*, Vols. 1–3 (Berkeley: University of California Press, 1977).

Kelley, Robin D. G. "'We are Not What We Seem': Rethinking Black Working Class Opposition in the Jim Crow South," *Journal of American History*, 80 (June 1993): 75–112.

———. *Race Rebels: Culture and Politics of the Black Working Class* (New York: Free Press, 1994).

Kirk, Joyce. "A 'Native' Free State at Korsten: Challenge to Segregation in Port Elizabeth, 1901–1905," *International Journal of African Historical Studies*, 17, 2 (June 1991): 309–336.

———. *Making a Voice: African Resistance to Segregation in South Africa*. Boulder: Westview Press, 1988.

Khosa, Meshack M. "Changing Patterns of 'Black' Bus Subsidies in the Apartheid City, 1944–198," *Geo Journal*, 22 (1990): 251–259.

———. "Routes, Ranks and Rebels: Feuding in the Taxi Revolution," *Journal of Southern African Studies*, 18, 1 (March 1992): 232–251.

Killingray, David Killingray. Significant Black South Africans in Britain before 1912: Pan-African Organisations and the Emergence of South Africa's First Black Lawyers, *South African Historical Journal*, 64, 3 (2012): 393–417.

Kuper, Leo. *An African Bourgeoisie: Race, Class and Politics in South Africa* (New Haven: Yale University Press, 1967).

———. *Passive Resistance in South Africa* (New Haven: Yale University Press, 1957).

Kuumba, M. Bahati. "You've Struck a Rock:! Comparing Gender, Social Movements, and Transformation in the United States and South Africa." *Gender and Society*, 4, 16 (August 2002): 503–523.

Kuzwayo, Ellen. *Call Me Woman* (London: The Women's Press, 1985).

LaHausse, Paul. *Brewers, Beerhalls and Boycotts: A History of Liquor in South Africa*, History Workshop Topics Series 2 (Johannesburg: Ravan Press, 1988).

Lefebvre, Henri. *The Production of Space*, Translated by Donald Nicholson-Smith. (Massachusetts: Blackwell Publishing, 1974, 1984).

Lerumo, A. (pseudonym for Michael Harmel). *Fifty Fighting Years: The Communist Party of South Africa, 1921–1971* (London: Inkululeko Publications, 1971).

Lewis, Desiree. Introduction: African Feminisms, *Agenda: Empowering Women for Gender Equity,* 16, 50 (2001): 4–10.

Lindfors, Bernth. *Early African Entertainments Abroad: From the Hottentot Venus to Africa's First Olympians* (Africa and the Diaspora: History, Politics, Culture) (Madison: University of Wisconsin, 2014).

Lodge, Tom. *Black Politics in South Africa since 1945* (London: Longman, 1983).

Luthuli, Albert. *Let My People Go* (New York: McGraw Hill, 1962 Reprint ed. New York: Meridian Books, 1969).

Mabin, Alan. "Comprehensive Segregation: The Origins of the Group Areas Act and Its Planning Initiatives," *Journal of Southern African Studies*, 18, 2 (June 1992): 405–429.

Mandela, Nelson. *The Long Walk to Freedom* (Johannesburg: Ravan Press, 1994).

Marcus, Harold G. *A History of Ethiopia* (Los Angeles: University of California Press, 2002).

Marks, Shula. *The Ambiguities of Dependence in South Africa: Class, Nationalism, And the State in Twentieth Century Natal* (London: Longman, 1986).

———. *Not Either an Experimental Doll: The Separate Worlds of Three South African Women* (Bloomington: Indiana University Press, 1987).

Martin, Maria, "More Power to Your Great Self": Nigerian Women's Activism and the Pan-African Transnationalist Construction of Black Feminism, *Phylon*, 53, 2 (Winter 2016): 54–78.

Marx, Anthony. *Making Race and Nation: A Comparison of South Africa, the United States and Brazil* (Cambridge: Cambridge University Press, 1998).

———. *Lessons of Struggle: South African Internal Opposition, 1960–1990* (New York: Oxford University Press, 1992).

Mashala, Keona. *Were women hidden from South Africa's political history?: A Life History of Mina Thembeka Soga.* MA thesis, University of Johannesburg, Johannesburg, South Africa, 2020.

Masola, Athambile, "Bantu women on the move": Black women and the politics of mobility in The Bantu World, *Historia*, 63, 1, (May 2018): 93–111.

Mathabane, Mark. *Kaffir Boy: The True Story of A Black Youth's Coming of Age in Apartheid South Africa* (New York: Free Press, 1986).

Mather, C. T. "Racial Segregation and Johannesburg's 'Location in the sky,'" South African *Geographical Journal*, 69, (1987): 119–128.

McCarthy, Jeff and Mark Swilling. "Transport and Political Resistance," *South African Review*, 2 (1984): 26–44.

McCarthy, Jeff. "SA's Emerging Pattern of Bus Transportation," *Political Geography Quarterly*, 5 (1985): 235–249.

McCord, Margaret. *The Calling of Katie Makanya* (Cape Town: David Philip, 1995).

McGee, Holly Y., McGee. *Radical Antiapartheid Internationalism and Exile: The Life of Elizabeth Mafeking* (London: Routledge Press, 2019).

Mokonyane, Dan. *Lessons of Azikhwelwa* (London: Nakong ya Rena, 1994).

Mooney, Katie. Katie Mooney, Amadodakazi – Baradi Ba Africa (Daughters of Africa) Overview and Archival Records at NARSSA, unpublished paper, 2018.

Morrell, Robert. "Of Boys and Men: Masculinity and Gender in South African Society." *Journal of Southern African Studies*, 24, 4 (December 1988): 605–630.

Mufson, Stephen. *Fighting Years: Black Resistance and the Struggle for a New South Africa* (Boston: Beacon Press, 1990).

Ngcukaitobi, Tembeka. *The Land is Sours: South Africa's First Black Lawyers and the Birth of Constitutionalism* (Century City: Penguin Random House, 2018).

Odendaal, Andre. *Vukani Bantu! The Beginnings of Black Protest Politics in South Africa to 1912* (Cape Town and Johannesburg: David Phillip, 1984).

Odim, Cheryl, and Nina Emma Mba. F*or Women and the Nation: Funmilayo Ransome-Kuti of Nigeria* (Chicago: University of Illinois Press, 1997).

Olwage, Grant. John Knox Bokwe, Colonial Composer: Tales about Race and Music, *Journal of the Royal Musical Association*, 131, 1 (2006): 1–37.

Opland, Jeff. *The Nation's Bounty: The Xhosa Poetry of Nontsizi Mgqwetho* (Johannesburg: University of Witwatersrand Press, 2007).

Painter, Nell Irvin. *Sojourner Truth: A Life, A Symbol* (New York: W. W. Norton, 1996).

Parnell, Susan. "Public Housing as a Device for White Residential Segregation in Johannesburg, 1934–1953." *Urban Geography*, 9, 6 (November–December 1988): 345–360.

———. "Creating Racial Privilege: The Origins of South Africa Public Health and Town Planning Legislation," *Journal of Southern African Studies*, 19, 3 (September 1993): 471–488.

Town Planning Legislation. "Sanitation, Segregation and the Natives (Urban Areas) Act: African Exclusion from Johannesburg's Malay Location, 1897–1925," *Journal of African Historical Geography*, 17, (July 1991): 271–288.

———. "Racial Segregation in Johannesburg: The Slums Act 1934–1939," *South African Geographical Journal*, 70 (1986): 112–126.

Patterson, Orlando. *Slavery and Social Death: A Comparative Study* (Cambridge: Harvard University Press, 2018).

Pile, Steve and Michael Keith. *Geographies of Resistance* (London: Routledge, 1997).

Pirie, G. H. "Ethno-linguistic Zoning in South African Black Townships", *Area*, 16, 4 (1988): 462–523.

———. "Rolling Segregation into Apartheid: South African Railways, 1948–1953," *Journal of Contemporary History*, 27 (October 1992): 671–693.

———. "The Transformation of Johannesburg's Western Areas," J*ournal of Urban History*, 11 (August 1985): 387–410.

———. "Urban Population Removals in South Africa," *Geography*, 68, (1983): 347–349.

Piven, Frances Fox. *Poor People's Movements: Why They Succeed, How They Fail* (New York: Vintage, 1979).

Plaatje, Solomon T. *Native Life in South Africa Before and Since the European War And the Boer Rebellion* (London: P. S. King and Sons, Ltd, 1920).

Platzky, L. and Cherryl Walker. *The Surplus People: Forced Removals in South Africa* (Johannesburg: Surplus Peoples Project 1985).

Posel, Deborah. "Rethinking the 'Race-Class Debate' in South African Historiography," *Social Dynamics*, 9, 1 (1983).

———. "The Meaning of Apartheid before 1948: Conflicts of Interests and Powers Within the Afrikaner Nationalist Alliance," *Journal of Southern African Studies*, 14, 1, (1987): 154–166.

———. *The Making of Apartheid* (Oxford: Oxford University Press, 1991).

Prashad, Vijay. *The Darker Nations: A People's History of the Third World* (New York: The New Press, 2007.

Ranger, Terrence. Thompson Samakange: Tambaram and Beyond, *Journal of Religion in Africa*, 23, 4 (1993): 318–346.

Rich, Paul. "Ministering to the White Man's Needs: The Development of Urban Segregation in South Africa, 1913–1923," *African Studies*, 37, 2 (1978): 444–465.

———. "Apartheid Theory, 1930–1939," *Journal of Southern African Studies*, 7, 2 (Summer 1980): 120–134.

Robeson, Eslanda. *African Journey* (New York: The John Day Company, 1945).

Robinson, Jennifer. "A Perfect System of Control? State Power and 'Native Locations' in South Africa"; Environment and Planning, *Changing Society and Space*, 8 (1990): 135–162.

———. *The Power of Apartheid: State, Power, and Space in South African Cities* (Oxford: Heinemann, 1996).

Robnett, Belinda. *How Long? How Long?: African American Women in the Struggle for Civil Rights* (Oxford: Oxford University Press, 1997).

Rogaly, Joe. "The Bus Boycott," *The Forum*, (March 1957): 11–15.

Roux, Edward. *Time Longer than Rope: A History of the Black Man's Struggle for Freedom in South Africa* (Madison: University of Wisconsin Press, 1966).

Rule, Peter. *Nokukhanya: Mother of Light* (Braamfontein: The Grail, 1993).

Sapire, Hilary. "Apartheid's Testing Ground: Urban 'Native Policy' and African Politics in Brakpan, South Africa, 1943–1948," *Journal of African History*, 35, 1 (1994): 99–123.

Savage, Michael. "The Imposition of the Pass Laws on the South African Population in South Africa," *African Affairs*, 85, 339 (April 1986): 181–205.

Scott, James. C. *Weapons of the Weak* (New Haven: Yale University Press, 1985).

———. *Domination and the Arts of Resistance*: Hidden Transcripts (New Haven: Yale University Press, 1990).

———. *Seeing Like a State: How Certain Schemes Have Failed* (New Haven: Yale University, 1999).

Scott, Joan Wallach. Gender: A Useful Category of Historical Analysis, *The American Historical Review*, 91, 5 (December 1986): 1053–1075.

Seabury, Ruth Isabel. *Daughter of Africa* (Boston: Pilgrim Press, 1945).

Simons, H. J. & R. E. Simons. *Class and Colour in South Africa 1850–1950* (Baltimore: Penguin Books, 1969).

Sithole, Nkosinathi. Beyond African nationalism: Isaiah Shembe's Hymns and African Literature, *Literator*, 35, 1 (November 2014): 1–8.

Stadler, Alfred. "Birds in the Cornfield: Squatter Movements in Johannesburg, 1944–47," *Journal of Southern African Studies*, 6, 1 (1979): 360–372.

———. "A Long Way to Walk: Bus Boycotts in Alexandra, 1940–1945." In Phil Bonner (ed). *Working Papers in Southern African Studies*, (1981): 228–257.

Swanson, M. "The Sanitation Syndrome: Bubonic Plague and Urban Native Policy in the Cape Colony, 1900–1909," *Journal of African History*, 18 (1977): 44–56.

———. "The Politics of Subsistence: Community Struggles in War-time Johannesburg." In D. Hindson (ed.), *Working Papers in Southern African Studies* (Johannesburg, Ravan Press, 1983).

Switzer, Les. "The Ambiguities of Protest in South Africa: Rural Politics and the Press During the 1920's," *International Journal of African Historical Studies*, 23, 1 (1990): 87–109.

———. "Bantu World and the Origins of a Captive African Commercial Press in South Africa," *Journal of Southern African Studies*, 14, 3 (April 1988): 352–370.

———. (ed.). *South Africa's Alternative Press: Voices of Protest and Resistance, 1880's-1960's* (Cambridge: Cambridge University Press, 1997).

——— and Mohamed Adhikari (eds.). *South Africa's Resistance Press: Alternative Voices in The Last Generation Under Apartheid* (Athens: Ohio University Center for International Studies, Research in Regional Studies Africa Series no.74, 2000).

———. and Donna Switzer, The Black Press in South Africa and Lesotho: *A Descriptive Bibliographic Guide to African, Coloured and Indian newspapers, newsletters, and magazines 1836–1976* (Boston: G. K. Hall & Company, 1979).

Tamboukou, Maria. Power, Desire and Emotions in Education: Revisiting the Epistolary Narratives of Three Women in Apartheid South Africa, *Gender and Education*, 18, 3 (2006): 233–252.

Taylor, Ula Yvette. *The Veiled Garvey: The Life & Times of Amy Jacques Garvey* (Chapel Hill: University of North Carolina Press, 2002).

Thompson, Leonard. *The Unification of South Africa 1902–1910* (Oxford: Clarendon Press, 1960).

———. *The Political Mythology of Apartheid* (New Haven: Yale University Press, 1985).

———. *History of South Africa* (New Haven: Yale University Press, 1990).

Umoren, Imaobong D. *Race Women Internationalists: Activist-Intellectuals and Global Freedom Struggles* (Los Angeles: University of California Press, 2018).

Vinson, Robert. *The Americans Are Coming!: Dreams of African American Liberation in Segregationist South Africa* (New African Histories) (Athens: Ohio University Press, 2012).

———. *Albert Luthuli* (Athens: Ohio University Press, 2018).

——— and Robert R. Edgar. Zulus Abroad: Cultural Representations and Educational Experiences of Zulus in America, 1880–1945, *Journal of Southern African Studies*, 33, 1 (March 2001): 43–62.

Walker, Cherryl (ed.). *Women and Gender in Southern Africa to 1945* (Cape Town: David Philip and London, 1990).

———. *Women and Resistance in South Africa* (New York: Monthly Review Press, 1982).

Walshe, Peter. *The Rise of African Nationalism in South Africa: The African National Congress, 1912–1952* (London: C. Hurst & Co, 1970).

Wells, Julia C. *We Now Demand! The History of Women's Resistance to Pass Laws in South Africa* (Johannesburg: University of the Witwatersrand Press, 1993).

———. "Why Women Rebel: Women's Resistance in Bloemfontein (1913) and Johannesburg (1956)," *Journal of Southern African Studies*, 10, 1 (1983): 55–70.

Welsh, David. *The Roots of Segregation: Native Policy in Colonial Natal, 1854* (Cape Town: Juta Press, 1971).

Williams, John A. *From the South African Past: Narratives, Documents and Debates* (New York: Houghton Mifflin Company, 1997).

Theses and Dissertations

Brooks, Alan K. "From Class Struggle to National Liberation: The Communist Party of South Africa, 1940–1950." MA thesis, Sussex University, 1967.

Carter, Charles E. "Comrades and Community: Politics and the Construction of Hegemony in Alexandra Township, South Africa 1984–7," unpublished PhD thesis, Oxford University, 1991.

French, Kevin J. "James Mpanza and the Sofasonke Party in the Development of Local Politics in Soweto," MA Dissertation, University of the Witwatersrand, 1983.

Glaser, Clive. "Anti-Social Bandits, Juvenile Delinquency and the Tsotsis: Youth Gang Subculture on the Witwatersrand 1936–1960," unpublished MA dissertation, University of the Witwatersrand 1995.

Hindson, Doug. "The Pass System and the Formation of an Urban African Proletariat: A Critique of the Cheap Labour Thesis." Ph.D. dissertation, University of Sussex, 1983.

Jeffrey, Ian. "Cultural Trends and Community Formation in a South African Township: Sharpeville 1943–1985," MA Dissertation, University of the Witwatersrand 1991.

Khan, Umehani. A Critical Study of the Life of Sibusisiwe Makanya and Her Work as Educator and Social Worker in the Umbumbulu District of Natal 1894–1971, MA, University of KwaZulu/Natal, 1995.

Kramer, J. "Self Help in Soweto: Mutual Aid Societies in A South African City" MA dissertation, University of Bergen, Norway, 1976.

Kros, Cynthia. "Urban African Women's Organizations and Protests on the Rand from the Years 1939 to 1956," unpublished BA Honours thesis, 1978.

Manoim, I. "The Black Press 1945–63," MA dissertation, University of the Witwatersrand, 1983.

Mariotti, Amelia Marte. "The Incorporation of African Wage into Wage Employment in South Africa, 1920–1970," PhD Thesis, University of Connecticut, 1980.

Nauright, John. "Black Island in a White Sea," Ph.D. Thesis, Kingston: Queens University, 1992.

Sarakinsky, Mike. "From Freehold Township to Model Township: A Political History of Alexandra 1905–1983," unpublished honours dissertation, University of the Witwatersrand 1984.

Thomas, Brandy. "Give Them Their Due:" Black Female Missionaries and The South African-American Nexus, 1920s–1930s, B. A. Thesis, The Ohio State University, Columbus, Ohio, 2011.

Tourikis, P. "The Political Economy of Alexandra Township, 1905–1958," BA Honours Dissertation, Sociology, University of Witwatersrand, Johannesburg, 1981.

Online Sources

Blain, Keshia N. Blain. Teaching Black Internationalism and Amerikanah, https://ir.uiowa.edu/cgi/viewcontent.cgi?article=1029&context=history_pubs.

Feinberg, Harvey. A. B. Xuma: "Bridging the Gap between White and Black in South Africa" (1930) Commentary by Harvey Feinberg, Connecticut State University https://www.milestonedocuments.com/documents/view/a-b-xumas-bridging-the-gap-between-white-and-black-in-south-africa/.

Mgqwetho, Nontsizi, We're Stabbing Africa, https://www.poetryinternational.org/pi/poem/11272/auto/0/0/Nontsizi-Mgqwetho/Were-Stabbing-Africa/en/nocache, date accessed 28 December 2020.

Opland, Jeff and Nontsizi Mgqwetho, Listen Compatriots!, 176. Nontsizi (Cizama, Imbongikazi yakwaCizama) Mgqwetho https://www.sahistory.org.za/people/nontsizi-cizama-imbongikazi-yakwacizama-mgqwetho, date accessed 24 December 2020.

South Africa's national anthem, with English translation, https://kairossouthernafrica.wordpress.com/2011/08/10/south-africas-national-anthem-with-english-translation/.

"Word Painting in Songwriting," https://www.thesongwritingdesk.com/word-painting.html.

Index[1]

A

B

[1] Note: Page numbers followed by 'n' refer to notes.

D. Y. Curry, *Social Justice at Apartheid's Dawn*, African Histories and Modernities, https://doi.org/10.1007/978-3-030-85404-1

K

L

M

N

P

R

S